Bernard Haitink

Bernard Haitink

A Working Life

Simon Mundy

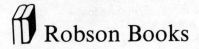

Robson Books

'For my children and all guardian angels who have made this impossible life possible.'

BERNARD HAITINK

First published in Great Britain in 1987 by Robson Books Ltd,
Bolsover House, 5–6 Clipstone Street, London W1P 7EB.

British Library Cataloguing in Publication Data

Mundy, Simon
   Bernard Haitink: a working life.
   1. Haitink, Bernard   2. Conductors (Music)
   — Netherlands — Biography
   I. Title
   785'.092'4   ML422.H/

ISBN 0-86051-445-5

Phototypeset by AKM Associates (UK) Ltd,
Ajmal House, Hayes Road, Southall, London
Printed and bound by Adlard & Son Ltd.
The Garden City Press, Letchworth, Herts.

Contents

CONTENTS

Preface

BERNARD HAITINK HAS been a valued conductor for many years, but it is perhaps only now that his true status is beginning to be appreciated. Inevitably, then, this book must have the characteristics of an interim report. However, certain aspects of his life have now reached a stage where an evaluation is possible and useful. His periods in charge of the Netherlands Radio Philharmonic Orchestra, the London Philharmonic Orchestra, the Concertgebouw Orchestra and Glyndebourne Festival Opera have been – or are about to be – completed. With 280 or so works recorded for the gramophone (a figure that includes some pieces recorded two or three times), his position as a major figure in the history of the medium is secure. Moreover, it is the experience gained from such an impressive range of activities that will make his tenure as Music Director of the Royal Opera House, Covent Garden, so intriguing to follow.

To write this book – not only the first to be devoted to Haitink, but also to any of the four conductors of the Concertgebouw Orchestra in its first century – has been a privilege. That it has also been a pleasure is largely due to Bernard Haitink himself, whose help, kindness and good humour in the face of tedious and sometimes uncomfortably personal questioning have been invaluable. I am equally in the debt of his family, especially his sister Laura In't Veldt and his daughter Marianne, both of whom have provided me with as much encouragement as information.

For much of the verbatim reporting included here I have drawn on material from interviews conducted by myself and also by Alan Blyth, who spent a considerable time compiling them between 1979 and 1982, although they have remained unpublished. I am grateful for his generosity in allowing me to use them freely.

Many people have contributed time and information, without which this book would have taken longer to compile and been poorer in result. Ben Joppe, Bernard Haitink's assistant in the Netherlands, and Diana Rix, his agent at Harold Holt Ltd, have been my mainstays. Marius Flothuis, Sir Peter Hall, Alfred Brendel and Dolf van Dantzig have been generous with their time.

My thanks are also due to the members and former members of the LPO, in particular Nicholas Busch, Alexander Cameron, Alan Cumberland and Judith Swan, and, from its staff, Frances Cook and

7

Judy Grahame; Helen O'Neill and Joanna Townsend at Glynde-bourne; Katharine Wilkinson and Betty Scholar at the Royal Opera House, Covent Garden; Eleanor Hayes, Jan Rubinstein and Michael Sage at Philips; Marius Carboni at Decca; Katharine Copisarow at EMI; Hein van Royen and the staff of the Concertgebouw Orchestra. Their help has been much appreciated, as has that of many friends and colleagues.

SIMON MUNDY

Gladestry, Powys

April 1987

I
Amsterdam, childhood and war

I N THE EARLY spring of 1959 there was a small meeting in
Amsterdam at the apartment belonging to Eduard van Beinum,
the conductor of the Concertgebouw Orchestra since the end of the
Second World War. With van Beinum were Marius Flothuis, the
composer and the orchestra's Artistic Director, and Bernard Haitink,
the young conductor of the Netherlands Radio orchestras. Haitink had
been approached by the Rotterdam Philharmonic Orchestra and was
considering whether to accept the post of conductor there. It would
have been a sensible move at the age of thirty, giving him control of one
of the best orchestras in the country and moving the greater part of his
work from the radio studio to the concert hall. Van Beinum, however,
was unenthusiastic, urging Haitink not to take any decision without
contacting him first. To Flothuis the meaning of that was clear. In
effect van Beinum had named his successor.

A few weeks later, on 13 April, van Beinum died of heart failure. His
death was sudden, but not unexpected by those close to him who had
known for years that his condition made each day a potential hazard.
For the orchestra, however, it meant that the continuity of sixty years
in which only two men had served in the post of Conductor had been
broken. For whatever van Beinum's indication in private, to the
outside world his successor was by no means an obvious choice. Even
so, on 1 September 1961, Bernard Haitink officially assumed van
Beinum's title, at first jointly with the older and more experienced
Eugen Jochum, but after three years with sole authority. For over a
quarter of a century Haitink headed the Concertgebouw Orchestra,
lifting its reputation from that of a respectable but unfashionable
ensemble to the position of one of the finest half-dozen in the world.
From 1967, before he was forty, he was achieving similar success with
the London Philharmonic Orchestra. It is as much due to Haitink as to
anyone else that two capital cities that were long regarded as part of the
provinces of the musical world are now firmly at its centre.

For Haitink to have made such an impression within so few years, in a
profession with a well-developed reverence for age, it might be

assumed that his background and upbringing groomed him for musical stardom from early childhood. A family steeped in music with the awareness and intention to nurture a prodigy would seem to be the main requirement. In fact, though his parents were neither inartistic nor antagonistic to his interests, he could hardly have had a more normal childhood in Amsterdam in that generation.

Willem Haitink, his father, had been born in 1885 in Delft. Haitink's grandfather had been an engineer, and although Willem did not follow him, deciding instead to study law at Leiden University, he never moved far from the engineering industry, working as an administrator first for the railways and then for the Electricity Board, of which he eventually became Director. He was a solid man, conventional in his beliefs and behaviour to an extent that was occasionally to prove stultifying for his children. He was quiet, ordered in every aspect of his life, but was also gracious in his dealings with people – all qualities which stood him in good stead in his professional life. Change for Willem Haitink was not a state to be encouraged and he avoided marriage until the age of thirty-seven.

When he did marry, in 1922, it was to someone with very different characteristics from his own. Anna Verschaffelt was twelve years younger than Willem and came from a family that, while rooted in the sciences, belonged more to the intelligentsia than her husband's. Anna's father was Flemish – his brother lived in Ghent – but had settled in Amsterdam three years after she was born, to teach at the University. There he held the post of Professor of Botany, and Anna, the only child, grew up in a lively and inquisitive household where music, history and literature were part of the fabric. Her mother was Jewish – a fact which might have proved dangerous later on – and had a lifelong passion for French culture that stemmed from her Belgian background. It was a passion that Anna inherited, and when she enrolled at Amsterdam University, at her father's urging, it was to read French. For years after her marriage she maintained those contacts as Secretary of the Alliance Française in Amsterdam.

Two years after she married Willem Haitink her first son, Eduard, was born. A daughter, Laura, followed in 1927 and on 4 March 1929 her third child arrived. He was christened Bernard Johan Herman.

The family home expressed all the ambitions of the modern Dutch middle class. The house Willem Haitink bought at 76 Reijnier Vinkeleskade was part of a comfortable new terrace, brick-built but in the most up-to-date Bauhaus style. The starkness of the flat-roofed 1920s design was softened by its position on the southern edge of the old south side of the city. A small front garden, the street itself and a thin strip of lawn separated it from the North Amstel Canal which links the Nieuwe Meer with the Amstel river. Much of the land across the canal was still undeveloped and, where the suburban sprawl of New South Amsterdam now stretches, the fields had not yet been completely swallowed up. Amsterdam was still a small city, only slowly expanding from the kernel of its seventeenth- and eighteenth-century canals which enclose the earlier town in an irregular hexagon. A few minutes' walk from Vinkeleskade to the north are the municipal buildings of the late nineteenth century that made the Old South such a fashionable area in which to live – among them the Concertgebouw (literally 'Concert Building') and the Rijksmuseum, home for much of the Netherlands' collection of Rembrandt's work.

For Laura and Bernard the choice of their first school reflected both the modernism of the area and the radical intellectual outlook of their mother. Across the North Amstel Canal and a few hundred yards down Rubens Straat is the Open Lucht ('Open Air') School in Cliostraat. Now it sits in a square, confined and almost hidden by subsequent building, but at that time its name was indicative of its position and liberal teaching philosophy. The school itself is a remarkable structure, an essay in the avant-garde architectural principles of the early 1930s which is still startling to the eye today.

For the first ten years of his life Bernard's home was the epitome of stable ordinariness. Schooldays kept him in suburban Amsterdam; the Easter and summer holidays were spent in North Holland at Bergen aan Zee, where the Haitinks rented a house for the season. Otherwise there were occasional excursions to France or Belgium, and once in a while to Switzerland, but his father was happiest with a fixed pattern to his life and ambitious travel was not one of his interests. From those days, though, a fascination with and love of the sea was kindled in Bernard which has never left him, and it is at Bergen that he still keeps his home in Holland. It was a sheltered childhood which protected the children from extremes of wealth or poverty and allowed little to disturb the calm of routine. Willem Haitink approached his family with the gentle detachment which he brought to his work as a civic administrator and, though his wife was by nature far more temperamental, she was happy to abide by the secure conventionality of his expectations. For the young Bernard life was settled but dull. While he possessed his father's ability to concentrate and work in a steady unhurried way, he also had his mother's sense of enquiry and the natural rebelliousness of her early years which she later suppressed. The aloof rigidity of family life irritated him and he came to be seen as the moody rebel of the household, something of a loner who fitted badly into the unit and preferred to build his own life without reference to the others. At school shyness held him back and he encouraged few close friendships. Those he did develop, however, were held loyally.

For such a family the outbreak of war had a particularly traumatic effect. From the first attack by German forces on Moerdijk on 10 May 1940 it was clear that the Dutch would be unable to hold back the invasion for any length of time. Within three days General Winkelman, faced with the German threat to bomb Rotterdam and Utrecht, was forced to surrender. The Luftwaffe bombed Rotterdam anyway, but by that time the occupation was an accomplished fact. The repression that began immediately was obvious even to the eleven-year-old Bernard Haitink. He had become aware of what Nazism meant two years earlier when he had read about the Anschluss, but now the effects could be felt in the details of his own life.

The outbreak of war coincided with his move from the 'Open Air' School in Cliostraat to the Lycée, where his mother's enthusiasm for all things French could be passed on. At school the Jews, both teachers and pupils, began to be weeded out. Amsterdam had always boasted a large and vigorous Jewish population, many of them descended from Portuguese and Spanish refugees who had fled to the emerging Dutch Republic, with its tolerance for religious and political dissent, during the Inquisition at the end of the sixteenth century. By the 1940s they had become one of the most integrated and accepted Jewish communities in Europe, but persecution inevitably began with the occupation. At the Lycée they were at first segregated and then removed altogether. Gradually friends disappeared and their houses were sealed.

At home there was the danger that Anna Haitink's Jewish parentage would be unearthed but, although the occupying forces came to the house several times to question her about her activities as Secretary of the Alliance Française, they never discovered the more perilous connection. It was not only Jewish households, of course, that felt the terror of the German regime, and the times were especially worrying for anyone who had links with public life. A close colleague of Willem Haitink's at the Electricity Board had been one of those who had toured Germany before the outbreak of war and returned impressed by the advances in engineering and efficiency. In July 1940 his sons were among the first to be executed for acts of 'sabotage'. There were few Dutch families which did not have similar stories to tell about their friends and relations over the following five years.

In 1941 the fear touched the Haitink household directly. After the bombing of a pro-Nazi bookshop, the Gestapo took hundreds of hostages. In the early hours of the morning two 'civilians' came to Vinkeleskade. Willem Haitink took off his wrist-watch and was taken away. For four weeks the family had no news of him and the Gestapo refused to reply to questions. Then a letter came from Amersfoort. It was heavily censored, but Willem managed to include a reference to the score of Beethoven's *Fidelio*. It pointed to the Prisoners' Chorus, and the family knew from that, and from the letter's place of origin, that he was in the concentration camp used mainly for Russian soldiers captured on the Eastern Front. After four months, on the anniversary of Hitler's birth, the hostages were released and Willem emerged, his previously round figure reduced to little more than a skeleton. Throughout the war, however, he managed to retain his job, though at the cost of frequent threats from the occupying forces on the one hand and the Dutch underground on the other.

Bernard's reaction to the turmoil was to withdraw even more into himself than he had before. With his friendships disrupted by the combination of a new school and war, and family life shaken from its formerly impermeable security, he began to feel ever more isolated. The main school building had been commandeered by the Germans, so even here there was no sense of normality and he increasingly found reasons not to attend or to ignore the work which was expected of him.

The avenue of escape was music. It was not one which he discovered suddenly, or even very early, but as the rest of his life became more uncertain, so he found that music could supply him with a world of feeling and expression that was his own. Bernard had begun to take an interest when he was nine, starting lessons on the violin and attending his first concert at the Concertgebouw. Willem Mengelberg, then the orchestra's undisputed ruler, conducted Bach's *St Matthew Passion*. Bernard sat behind the chorus, from where he could watch all the conductor's expressions. He was fascinated by the small man, sturdy and grey-haired, who directed the orchestra with imperious authority. On that occasion the music made less of an effect than the interpreter, but later in the season Mengelberg conducted Tchaikovsky's 'Pathétique' Symphony and from that moment on Bernard was addicted.

Music was not unknown in the household – his mother played the piano and enjoyed singing Schubert songs – although the real excitement was generated from other sources. Rummaging in a cupboard at the age of twelve, he discovered a couple of miniature orchestral scores: one of Beethoven's Violin Concerto, the other of Schubert's Eighth Symphony, the 'Unfinished'. They had belonged to his grandfather on his father's side who had balanced his engineering

interests with a talent for singing and a general love of music. From
then on Bernard gathered as many scores as he could, often presenting
the bills from the music stores to his mildly shocked but uncomplaining
father. With the scores at hand Bernard devoured whatever music was
to be heard on the radio. At first the books seemed indecipherable but
gradually, as his own knowledge of the orchestra increased and his
violin lessons progressed, the pages of notes began to make sense.

With the wartime disruption of musical life in Amsterdam, the radio
became his most important source. Apart from local broadcasts, he
tuned in to the concerts on the BBC, in itself an act of resistance since
any contact with England was banned during the occupation (at school
the teaching of English was forbidden too). From the Proms he heard
music every evening in the summer months, at first relayed from the
Queen's Hall and then, after it was destroyed by a bomb in 1941, from
the Albert Hall. He still remembers the effect of the Wagner nights,
Bach and Handel evenings and the Fridays devoted to Beethoven,
conducted by Sir Henry Wood. Basil Cameron and Sir Adrian Boult
also made a lasting impression, as did the piano-playing of Myra Hess
and the violin of Ida Haendel.

His own teacher was Charles van de Rosier, a member of the second
violin section of the Concertgebouw Orchestra, who regarded Mengelberg as the ideal conductor. As the war went on, however, Mengelberg
appeared less and less frequently, rarely venturing from his base in
Switzerland, and his duties were assumed by van Beinum. Mengelberg's attitude to the German occupation was considered at best
ambivalent in Amsterdam and he never again won the appreciation he
had enjoyed before the war. It was regarded as particularly in-
comprehensible that he put up such little opposition to the banning of
almost all composers not regarded as suitably patriotic by the Nazi
authorities, especially Mahler, whose reputation as a great symphonist
Mengelberg had been responsible for building almost single-handed
since the early years of the century. The banning orders invariably
made nonsense of the orchestra's programmes, and their absurdity was
pointedly revealed when Mengelberg was given special dispensation to
conduct two performances of Tchaikovsky's 'Pathétique' Symphony
(one in Amsterdam, the other at The Hague) for the ludicrous reason
that it was a particular favourite of the wife of the military governor.
Despite the truncated repertoire to be heard, the young Haitink
attended the concerts as often as he was able. His parents at first tried
to prevent him from going, appalled by the way in which all Jewish
members of the audience were refused entry and the seats in the hall,
which untypically for the Concertgebouw remained half empty, were

taken up by German officers. To be able to hear music live was becoming so obviously important to their son, however, that they eventually relented, although they themselves stayed away.

During the last year of the war, conditions in Amsterdam worsened as the occupying forces came under increasing pressure from the Allies. As the Germans sequestered supplies to meet the needs of their retreating armies and the farmland to the south was wrested from their control, so food and fuel became scarce. To find anything adequate, even on the black market, meant cycling all over the city, and on more than one occasion the Haitink family, like many others, was reduced to eating tulip bulbs. Electricity was unavailable much of the time – whatever the efforts of Willem Haitink – and at the Concertgebouw the players' desks were placed to catch what natural light they could for the last concert of the war, as the Canadian army drew closer to the city. Van Beinum conducted, convinced that his doing so would condemn him to be hanged at the end of the occupation. Two months later he and the orchestra returned to the Concertgebouw for the first concert in liberated Amsterdam. Mahler, banned since the German invasion, was the composer closest to the orchestra's heart and his Second Symphony, the 'Resurrection', expressed better than any other the trials of the war years and the exultant hope for the future of the freed city.

In many ways, however, the period after the liberation was as difficult as that of occupation. The atmosphere of revenge against those accused of collaborating with the Nazis brought unaccustomed civil violence to the streets as the frustration and hate were vented. For the Haitink children, brought up even in wartime with a peculiarly sheltered view of the outside world, coming to terms with the bitterness was hard. Even though they were not directly affected, the atmosphere of recrimination, the blurring of the definitions of right and wrong, was difficult to comprehend. For Bernard, painfully shy at the best of times, it provided yet further reasons for withdrawal into his own world of imagination and music.

At least now the musical diet was not restricted by the politics of war and the radio could provide the broadening of musical experience that he needed, without the necessity of illegal listening. So Boult's interpretations of the symphonies of Elgar and Vaughan Williams, Beecham's Haydn and Mozart, and the works of Mendelssohn, Tchaikovsky and Mahler could be explored without hindrance. Sir Adrian Boult was the first foreign conductor to work with the Concertgebouw Orchestra after the war. On 4 November 1945 they performed John Ireland's London Overture, Elgar's 'Enigma' Vari-

ations and, in the evening but not at the same day's matinée, the
Dances from *Checkmate* by Arthur Bliss. Five years earlier, six months
into the war, Boult had been one of the last to risk travelling to Holland
before the invasion when, on 29 February 1940, he had also conducted
the 'Enigma' Variations. His account (in *My Own Trumpet*) of the
postwar visit gives a clear idea of the state of Amsterdam only a few
months after liberation.

> ...things were still *very* difficult. A small airfield near Leiden was all
> that civilian traffic could use, and I was fetched from there by a
> member of the Concertgebouw staff in a car which he had taken to
> pieces and dispersed in a dozen different friends' houses during the
> war. He had only just assembled it, and it was still one of the very few
> private cars in Amsterdam. As the railway had not been repaired, I
> should, without him, probably have been unable to reach Amster-
> dam till next day. The orchestra had suffered serious losses, and the
> wartime replacements were naturally of a different calibre from their
> older colleagues, though Eduard van Beinum was quickly effecting
> amazing improvement.

In June 1947 Boult returned with his own BBC Symphony Orchestra
and an ambitious programme in which they played the Overture *The
Taming of the Shrew* by the Dutch composer Johan Wagenaar,
Vaughan Williams's Concerto for Two Pianos (with Cyril Smith and
Phyllis Sellick as soloists), Stravinsky's *Scherzo fantastique* and
Schubert's Ninth Symphony, the 'Great' C major. Meanwhile, in 1946,
Bernard Haitink had made his first trip in the opposite direction,
travelling to England for a fortnight's holiday with a family near
Epsom in Surrey. London and the surrounding towns were in not
much better shape than Amsterdam (worse in many ways, since the
latter had escaped any large-scale bombardment) but it was a
refreshing change of scene, and for the first time Bernard felt that his
fascination with music was regarded as normal rather than as a little
eccentric.

At home in the Netherlands there were changes in the household that
year when his sister, Laura, at the age of nineteen married Chris In't
Veldt, ten years her senior. In 1949 they left Holland altogether,
travelling to a post in the Colonial Service in the Dutch East Indies, a
move that made her settled and safety-conscious parents thoroughly
anxious.

On Bernard's return from England in the summer of 1946 his
dissatisfaction with life in Vinkeleskade gradually came to a head. His

schooldays at the Lycée had been inevitably tainted by the war and his enthusiasm for the business of everyday lessons was minimal. This was partly due to normal teenage rebellion, but also to a growing awareness that such talents as he possessed were not likely to be best developed through the usual processes of academic matriculation. Whatever he was to become, he knew by then, would be as a result of his love for music. Quite what his sphere of accomplishment would be was rather less clear. He was an able, but not particularly gifted violinist and his prospects as a musician were hardly those of a child prodigy. Nevertheless, after a certain amount of argument and persuasion, the seventeen-year-old Bernard was allowed to leave school without taking his final examinations. It was a risky decision but, in a world emerging from war, hardly less uncertain a course than any other. From then on, at least, there was to be no doubting where his dogged energy was to be directed.

II
Apprentice and radio man

I N 1947 BERNARD Haitink arrived at the Amsterdam Conservatory
of Music. For his first year as a student the loftier ambitions had to
be put behind him as he grappled with the fundamental rules of
musical theory. Until then he had relied on the unsystematic information he had been able to glean from violin lessons and self-taught
score-reading. His knowledge of the music itself was already extensive.
Even when he was ten, his sister remembers, he could identify works
played on the radio with, as it seemed to Laura, amazing ease, and
concert-going during the war had improved the range of his listening,
although there were still unsatisfactory gaps. Violin lessons continued,
though it was clear that a new Dutch virtuoso was not in the making.
Nevertheless, work occupied him to rather greater purpose than it had
at the Lycée.

The emerging extent of his ambitions became evident with his first
personal encounter with a musician of world stature the following
year. At the beginning of 1948 Sir Adrian Boult returned to the
Concertgebouw to conduct four concerts: two performances of
Vaughan Williams's masque for dancing, *Job* (on 29 and 30 January),
and, on 1 and 2 February, two performances of Elgar's *The Dream of
Gerontius*. Since the First World War, when – as in the Second –
English music had been banned in Germany, Elgar's reputation
outside Britain had diminished to the extent that his major works
hardly ever appeared on concert programmes. In Amsterdam, though,
the Toonkunst Choir arranged the *Gerontius* performances as a gesture
of thanks to England for her help during the war. As well as Boult, the
soloists Mary Jarred, Parry Jones and Harold Williams were brought
over – a rare event at a time when English singers were regarded on the
Continent as being almost as lowly as English composers. Sir Adrian
later wrote:

[We] were given a wonderful reception. I particularly remembered
Eduard van Beinum's comment in the interval: 'But this is a
masterpiece!' I was able to remind him that fifty years before, fifty
miles away, Richard Strauss had said exactly the same thing after a
performance in the Lower Rhenish Festival at Düsseldorf.

After the concert the Anglo-Dutch Society held a celebratory dinner at which Boult was the guest of honour. Next to him sat Bernard Haitink, who plucked up the courage during the meal to admit that he too wanted to become a conductor. Boult's reaction was non-committal.

The following summer Haitink went across the North Sea again, this time travelling to Scotland for the second Edinburgh Festival with a fellow student, Otto Hamburg. There they heard van Beinum conduct the Concertgebouw Orchestra, making its first overseas tour since the war, in Bartók's Concerto for Orchestra and Debussy's *La mer* at the Usher Hall, the only building in Britain at the time with acoustics good enough to rival those of the orchestra's own home. More importantly for the future, however, Haitink was exposed to opera for the first time when he saw Rafael Kubelik conduct Mozart's *Don Giovanni* at the King's Theatre.

The production, by Carl Ebert, with Paolo Silveri as Giovanni, Vito de Taranto as Leporello, Ljuba Welitsch as Donna Anna and Ian Wallace as Masetto, had been brought up from Glyndebourne for the festival, and for Haitink there were very clear pre-echoes of the future. Thirty years later Glyndebourne was to provide him with his first post in an opera house, and *Don Giovanni* was to be one of the most successful productions he conducted during his tenure as music director. In 1948 the two students were determined to attend a rehearsal as well as the performance. At first they were told that it was impossible, but they persisted and eventually Ian Hunter, assistant to the general manager, Rudolf Bing, was persuaded to smuggle them into the auditorium. Two decades later Hunter, by then head of Harold Holt in London, became Haitink's agent.

Once back in Amsterdam after the summer's discoveries, he resumed his studies. It was clear by now that Haitink's ability with the violin was unlikely to equip him as a soloist for he was, on his own admission, a mediocre player. If that instrument was to be his only means of expression, then the most he was likely to achieve was a life at one of the lesser desks in one of the minor orchestras. Chamber music was more attractive, however, and some of his most enjoyable moments as a student were spent playing quartets, usually as the second violin.

Spurred on by his passion to make music but faced with the obvious limitations of the violin, Bernard Haitink was increasingly convinced that his blurted confession to Boult was correct and that he should concentrate on trying to become a conductor. The conviction was reinforced the next summer, 1949, when his parents agreed to finance his first trip to Austria for the Salzburg Festival. It proved to be even more of an inspiration than Edinburgh had been the year before, as it gave him his first opportunity to watch Wilhelm Furtwängler conduct. The main opera production that year was Beethoven's *Fidelio* and for Haitink it was an unforgettable experience, though interestingly it was the orchestra's contribution rather than that of the singers that left the most lasting impression.

'At first I thought the overture was pedestrian,' he recalls. 'Then, when the Quartet started, the magic began. I'll never forget the first six bars, the way the violins and cellos sounded. From then on there was a feeling in the Festspielhaus that I will always remember. The next morning I went into the rehearsal of Bruckner's Eighth Symphony, also with Furtwängler. After that I walked along the Salzach in another world, I was so carried away. I can only say his interpretation was like a laser beam to the music – you suddenly understood why it had been written.' A few days later Haitink heard Herbert von Karajan conduct Beethoven's Ninth Symphony, but it was Furtwängler's art which he cherished most on his return to Amsterdam.

At the Academy Haitink was determined to take further the idea of conducting. As with most things in his life, however, he decided to shortcut the usual means of approach and consulted the most interesting rather than the most proper person. Instead of enrolling in the official conducting class, which was generally regarded as un-inspiring, he contacted the stimulating but controversial conductor of the Academy orchestra, Felix Hupka. The response was not en-couraging, since Hupka refused either to give him lessons or to allow him a trial with the orchestra.

That effectively marked the end of Haitink's progress for two years for, in 1949, he was called up to do his compulsory military service. The nineteen months spent in uniform he regarded as a waste of time and – on the part of the taxpayer – money. For someone already excessively shy, short of stature and not mechanically minded, the business of soldiering was unlikely to be of great benefit. He was among the first group of conscripts that did not have to do a tour of duty in Indonesia and, grateful as he was for that, he was not inspired by the exercises in drill that were required instead.

When he emerged from the army at the age of twenty-one, Haitink returned to his studies at the Academy and continued his relentless progress towards the lesser reaches of the orchestra. Hupka was still ostensibly uninterested in teaching him conducting and the college authorities regarded his prospects as less than glorious. One morning, however, Hupka gave him the chance that he needed. The orchestra was rehearsing the Tchaikovsky Violin Concerto. A few minutes into the session, Hupka stepped down from the podium and asked Haitink to take charge of the orchestra for the first movement. Afterwards, the sudden test over, the long-sought lessons were agreed to. They were, however, unofficial, since they fell outside the normal arrangements of the conducting-class curriculum, but this did at least mean that Haitink had the benefit of his idiosyncratic teacher's undivided attention.

Much to the new student's surprise, the main instrument that he was required to take to the conducting lessons was not the baton but the violin. Hupka realised that what was missing was not stick technique – that could be tackled later – but the consistent ability to be able to express and control a musical phrase with the confidence of an executant rather than the passivity of the listener. At the same time he worked on Haitink's awareness of the detail and variety of inter-pretation. With his teacher, a 'fanatical' concert-goer anyway, Haitink went to hear as much music as he could, the two of them examining and discussing the minutiae of the performance at length afterwards. In the meantime, as far as the rest of his tutors were concerned, he was merely continuing with his violin lessons. To Haitink, Hupka was an extraordinary man, so great was the force of his personality when he took the orchestral classes each Wednesday and Saturday. His student became a tremendous admirer, fascinated to be, as he saw it, very close to 'a clear source of music' for the first time.

However interesting the discussions, the hours of work on phrasing, and observation from the second violin section, Haitink had as yet almost no experience of actually standing up in front of an orchestra. Since his work with Hupka was unofficial, it was difficult for him to achieve anything within the framework of the Academy curriculum. So in 1953 it was suggested that he enrol in the conducting course held every summer by Netherlands Radio at the broadcasting headquarters in Hilversum, twenty miles east of Amsterdam. Haitink passed the examination in music theory which was the entrance requirement, attended, conducted – and impressed nobody.

Among the adjudicators, however, was Ferdinand Leitner, at that time Music Director of the opera at Stuttgart. Felix Hupka had noticed that there was something about the way Haitink used his hands that, despite his diffidence and inexperience, marked him out from the rest. Leitner, too, felt that there was a spark that needed kindling and at the end of the course suggested that, instead of returning to his studies at the Academy, Haitink should join the violin section of the radio orchestra as a student member. This would give him the opportunity to

broaden the repertoire that he encountered as a musician and to watch
a greater range of conductors at work from a position where he could
learn the practical use of their methods. The advantage of playing in a
radio orchestra was that it covered a far greater range of works in the
course of a season than a conventional symphony orchestra and, with
the performances divided between the studio and concert halls around
the country, enabled Haitink after a year to feel at home in a variety of
professional fields. The Netherlands Radio Philharmonic Orchestra's
chief conductor at the time was Paul van Kempen, a figure who was
controversial in his approach and by no means universally popular
with the players. Nevertheless, Haitink found him an able and
interesting musician to play for.

At the end of the season, in the summer of 1954, Haitink left his place
in the orchestra – for the last time, as it turned out – and rejoined the
conductors' course. Once again Ferdinand Leitner was the principal
adjudicator, and at the end of the six weeks of study he asked Haitink
what he wanted to conduct at the final concert. Despite his year in the
profession, Haitink was still a diffident and unassertive man and could
not summon up the confidence to choose anything himself. In the end
Leitner picked for him, choosing the Prelude and 'Liebestod' from
Wagner's *Tristan und Isolde*, to be presented to an invited audience on
the last day. To prepare for the concert, Haitink conducted while
Leitner played the music through on the piano before the orchestra and
audience were faced.

Whatever his misgivings, Haitink's first trial in front of an audience
was a considerable success, and by then Leitner was sure enough of his
talent to know that there was a great deal of potential to be exploited.
He was able to offer Haitink two possible alternatives: either he could
be recommended for a staff conductor's job with Netherlands Radio
or, if that did not materialise, Leitner was prepared to take him to
Stuttgart as his assistant at the opera. Had Haitink taken the latter
course, he would have worked in a major theatre almost twenty years
before he did in fact do so and his advancement as a symphonic
conductor would probably have been delayed by several years.

In the event, he was offered a post with the radio orchestras for the
1954–5 season. Apart from the Radio Philharmonic there were four
other groups on which Haitink could cut his professional teeth: the
Broadcasting Orchestra, the Broadcasting Chamber Orchestra, the
Promenade Orchestra and the Broadcasting Choir. On top of the
business of preparation, he was given four studio concerts of his own in
the first season. Considering the punishing schedules of later years,
such a small number might seem paltry in comparison. But for him at

the time it was a daunting prospect, since all the music had to be learned, studied and rehearsed for the first time. The process of preparing a score for performance is far more time-consuming and complicated than most members of the audience – or the orchestra, for that matter – realise. The difference between mastering the second violin part of a symphony and having the complete score known and understood, so that tempi, balance and detail can be judged and communicated, is as different as riding a bicycle is from piloting an airliner.

The following season he continued to accumulate experience, and this time was entrusted with twelve programmes and the title Permanent Conductor. As well as being shy, Haitink is by nature a cautious person and he found the speed of his progress hard to come to terms with. He hates to commit himself to a decision or to conduct a work until he is certain in his own mind that he has prepared the groundwork thoroughly. This can be a slow and rather deliberate process. The dictates of a radio station, which consumes performances with an insatiable appetite, are such that speed and competence are greater virtues in a conductor than ponderous care and unhurried method. There was no time for perfectionism and Haitink continually felt himself rushed, a state which unsettles him more than almost any other.

Nevertheless, he found that he quickly built a close and happy relationship with the broadcasting orchestras, partly, perhaps, because the players found him a refreshing change from their unpopular principal conductor, van Kempen. As a result the occasion picked for his first public concert with the Netherlands Radio Philharmonic Orchestra was a prestigious one: a performance at the Holland Festival in The Hague of Cherubini's C minor Requiem in June 1956.

That year proved to be eventful for Haitink both personally and professionally. At the age of twenty-seven he married Marjolein Snyder, whom he had first met at music college, where she was studying piano. At the time they had taken little notice of each other but later, after a chance meeting in the unromantic surroundings of an Amsterdam tram, their friendship grew. At the same time it became clear that his father was terminally ill with cancer. Willem Haitink lived long enough, however, to see his son's marriage and his first major success in public at the Holland Festival.

That performance in The Hague led to what can be regarded, with hindsight, as having been perhaps the single most important engagement in Haitink's life. The Cherubini Requiem is neither heard frequently nor might it be thought a likely vehicle for the launching of a conductor's career. In 1956, though, the Requiem was not only due to be heard at the Holland Festival in the summer but was scheduled for the winter season at the Concertgebouw, with the same choir but with Carlo Maria Giulini conducting. Shortly before the concert Giulini pulled out, leaving the orchestra's management with a problem. There was too little time for van Beinum to learn the unusual score, yet it was too late to change the programme. Marius Flothuis, the Concert-gebouw Orchestra's Artistic Director, and van Beinum took the obvious course and called Haitink in to see them at the orchestra's offices. Since he had just performed the Requiem with the same choir, would he take over the Amsterdam concert, they asked. The first half was to consist of Vivaldi's *Four Seasons*, with Theo Olof playing the solo violin part, so that would pose no problems for the conductor, however young.

To their astonishment, Haitink refused. He gave two reasons. First, the number of scores he had to learn for the radio orchestras' season meant that he was unwilling to take on any extra engagements. Second, and more important, he felt that, with only two years' professional conducting experience behind him, he was not ready to take on the country's most influential orchestra. A concert with the Concert-gebouw was not something to be rushed into and he simply did not feel it would be anything but a 'foolish undertaking'. Neither van Beinum nor Flothuis was prepared to allow the matter to drop that easily. Eventually, against his better judgement, Haitink was persuaded to accept. There were to be two performances, on 7 and 8 November at 8.15 in the evening. As Haitink walked down the steps that lead from the conductor's room, through a section of the audience and the orchestra, all his misgivings seemed justified as he heard a woman mutter 'My goodness, what a schoolboy!' For the twenty-seven-year-old, well aware of his own limitations, it was hardly an auspicious beginning.

The performance removed everybody's doubts, except perhaps those of Haitink himself. There was no applause, since the Hungarian Uprising had just been put down by Soviet tanks and it was decided to greet the Requiem in silence as a mark of respect. Haitink was mildly grateful for that, since it meant that, however he had fared, he would not be able to judge his reception from the clapping and the audience was bound to be moved by the sense of occasion. None the less, as far as Flothuis and the orchestra were concerned, the new man had proved himself a worthy interpreter. There was a sense that at last there was a Dutch conductor on the horizon capable of developing into, at the least, a regular guest with the orchestra. Haitink's youth, obvious ability (even at such an early stage of his career) and seriousness of purpose impressed Flothuis considerably. It is usual practice at the Concertgebouw for a conductor who deputises at short notice to be invited back the following season to give a programme in his own right. But in Haitink's case Flothuis fulfilled the obligation with unusual enthusiasm and a feeling that there was likely to be something special and unexpected about the emerging partnership.

Given the fact that he was largely unknown and almost untried, Haitink might have thought it reasonable to expect to direct the Concertgebouw Orchestra once or twice the following year. In the event, and still certain that he was taking on too much, too soon, he was engaged for seven concerts in the 1957–8 season. In November his programmes contained the mixture of new music, French music and the classical German repertoire that was to characterise his concerts with the Concertgebouw Orchestra for the next decade. The first, on 12 November, contained a Mozart overture, Mendelssohn's Scottish Symphony, Three Slavonic Dances by Dvořák and Saint-Saëns' Fifth Piano Concerto with Marie-Thérèse Fourneau as soloist. That, and the programme that was played five days later, was an afternoon concert. In the second Haitink conducted the Overture to *Il matrimonio segreto* by Cimarosa, the Organ Concerto Op.4 No.2 by Handel (with Piet van Egmond as soloist) and Brahms's *German Requiem*.

Later that month (on 21 November 1957) Hans Henkemans played Mozart's Piano Concerto K.488, and before the interval Haitink conducted the world première of a symphony by his near contemporary Robert Heppener. Brahms's Second Symphony ended the evening. Two nights later the Cimarosa, Heppener, Saint-Saëns and Mendelssohn works were given at a gala performance to mark the International Congress of the European Cultural Foundation, and on the next evening (24 November) Haitink was on the rostrum again for Bach's Cantata No.169 – with the alto Annie Hermes – and, significantly for the future, the Second Symphony by Anton Bruckner. For his last appearances of the season (on 7 and 8 March 1958) he conducted the Mendelssohn Scottish Symphony again, Bartók's Concerto for Orchestra and a violin concerto by Bach, for which he was joined by Yehudi Menuhin. Already he was being entrusted with prestigious events and repertoire that was sufficiently important to be the usual prerogative of the orchestra's principal conductor, rather than that of a novice guest.

By this time, however, others beside the Concertgebouw had noticed that an artist of some stature was beginning to emerge. In 1956 the chief conductor of the radio orchestras, Paul van Kempen, had died and

Bernard Haitink had been asked to succeed him. Haitink had been the choice of the players for some time, but the new role carried with it responsibilities which filled him with some apprehension. From the beginning of the 1957 season he was officially in charge of all four orchestras and chorus of Netherlands Radio, with the duty to conduct a considerable proportion of the output himself, much of which had to be learned from scratch.

Haitink approached his new post with a mixture of excitement and trepidation. While the appointment gave him the chance to launch his career with a flourish, no one knew better than he did the depth of his inexperience. Bruno Walter's dictum that it takes ten years to make a conductor and another ten to make a good one seemed all too obviously applicable. It was only eight years since he had first admitted to Hupka that he wanted to take lessons, four since he had stood in front of an orchestra for the first time and been quietly discouraged about his prospects. Now, at the age of twenty-eight, he was expected to play his part in planning programmes, auditioning players, supervising the work of the orchestras and, of course, take the lion's share of the conducting. There were – and are – plenty of precedents for a conductor in his twenties becoming the principal of an orchestra. Henry Wood started the Promenade Concerts at twenty-five, Mengelberg was a year younger when he inherited the Concertgebouw Orchestra, and Simon Rattle was also twenty-five when he assumed control of the City of Birmingham Symphony Orchestra. However, there can be few examples of a conductor taking over the direction of four orchestras, a chorus and a sizeable chunk of a major national broadcasting organisation with such a thin curriculum vitae.

The qualification that made Haitink the right choice, and in which he had least confidence, was the trust of the players. They knew and liked him, had watched his talent emerge and had seen him rise from within their own ranks. However, respect – as distinct from co-operation – had to be won and Haitink felt that they soon realised just how inexperienced and disorganised (never a term one would normally associate with him) he was. The turning-point came with the decision to schedule Stravinsky's *The Rite of Spring*. Haitink had never tackled the work before, and while it is not as complex as some music of the postwar avant garde, once learned and in the blood, the *Rite* remains one of the trickiest scores in the day-to-day orchestral repertoire to master. Haitink, though, locked himself away with the music and had it ready for performance in only two weeks. The Radio Philharmonic Orchestra – not a group of musicians to suffer young conductors gladly – was impressed and the performance in Amsterdam, given as part of the Holland Festival, confirmed Haitink's success.

Whatever his own fears about his appropriateness for the role, the principal conductorship gave him a chance to explore an immense range of music, from Bach to the output of the most up-to-date Dutch composers. More importantly for his development, it allowed him to identify those areas of the repertoire with which he felt most comfortable. As both Boult and Otto Klemperer pointed out, it is dangerous for a conductor to be too much of a specialist. Too narrow a diet limits the extent of musical awareness and eventually constricts the breadth of expression. On the other hand, any musician will have more to say about some works – or categories of works – than about others, and Haitink was beginning to be able to mark out the boundaries of his enthusiasms. There were plenty of obscure pieces to present, which would have been uncommercial in the concert hall and which the radio station therefore had a duty to perform. But Haitink was also able to try his hand at repertoire that was to be increasingly important to him. He conducted Bruckner's *Te Deum* and Ninth Symphony, as well as the major works of Stravinsky, Ravel and Debussy. Perhaps not surprisingly, given his mother's love of French culture and her secretaryship of the Alliance Française (though he and his sister were nearly put off the entire subject as children through their forced attendance at the French Consulate parties), Haitink was developing an affinity with that country's music. Interestingly, he even tackled opera for the first time, directing a studio performance of Mozart's *Die Entführung aus dem Serail*, the work which fifteen years later was to provide his first opportunity to conduct at Glyndebourne.

Away from the concert hall and the radio station, the autumn of 1957 was dominated by a domestic event of significance. In October his first child, a daughter, was born and named Marianne. Over the ensuing years the family grew steadily until, by the early 1970s, there were five children to support.

The year 1958 was one of remarkable progress for Bernard Haitink. As well as his continuing work for Netherlands Radio at Hilversum, he was starting to be a frequent guest in the concert hall. There were appearances with the Concertgebouw Orchestra, but he also conducted the Rotterdam Philharmonic and orchestras in Haarlem (just outside Amsterdam) and, in the far north of the country, Groningen. At the Holland Festival in the early summer he performed Honegger's *King David* with his own NRPO and Carl Orff's popular choral work *Carmina Burana* with The Hague Philharmonic (usually known in the

Netherlands as the Residentie Orchestra).

The year had begun, however, with an engagement that was something of a landmark in his life when he conducted outside the Netherlands for the first time. Eduard van Beinum, as well as being conductor of the Concertgebouw Orchestra, held a similar position with the Los Angeles Philharmonic, and at his suggestion Haitink was booked to make his United States début in January 1958. For the public the main reason for attending was likely to have been the performance of Yehudi Menuhin in the Brahms Violin Concerto, though the *Los Angeles Times* was perceptive enough to notice that it was for Haitink's contribution that the concert would be remembered. The music editor, Raymond Kendall, wrote:

He took his place before the Los Angeles Philharmonic like a veteran, and turned off two other Brahms works – the *Tragic* Overture and the Fourth Symphony – so intensely and so well as to set off his first appearance in the United States as more than good: it was noteworthy. Given consistent chances to mature and to gain experience in all facets of a conductor's responsibilities, he may well become one of the most significant conducting talents this generation has produced.

Haitink would have been surprised to read that 'he comes from the province of Limburg' and perhaps not thrilled to be told that 'his conscious or unconscious emulation of Van Karajan (*sic*) is overevident'. Nevertheless, the descriptive assessment was more than encouraging.

Outstanding characteristics of his conducting are the intensity and vitality with which he kindles a fire under the orchestra. Then, just before its passionate outburst becomes too extreme, he tempers his beat, nurturing the orchestra from climax to climax without a hurried tempo or any harsh overplaying. The sound is firstrate, and the cumulative effect is never fractured into too small units; he has a sense of proportion, of musical architecture in unusual degree.

The rival *Herald Examiner* rather spoiled the impact of its headline by misspelling the conductor's name. 'Thrill to Hartink, Menuhin,' it read. But it finished with a valid point. 'In a first concert appearance with the orchestra, that he should command such response and variety of tone from musicians strange to him was the mark of a maestro on the march to greatness.' Alma Gowdy was plainly a critic who believed in alliteration.

During the summer he ventured abroad again, this time only as far as Brussels, however, where he conducted the Residentie Orchestra at the World's Fair. Soon he was to be seen in Germany as well, directing the Bavarian Radio Symphony Orchestra in Munich and, courtesy of his old mentor Ferdinand Leitner, the Württemberg Staatstheater Symphony Orchestra in Stuttgart.

The season that began in the autumn of 1958 saw Haitink reinforcing his contact with the Concertgebouw Orchestra, both at home and overseas. On 29 and 30 October in Amsterdam he conducted Three Dances from *The Bartered Bride* by Smetana, the Viola Concerto by Bartók, with Klaas Boon – the orchestra's principal – as soloist, and Tchaikovsky's Fifth Symphony. For the concert in The Hague on 1 November he replaced the Bartók with Bruch's First Violin Concerto, in which Sylvia Rosenberg played the solo part. Later, still with bits of *The Bartered Bride* opening the evening, he was back in the hall for Haydn's Symphony No.99 and the third concerto of the week: Beethoven's for violin, this time, with Jacob Krachmalnick. In September he had conducted his own orchestra, the Radio Philharmonic, there in the Piano Concerto K.453 by Mozart (with Ingrid Haebler) and Bruckner's Fourth Symphony; his first chance to present in public a work to which he felt increasingly close.

Haitink's experience as a concerto accompanist was growing with each engagement. With him and the Concertgebouw at home Bram de Wilde performed Weber's First Clarinet Concerto on 5 January 1959, and on 18 March the orchestra's principal cellist, Tibor de Machula, played Ernest Bloch's *Schelomo*. Dvořák's Seventh Symphony (in those days labelled No.2) was also added to his repertoire.

In May 1959 the Concertgebouw entrusted him with a touring date abroad for the first time. That spring van Beinum was to appear in Britain, directing his Dutch orchestra in the provinces as well as at the Royal Festival Hall in London. However, he ceded one engagement to his younger colleague, and so Bernard Haitink made his English début on 5 May at 7.15 pm in Huddersfield Town Hall. The programme was similar to the one he had given in Amsterdam in January. It opened with Haydn's Symphony No.99, finished with Dvořák's Seventh, and in the middle was placed Stravinsky's *Firebird* Suite, a piece that orchestras love to take on tour to show off their prowess. For Haitink the experience was a memorable one and it marked an association with the North of England which was to be cemented further before he made his first appearance in London.

Once back in the Netherlands, he went with the Concertgebouw Orchestra on some of its out-of-town duties, conducting Richard Strauss's *Don Juan* and Brahms's Second Symphony in Eindhoven in early June. A month later the Second Symphony joined the Bruckner works on his list when he performed it in Leiden and, two evenings afterwards, in Amsterdam; on the latter occasion as part of the Holland Festival. In the first half was Handel's Utrecht *Te Deum*, with the young Elly Ameling as soprano soloist.

The death in April of Eduard van Beinum had left the orchestra without an official conductor. While his death was not unexpected, it was sudden. His medical condition had been no worse than in previous years and, even though his health had been a matter of concern, somehow the players and administrators had become used to the idea. Consequently, when he died they were little better prepared than they would have been had van Beinum never been ill. The problem of choosing a successor was a considerable one. Van Beinum had clearly been grooming Haitink for the post, and he had obligingly turned down approaches from, among others, the Minneapolis Symphony and Rotterdam Philharmonic Orchestras. His period at Netherlands Radio was generally agreed to have been a success and he was slowly beginning to make his presence felt outside his country and, indeed, continent. However, within the Concertgebouw there were many people who had reservations about appointing him to the conductorship. His talent was recognised and accepted, but the Concertgebouw Orchestra is a conservative body by nature and was, at that time, a somewhat elderly one too. The idea of appointing a man who had only just turned thirty was not one that came naturally. The fact that van Beinum himself had been a similar age when he became Mengelberg's deputy was conveniently put aside. For those players van Beinum had been a mature conductor, at home with and master of the great classics, and as yet Haitink simply was not. Against that was the argument that the orchestras had always had a Dutch conductor and there was no one other than Haitink with comparable abilities. His five-week spell with the orchestra that season had made him one of its most frequent and regular guests.

The deliberations continued during the summer and autumn of 1959. In the meantime, Haitink fulfilled the rest of his engagements for the season and continued his work with the radio station. Then, in September, he returned to the Concertgebouw for an occasion which was to be the start of a familiar routine over the following years: his first session for Philips Records. The company was only a few years old and in 1954 had wrested from Decca the right to record the orchestra. It was sensible, therefore, to add to its artists' list the man who was now regarded as the most promising Dutch musician of his generation. Haitink was also, of course, no stranger to the microphone, since most of his work with the radio orchestras had been done under studio conditions.

The first disc to be recorded was of the work he had brought to Huddersfield the previous May, Dvořák's Seventh (second) Symphony. To this were added four of the Slavonic Dances Op.46 (Nos. 1, 3, 7 and 8). The producer on that occasion – and on virtually all others with Haitink over the ensuing decade – was Jaap van Ginneken. A dozen years later he wrote about the first day's work:

> A young man came into our control room . . . He told me he would leave it entirely up to me how to proceed. His behaviour seemed almost carefree. He trusted himself and everybody. There were no real problems during his first session – any more than there had been with his first concerts. Everything was right; there was hard work but no perfectionism. The result was good music.

Van Ginneken went on to point out the qualities that, over the years, had consolidated Haitink's ability to command respect.

> He is exactly the same man and the same musician who plants his feet stably on the rostrum; who never loses contact with the reality of orchestra members as flesh-and-blood people struggling with stubborn instruments. He is still the same creative but patient craftsman.

The session was to be the first of hundreds, so that Bernard Haitink now has one of the longest discographies of all musicians throughout the world.

The 1959–60 season was one of transition. Whatever was to be the result of the Concertgebouw's search for a new conductor, Haitink was still principal of the Netherlands Radio Philharmonic Orchestra and his guest engagements for the year were numerous enough to confirm his status as an artist of truly international calibre. There were dates in Lisbon and Paris (with the Pasdeloup Orchestra), with the symphony orchestra in San Francisco and the radio orchestra in Berlin.

Haitink spent January 1960 with the Concertgebouw, in both Amsterdam and The Hague. He accompanied Yehudi Menuhin in violin concertos by Bartók and Brahms, and – an indication of the catholicity of his taste at the time (or perhaps that of Marius Flothuis who, as Artistic Director, was the main guiding force behind the programming) – Strauss's *Don Juan*, Mozart's Linz Symphony and Lutoslawski's Concerto for Orchestra were also included. In February he added Ravel's *Daphnis et Chloé* Suite No.2 to his list, which was to become something of a staple piece over the following seasons, and performed Rachmaninov's Second Piano Concerto with Daniel Wayenberg, who was also often to be found on the programmes at that time.

In March the Concertgebouw Orchestra finally announced its decision to appoint Haitink Conductor. However, it also decided to withhold complete control and to pacify the less adventurous contingent on the board by asking him to share the post with the German conductor Eugen Jochum. This, it was felt, would maintain the balance between experiment and innovation. Jochum, nearly thirty years older than Haitink, had first come to the orchestra during the wartime occupation – indeed, he had been one of the first artists Haitink had seen when he attended concerts as a boy – and he was one of the few people who had appeared in Amsterdam at that time with whom the orchestra still felt comfortable.

Just as had been predicted, the appointment of Haitink in any capacity caused some raised eyebrows in the Dutch musical establishment. The press release issued by Philips on 18 March reflected this by stressing the 'combination of youth and vast experience' and the fact that the orchestra's previous conductors had also taken up the post at a similar age. The General Manager of the orchestra, Piet Heuwekemeijer, was quoted as saying that the appointment was one with which van Beinum would have fully agreed and pointed out, as corroboratory evidence, that he had delegated one of his Los Angeles concerts to Haitink.

Haitink himself had been fully aware of the likely reaction and was not sure that the criticism was not right. 'Many of the concerts I should never have done,' he has said, 'but they were looking for a youthful conductor and a new approach. I think I was very immature. I managed all the work, but I don't think I really knew what I was doing.' However, the prospect of having a stable base in the concert hall from which to work with a band of players steadily, after several seasons in which most of his appearances around the world were as an infrequent guest, was one he could hardly resist, especially when the orchestra was the most prestigious in the country. He was equally aware of the disadvantages of staying too long as the conductor of the radio orchestras, happy as he was in Hilversum. 'I think the danger is that you perform so much music that you never really get inside any of it. I did an enormous amount of repertoire without ever being able to settle down. I am sure if I had stayed with the radio orchestras I would have stayed a mediocre conductor. I would not have had the chance to develop.'

Although the appointments were announced in March 1960, neither Haitink nor Jochum was able to take up the post until the autumn of 1961. During the intervening eighteen months, however, they shared much of the work in any case, while the orchestra made up the rest of its programmes from a roster of guest conductors that amounted to fourteen different names – 'horribly many', as Marius Flothuis recalls.

In the meantime, Haitink was still under contract to Netherlands Radio, but he did embark on several more recordings for Philips. In May he recorded five works: Violin Concertos by Tchaikovsky and Mendelssohn, together with Beethoven's Violin Romances, with Arthur Grumiaux as soloist; Mendelssohn's *Hebrides* Overture ('Fingal's Cave'); and one of the very few Dutch works, surprisingly, that he has preserved for that country's largest record company, the *Symphonic Etude* by Hendrik Andriessen.

Over the succeeding seasons Haitink was to perform a considerable amount of Dutch music in the concert hall, however; especially by those composers active in the 1920s, a period which marked something of a renaissance for music in the Netherlands after almost three centuries of undistinguished obscurity. In the 1959–60 season he included the *Hymne du grand Meaulnes* by Rudolf Escher and Music for Sophocles' *Electra* by Alphons Diepenbrock, which formed the second half of his Holland Festival concert on 30 June.

When the 1950s began Bernard Haitink had been disenchantedly square-bashing as a conscripted member of the Dutch army. Even when he was able to resume his musical training, the likely outcome seemed to be that he would either spend his life in the lower ranks of the orchestra (a fate little different from that of the lower ranks of Her Majesty's forces!) or be driven into a less than thrilling occupation teaching the violin. Only he took his ambition to be a conductor seriously. In the end it was probably because he was so obviously serious about that – and so dismissive of any other path into which more cautious members of his family or his tutors tried to steer him – that persuaded Felix Hupka and Ferdinand Leitner (figures of musical distinction not inclined to encourage day-dreaming and whimsy among their students) to allow this small, baby-faced and excruciatingly retiring young man to take his chance. In most instances where a musician comes to the fore at an unusually early age, the one quality which stands out is confidence in his or her own ability. Yet, for Haitink, standing in front of an orchestra – even suggesting a piece of music that he would like to conduct – was initially a torturing ordeal. His strength came from the knowledge that the only thing that mattered for him was the expression of music, and his only satisfactory method of achieving that was as a conductor. It was not his ability in which Bernard Haitink had faith as a student, but his need to find that ability. It was others, notably Leitner and his colleagues at Netherlands Radio, later Eduard van Beinum and Marius Flothuis, who realised not only that he was capable of conducting but that he had both the determination to achieve technical excellence and the musical insight to become an artist of whom Holland had great need. By the time the 1950s ended Haitink was Principal Conductor of the Netherlands Radio Philharmonic Orchestra – and had been for three years – Joint Conductor Designate of the Concertgebouw Orchestra, and a welcome guest in cities as far apart as Leiden and Los Angeles. Not only could he now afford to take his ambitions seriously, he had convinced much of Europe and America.

III
Control at the Concertgebouw

WHILE NEITHER EUGEN Jochum nor Bernard Haitink was officially in control at the Concertgebouw until the autumn of 1961, the vacuum caused by the orchestra's lack of a conductor had to be filled, and in the event both men found themselves filling the role, graced with the inaccurate but euphemistically convenient title Permanent Conductor. Haitink, still running the music at Netherlands Radio, in theory now had responsibility for five orchestras as well as a burgeoning catalogue of guest engagements at home and abroad. For the sort of young conductor whose chief aim is to be seen at as many airports and in front of as many different groups as possible, it would have been a glorious situation. For Haitink, never a man to rush and who values the patient development of understanding between musicians that comes above all from consistent contact, it was a less than satisfactory arrangement.

The season in Amsterdam had one overriding objective: to prepare a programme for a major tour of the United States in the spring of 1961 which would be directed by both incoming conductors. Although Haitink's occasional appearances, especially on the West Coast, meant that he was by no means unknown in America, this would be his first transatlantic tour with a European orchestra. His second concert of the season marked another point in his relationship with the Concertgebouw, when he conducted Mahler's Fifth Symphony for the first time with them (on 28 and 29 September 1960 in Amsterdam and 1 and 2 October in The Hague). In the first half Nathan Milstein, Horowitz's childhood travelling companion, played the Dvořák Violin Concerto.

For the first concert of the autumn (on 17 September) he included two of the pieces to be taken on tour: the Dance Suite by Bartók (which he recorded, together with the Concerto for Orchestra, the same month) and Stravinsky's *Firebird* Suite. He finished his 8 October concert with *The Rite of Spring*, now firmly in his mainstream repertoire. More concerts followed in February and March which continued the preparatory work. Dvořák's Seventh (second) Symphony, already recorded eighteen months before, was brought back, and the most unusual piece to be packed, the Second Symphony (*Piccola sinfonia*) by Léon Orthel, was played. Born in 1905, Orthel was

35

Professor of Composition at the Amsterdam Conservatory from 1949 until 1971 and his second symphony, written in 1940, was a useful example of Dutch work for Haitink and Flothuis to include. It contains sixteen minutes of accessible music which fitted quite happily into any spot on the programme.

Although touring puts a considerable strain on players, managers and conductors, it is an invaluable exercise, for not only does it enable an orchestra to reach out to a public that would never normally be able to hear it live, it also gives the players the chance to compare their style and standard with a fresh and different set of musicians in the local orchestras. A successful tour can lift morale and exhilarate an orchestra more effectively than any number of favourable reviews and standing ovations at home.

For its first tour of the 1960s the Concertgebouw Orchestra left Amsterdam at the beginning of April. Most of the concerts were due to be conducted by Jochum – no doubt regarded as the more 'bankable' of the pair because of his seniority and reputation in the classics. Haitink, however, had the opportunity to make his débuts in Washington DC and New York, as well as taking on a large proportion of the dates in the Midwest and South. Constitution Hall was the venue for his Washington concert on 10 April 1961. The programme played to his strengths. In the first half was Mendelssohn's *Hebrides* Overture, Beethoven's Eighth Symphony and the Prelude and 'Liebestod' from *Tristan und Isolde* by Wagner. After the interval came the Orthel Second Symphony and Ravel's Suite No.2 from *Daphnis et Chloé*. The same collection was used to demonstrate his skills in Carnegie Hall, New York, five nights later.

After that the orchestral train moved off again. At Bucknell University in Lewisburg, Pennsylvania, on 20 April Haitink delivered the Overture to *Oberon* by Weber, Dvořák's Seventh Symphony, Stravinsky's *Firebird* Suite and the Ravel once more. Eight days later he was in Grand Rapids, Michigan, with the same assortment except that the Stravinsky was replaced by the Orthel. For the next month the orchestra trekked round the continent. Haitink found himself giving concerts in places he had hardly known existed a few weeks earlier. Much the same programme was played in Ruston, Louisiana, and Shreveport in the same state; in Louisville and Lexington, Kentucky, and some better-known centres: Houston (13 May), Dallas (15 May), Phoenix, Arizona (20 May), and finally Long Beach, California, on 27 May. Within a month of his return Haitink had to conduct an all-Dutch programme in Amsterdam of music by Diepenbrock, Willem Pijper, Kees van

Baaren, Jan van Gilse and Guillaume Landré. It was not a schedule for an old man!

At the end of the season Haitink finished his contract with Netherlands Radio. Whatever his feelings about having been thrown in at the deep end, there is no doubt that his time with the NRPO was of immense use. Apart from the scope for developing repertoire and technique, it provided him with the only opportunity that he has so far had to direct a choir and a chamber orchestra on a regular basis. By the summer of 1961 he had spent eight years with the Radio Philharmonic: one as a player, one as Assistant Conductor, two as Permanent Conductor and four as Principal. He had climbed through the ranks, though at rather more mercurial speed than was quite comfortable.

Although the job description of his new post with the Concertgebouw was very similar, the role was actually a far more searching one. While in theory the duties were to be shared with Eugen Jochum, on the insistence of the orchestra's artistic committee which felt that it would be wrong to burden such a young director with total responsibility for the orchestra's affairs, much of the real work was left to Haitink. Jochum preferred to confine his duties to conducting the limited repertoire of great classics which was his speciality, while his younger colleague shouldered the tasks of auditioning new players, day-to-day orchestral training, and conducting Dutch music and the more unusual or un-German programmes.

For the thirty-two-year-old Haitink the greatest asset of, but also the greatest obstacle to, his relationship with the orchestra was its magnificent tradition. It had been – and is still – the pinnacle of Netherlands musical life, drawing its pedigree from a history of stability and excellence dating back to 1888. In April of that year the Concertgebouw opened its doors for the first time, a sober grey building, classical and unfussy by the standards of the period, set on wooden piles standing on isolated polder land on the south side of the city a mile or so from the centre. At the first concert an orchestra and choir of seven hundred was conducted by Henri Viotta who, despite his Franco-Italian name, was from Amsterdam. He conducted the Wagner Society, and went on to found the Residentie Orchestra in The Hague in 1903. Seven months after the opening, on 3 November 1888, the Concertgebouw Orchestra gave its first performance as an established ensemble. The conductor was the thirty-two-year-old Willem Kes, formerly the director of music in his home town, Dordrecht. Kes soon impressed and irritated his patrons by his firm discipline, aimed as much at the audiences as at the players. His rehearsals soon became renowned for his attention to detail and ensemble, while the concerts became more serious musical events than Amsterdam had ever known before. Until his arrival it had been customary to chat, take refreshments and treat the music purely as background entertainment to a social occasion. Listeners wandered in whenever they wanted, whether the music was playing or not. Kes forbade such behaviour, refusing latecomers admission, confining eating to the interval and bringing the performance to a halt if there was unwarranted noise in the auditorium. The result was that the Concertgebouw had one of the best-trained orchestras and audiences in Europe.

Kes stayed with the orchestra for seven years, leaving in 1895 to take over the Scottish Orchestra (now the Scottish National). He remained there only two seasons before moving to still colder quarters as conductor of the Moscow Philharmonic Society. His successor in Amsterdam was even younger. At twenty-four Willem Mengelberg was, if anything, even more ambitious in his determination to foster new music. Kes had championed Chabrier and Tchaikovsky; Mengelberg introduced the audience to Richard Strauss, who conducted the first performance of his tone poem *Tod und Verklärung*, and Mahler, who came to conduct his own First and Fourth Symphonies. Mengelberg also took the orchestra on tour for the first time, travelling to the Bergen Festival in 1898 at the invitation of Grieg, who had been so impressed the year before when he had heard it in Amsterdam that he himself had shouted for an encore. Composers continued to be frequent guests throughout Mengelberg's tenure up until the Second World War, and his taste did not confine itself to the late-romantic tradition. Stravinsky, Hindemith and Milhaud all appeared at one time or another. Holland had for the most part been bypassed by the ravages of the First World War and so the orchestra was in an enviable position to retain its standards unhindered during the first third of the century. With the Second World War and Mengelberg's gradual departure, the Concertgebouw began to lose its unrivalled position. Van Beinum was a loyal and popular musician, whose quiet integrity commanded respect and affection. His philosophy was to interfere as little as possible with either the score or the players – an admirable approach but one which assumed that the orchestra was always at its peak.

The Concertgebouw Orchestra which Haitink took over was very different from the one left to van Beinum by Mengelberg, although, paradoxically, a significant proportion of the players was the same.

This was part of the problem. The average age of the players was around fifty and, while morale was high, virtuosity and discipline had been replaced by middle-aged complacency. Training had not in any case been van Beinum's strongest area, though he himself had believed that nobody else was able to handle the orchestra properly. Because of this George Szell, who had taken on much of the work as a guest conductor during van Beinum's years of ill health, found it hard to achieve the sort of results that he was accustomed to in Cleveland, where the clarity and unanimity of the string playing had become famous under his leadership.

Haitink's first years as conductor were less than easy in consequence. The orchestra was used to and enjoyed working with him and other young conductors as guests, but as the boss his authority needed to be established. The initial attitude among the older players was a mixture of condescension and paternalism, neither conducive to a radical rejuvenation of musical standards. Haitink, conscious of the fragility of his own position, did not always react with complete tact. There were occasions when, in order to assert his pre-eminence, he was harsher than was really diplomatic. From the beginning there was an anti-Haitink faction. But, as Marius Flothuis pointed out, there was also an anti-Jochum faction, so he was not noticeably less favoured than anyone else. Matters did improve, however, and a new pension scheme, with compulsory retirement at sixty-five, gradually redressed the age balance in favour of the younger players.

The orchestra is lucky to have as its home one of the acoustically warmest halls in the world, and Haitink set about using it more effectively as the basis for the orchestra's sound. The usual practice of doubling the wind section to give extra richness to the romantic repertoire was discontinued in favour of a cleaner, better-defined sonority. Haitink is one of the few mainstream conductors who believe that doubling is never necessary. In the Concertgebouw, of all halls, he feels, it only clouds and blurs the texture. He worked hard, too, with the strings, aiming for greater purity of ensemble without losing the glow that gives the orchestra such a characteristic sound, especially in German music of the nineteenth century. During their three years in harness, it was Jochum who took charge of most Beethoven, Brahms and Bruckner performances and, of the two conductors, drew the fuller sound from the players. Haitink concentrated on the precision and accuracy necessary in new music, the French repertoire and lighter-textured works such as those of Dvořák and Mendelssohn.

The fact that he was comparatively young for the job was a matter for comment not only from the orchestra but from the subscribers and

critics as well. Despite its liberal image and reputation as a cosmopolitan city, Amsterdam is a relatively small town with a deep sense of
conservatism and a rigid social code. Haitink had been born in the city
and was seen as belonging to it, but because of this the audiences of
lawyers, civil servants and city worthies that still make up the list of
Thursday-evening subscribers (among whom seats are passed from
father to son with pompous solemnity as family heirlooms) were
inclined to regard their youthful compatriot as a patronised and
indulged investment for the future, not entirely ready to be their
musical guide.

However glamorous and impetuous the public considered Haitink
to be, his life in the autumn of 1961, when he began his tenure, was a
model of suburban Dutch propriety. He lived in a comfortable modern
house at Laren, just outside Amsterdam in the Gooiland, or garden
district, with his wife, daughter Marianne (by then aged four) and the
dog. In December a second daughter, Ingrid, was born. Marianne's
main memories of the time are of sounds emanating from the large
music room, her mother leaving to go to concerts and her father
returning to eat at odd hours near midnight. Haitink's mother still
lived in the house in Vinkeleskade, as she was to do until her death, but
he had little contact with the rest of the family – there was more than a
hint of truth in his uncle's comment that if the family wanted to know
what he was doing it was best to read the newspapers. However, the
solid order of his domestic scene (if a home with two children under
five can ever be called orderly) was a good base from which to
approach his new responsibilities and provided a far less frenetic
background to his personal affairs than most young conductors of
international status achieve. Bernard Haitink shields his home life with
considerable determination, making sure that private matters are kept
in a separate compartment from public ones. When this shield fails, or
the sheltered calm that he cherishes is disrupted, his emotions come to
the forefront with a force all the greater for their usual control. The
1960s, though, while he was establishing his position at the Concertgebouw, were in personal terms some of the most settled years of his
life.

The concert that opened his period at the Concertgebouw in 1961
was made up of works that had already been well rehearsed the season
before: Beethoven's Violin Concerto with Steven Staryk, Stravinsky's
Firebird Suite and Ravel's *Daphnis et Chloé* Suite No.2 (given on 18 and
19 September). However, ten days later the programmes shifted to
more challenging territory and he began to serve notice of the sort of
music the subscribers could expect from him over the next three years.

The main feature was a careful balance between the familiar classics and interesting twentieth-century works. The concerts given in late September and early October 1961 give a good picture of the range and diversity of his interests – or at least the areas which he was then prepared to explore – and are worth listing in some detail. On 27 September the evening opened with a Partita by Hans Henkemans, whose work as both composer and piano soloist was a regular feature of the orchestra's seasons. Then Wilhelm Backhaus played Beethoven's Fourth Piano Concerto, and finally came Bartók's Concerto for Orchestra. On 4 and 14 October Haitink combined Frank Martin's Violin Concerto (Jo Juda being the soloist) with Bruckner's Seventh Symphony. On 7 and 8 October violin concertos by Bach and Prokofiev were sandwiched between Mendelssohn's Italian Symphony and Honegger's Third, the *Liturgical*. The Honegger work would be brought back for Haitink's spell with the orchestra the following February.

Perhaps the most adventurous of the concerts, and one which must have sent quivers through the more conservative patrons, was given on 18 and 19 October. Beethoven's Fifth Symphony and the concert aria *Ah, perfido!* (the latter sung by Helga Pilarczyk) were followed by Henze's *Nachtstücke und Arien* and Ravel's *Rapsodie espagnole*. It was a programme that was something of a triumph of planning for Marius Flothuis, the orchestra's Artistic Director, and showed that in Haitink he had found a conductor capable of tackling whatever he believed the audience should hear. Haitink has been described as a 'progressive traditionalist', and indeed Flothuis realised that his preferred repertoire was not to be found among the more outlandish pieces. However, in 1961 Haitink was keen to lift the orchestra out of its rather elderly rut. 'He never was a conductor who was interested in the real avant garde,' says Flothuis, 'but at that time what he knew about repertoire was less than what I knew, so he listened to my suggestions. I had heard *Nachtstücke und Arien* at the ISCM Festival in 1959, and when Haitink said to me in 1960, when we were planning his first season, "I don't mind doing something really crazy", I put it on the programme.' It is not one of Henze's easiest works, and at that time the composer was considered to be in the vanguard of European experimentalists. Nevertheless, most young conductors would hardly have described it as 'really crazy'. For a firmly classical musician like Haitink, however, and even more for the conventional audience in Amsterdam which he served, it was a mark of considerable tolerance and open-mindedness.

Later the same month Haitink and Flothuis showed that they were not oblivious to the other end of the musical spectrum either, when they included Purcell in a programme that also saw repeats of the Henze and Henkemans works. Autumn 1961 was noteworthy, too, for another reason. On Tuesday 31 October Haitink directed an English orchestra for the first time, travelling to the Liverpool Philharmonic Orchestra for an evening that was to be typical of his British concerts: Mozart's Overture to *The Marriage of Figaro*, Beethoven's Violin Concerto with Henryk Szeryng and Bruckner's Seventh Symphony. He returned to Liverpool the following November and was a regular guest there until his contract with the London Philharmonic Society ruled out engagements with other British orchestras.

At home in the Netherlands in the new year, and after Jochum had provided the audience with fare which made fewer demands on its spirit of adventure, Haitink continued with Flothuis's experiments. Two concerts stand out, in both of which *Nostalgies* for tenor and orchestra by Rudolf Escher (celebrating his fiftieth birthday that year) was played. In the first (on 18 February) it was placed between Debussy's *La mer* and Mozart's 'Posthorn' Serenade. In the second the baroque and the contemporary were alternated: a concerto grosso by Pieter Hellendaal (1721–99) preceded the Escher. Afterwards a concerto for harpsichord and fortepiano by C.P.E. Bach led into Lutoslawski's Concerto for Orchestra, an imaginative piece of programming which would now be likely to surface only in the schedules of a radio orchestra and has certainly disappeared from Haitink's list. It is significant – and something of a tribute to Dutch audiences at the time – that the Concertgebouw Orchestra not only played these works in Amsterdam, where the subscribers could be expected to be reasonably sophisticated, but was prepared to take them in similar programmes to much smaller centres. During the course of the winter Haitink toured with them to 's Hertogenbosch, Tilburg, Groningen and Kerkrade, among other places.

Much of the preparation by Haitink and Jochum looked forward to the spring, when the two conductors led the Concertgebouw Orchestra on its first tour of Japan. A short trip to Switzerland preceded it (the main event taking place in Montreux), but Haitink's first concert in the Far East was given on 19 April 1962 in Osaka. Further performances were heard in Shizuoka, Koriyama, Hiroshima and, of course, Tokyo. As on the tour of America the previous year, the works taken reflected Haitink's main areas of enthusiasm. French music was represented by *La mer* and Berlioz's *Carnaval romain* Overture; Germany by Beethoven's Eighth Symphony and Mendelssohn's Italian; the twentieth century by the *Firebird* Suite and Bartók's Concerto for

Orchestra; and Dutch music by Hans Henkemans's Partita.

Two major festival dates loomed for Haitink and the orchestra on their return. On 6 June they took the Mendelssohn and Bartók works to Vienna and were joined by David Oistrakh for Mozart's Violin Concerto K.216; and at the Holland Festival on 21 June works by Diepenbrock, Beethoven and Wolf were heard alongside Mahler's Fourth Symphony. For Haitink his first season as joint conductor of a world-class orchestra had been an eventful one, but that which began in the autumn of 1962 was, if anything, even more so.

At the Concertgebouw the 1962 series started with a straightforward evening of Bach, Berlioz and Beethoven, with the local composer for the orchestra's tour to Japan, Hans Henkemans, joining it in the role of concerto soloist. At the beginning of October, however, Haitink conducted the first two Dutch premières of the season: *Mascherata* by Hendrik Andriessen on 4 October and *Ombres* by Ton de Leeuw (a composer three years older than Haitink himself) on 7 October. That month the concerts were notable for a performance of Mahler's First Symphony, which he had recorded in September (the first of three versions that he has made), and an appearance in which he accompanied Artur Rubinstein in Brahms's Second Piano Concerto.

Even by the autumn of 1962 Haitink's discography for Philips was starting to look impressive. The previous year he had added four Ravel works – *Daphnis et Chloé* Suite No.2, *Pavane pour une infante défunte, Alborada del gracioso* and the *Rapsodie espagnole* – Smetana's *Vltava*, Tchaikovsky's *Capriccio italien* and Stravinsky's *Firebird* Suite. In July he recorded his first Beethoven disc – the Eighth Symphony – and Bruch's First Violin Concerto with Arthur Grumiaux, bringing to four the number of works they had recorded together. But September 1962 saw an extraordinary increase in his studio activity. That month alone, as well as the Mahler First Symphony, he conducted Mussorgsky's *Pictures at an Exhibition*, Dvořák's Fourth Slavonic Dance (to add to the set he had started to make in 1959), Berlioz's Overture *Carnaval romain* and the *Danse macabre* by Saint-Saëns.

At the end of October Haitink returned to the North of England, this time to Manchester, where he conducted the Hallé Orchestra (the oldest established in the country); and there, as in Liverpool, he was asked back in the succeeding season. Strangely, given his popularity with orchestras in Europe and America, he had never conducted in London which, with five first-rate symphony orchestras, was beginning to lay claim to having the richest, certainly the most voluminous, musical life of any capital city. However, this omission was corrected on 6 November 1962 when he faced the London Philharmonic

Orchestra for the first time at the Royal Festival Hall, in those days
standing in solitary splendour amid the wasteland of the South Bank.
It was appropriate that it should be the LPO that brought him to
London, for van Beinum had been its Principal Conductor in the late
1940s, ceding the post to one of Haitink's other important mentors, Sir
Adrian Boult.

The programme that Tuesday night certainly gave the audience
value for money, combining Beethoven's *Coriolan* Overture with
Rachmaninov's longest piano concerto, the Third, and Bruckner's
Third Symphony, by no means his shortest work either. The press the
next morning was generally appreciative, though only the *Daily
Express* allowed itself to indulge in purple prose, with the headline 'A
Romantic Climb up the Golden Mountains'. In the *Daily Telegraph*
Peter Stadlen admired Haitink's understanding of the Amsterdam
Bruckner tradition in his 'deeply considered performance', and *The
Times* (still in 1962 printing its reviews without crediting the writer)
respected him for 'conducting it with the assurance of faith'.

The only less than impressed critic was Neville Cardus, writing in the
Guardian. His review was, as ever, a model of the art but it was not one
to which the conductor's publicity agent would have given pride of
place in the file of clippings.

The concert for a long time offered no challenge to resourceful
musicianship . . . Mr Haitink began the proceedings with a
thoroughly competent if obvious presentation of the *Coriolan*
overture of Beethoven; then, despite Miss Lympany's excellencies,
the music until the interval failed consistently to keep my mind from
wandering, in spite of much loudness.

Now followed a performance of the third symphony of Bruckner,
more or less a strange work here, or anywhere else . . . The 1878
version, revised by Bruckner himself, was played. All the familiar
Bruckner 'fingerprints' could be detected in the performance
conducted by Mr Haitink and played by the LPO – conducted and
played with authority and some devotion, though Bruckner, even
more than Mahler, calls for richer, more plastic string tone than
English orchestras can give . . .

Miss Lympany was technically dexterous but more than a little
forthright with Rachmaninov, especially during the first movement
of the concerto . . . She rattled through the difficult cadenza –
difficult to the fingers – brilliantly, though not suggesting the
reserves of skill which go with the romantic grand manner. Mr
Haitink's handling of the score, too, was rather phlegmatic, the

transitions stark, the shading sometimes abrupt. So in the inter-
mezzo adagio, Miss Lympany's tone was too bright for nostalgia or
allurement of the senses. The finale had exuberance, not to say noise,
without the right broadening of tone at the 'run into the straight'.
Perhaps I am over-critical of Miss Lympany, who is an accomplished pianist. Rachmaninov concertos call for his own aristo-
cratically romantic treatment, or for the bedazzlements of Horowitz,
or the elegance and aroma of Moiseiwitsch at his best, or, in the D
minor concerto, the salon fascinations of Rubinstein – but I am
becoming unpardonably ungallant.

Whatever Cardus's reservations about Moura Lympany and the new
conductor, the LPO was happy enough with its guest to invite him back
the next year.

After Christmas at home in the Netherlands Haitink's second period
of the season at the Concertgebouw began on 9 January. It was a
particularly busy month, with eighteen different works filling ten
concerts. The variety of styles he was called upon to encompass was
once again extraordinary. While he undoubtedly feels that he found
himself conducting 'too many works not often enough' in his first years
with the orchestra, the sheer ingenuity of the programmes was
exhilarating. The audience may have missed the solid familiarity of
Jochum's concerts, but it could not have accused Haitink's of being
dull. The year was greeted with Handel's Music for the Royal
Fireworks, which the orchestra and Haitink were to record in
February, the *Symphony of Psalms* by Stravinsky and Mozart's Mass in
C minor, K.427. Three days later more Mozart (the symphony K.550)
was followed by Kees van Baaren's Variations for Orchestra, a work by
the fifty-six-year-old composer which was scheduled four times that
month. In the concerts at the end of February the Variations formed
part of what must have been one of the strangest programmes Haitink
has ever directed. It began innocuously enough with the Overture to
Bach's First Orchestral Suite and Debussy's *Ibéria*. Then came the van
Baaren work, after which a Dutch jazz group called the Diamond Five
improvised for a while before joining the Concertgebouw Orchestra in
Otto Ketting's (born 1935) Concertino for Symphony Orchestra and
Jazz Quintet.

The rest of the works played were less controversial but perhaps a
little more rewarding: the Brahms Concerto for Violin and Cello
performed with Yehudi Menuhin and Tibor de Machula, for example,
or the performances of the work he had taken to London, Bruckner's
Third Symphony. During February Haitink made his first recording of

a Mendelssohn symphony (No.4). He gave two concerts with the orchestra in May and one, a rather disjointed affair mainly devoted to arias sung by Renato Capecchi, in June. There was no major tour that season, though Haitink found he was busy enough. Apart from recording Dvořák's Eighth Symphony and two more Slavonic Dances (Nos. 2 and 6 – the remaining one, No.5, he did not get round to for another three years), Haitink travelled to Paris to make a disc there for the first time, of violin concertos by Stravinsky and Mozart (K.207) with David Oistrakh and the Lamoureux Orchestra. However, the most important event of the month was the birth of his first son, Willem. Given the increasing demands on his domestic economy, Haitink was at least in the lucky position, unusual for a conductor in his early thirties, of having a salaried position and a sheaf of royalty-earning discs to augment his freelance fees.

Bernard Haitink had heard the Concertgebouw Orchestra play away from Amsterdam for the first time when he had attended the Edinburgh Festival as a student in 1948. Fifteen years later he returned to the Scottish capital, this time in charge himself. He conducted two concerts in the 1963 Festival, programmes as striking in their diversity as those of earlier in the year. On 3 September the first half began with *Mouvements rétrogrades* by Ton de Leeuw. Then came Schumann's Piano Concerto with Eugene Istomin and, after the interval, Mahler's First Symphony; a performance which, *The Times* reported, 'carried immense conviction'. The next night Bartók's Dance Suite, the Stravinsky Violin Concerto (with Isaac Stern) and Brahms's Second Symphony were played.

The third year of Haitink's term as joint conductor was planned to be his most ambitious yet, both in the number of performances and in the scope of the music to be played. It was remarkable for the number of works by Dutch composers and also for the eminence of the soloists who were now being attracted to Amsterdam by the Concertgebouw's rapidly improving reputation. Haitink's records certainly helped (he laid down the Bruckner Third Symphony performance in October), but the main reason was the rejuvenation of the orchestra's sound effected by Jochum and Haitink since they had taken over. The result of having two conductors, both healthy and with strong views, after a period when the principal conductor was ill and too many guests had been employed – none of them in charge long enough to impose any particular style – meant that standards of ensemble, discipline and musicianship had all risen significantly. Fine as the Concertgebouw had always been, there was no doubt that, by the time it returned from Edinburgh, it had moved up a place or two in the world league of orchestras since the beginning of the decade.

The soloists who appeared with Haitink that season included the pianists Emil Gilels, Claudio Arrau, Rudolf Firkušný and Robert Casadesus, the baritone Gérard Souzay and the tenor Hugues Cuénod. Apart from the de Leeuw *Mouvements rétrogrades*, Dutch music that season was represented by works by Willem Pijper (the Piano Concerto, with Henkemans), Anthon van der Horst (the première of *Réflexions sonores*), Jan Felderhof and Henk Badings (his Tenth Symphony). On 5 May 1964 Haitink conducted an all-Dutch programme of music that, apart from Henkemans's Partita, was almost entirely unknown: the première of *Entrata* by Oscar van Hemel (born 1892), Sem Dresden's Second Violin Concerto, Matthijs Vermeulen's First Symphony and the *Nocturnes* by Louis Andriessen, then only twenty-five.

The mainstream programming was dominated by French music, Stravinsky (including his rarely performed cantata *A Sermon, a Narrative and a Prayer*) and an increasing awareness of the classics, which had been, until then, Eugen Jochum's province. Haydn's *The Seasons*, Schubert's Ninth Symphony (the 'Great' C major) and the Second and Fourth Symphonies of Brahms were given. More importantly, Haitink began to record a cycle of the Beethoven piano concertos with Claudio Arrau in April. The Fourth Concerto was recorded that month, with the First and Fifth following in June, the Second and Third having to wait until September.

In February 1964 Haitink cemented his growing reputation on the West Coast of America when he returned to the orchestra that had provided him with his first date on the other side of the Atlantic, the Los Angeles Philharmonic. The programme was not anything out of the ordinary – Mozart's Symphony No.29 (K.201), Tchaikovsky's Violin Concerto with Henryk Szeryng and the *Firebird* Suite – but the reaction of the newspapers was heartening, and gave an indication of the progress Haitink had made since his visit six years before. The *Los Angeles Times* reported on 28 February:

The big surprise of Thursday night's concert . . . in Philharmonic Auditorium was the conducting of Bernard Haitink, which was of major league status . . . He realizes his own strength by emphasizing the composers' individualities. His assurance comes from knowledge and perception, rather than from ego; he assists the music without obtruding on it and without inflicting himself into the picture. He exerts a firm command with a minimum of extraneous motion, and the clarity of his performance attests to an ear that hears everything that is going on in the orchestra. And, with all these sometimes negative virtues, he communicates. Stravinsky's *Firebird* Suite had a stunning performance, the best in a long time.

The *Citizen-News* managed not to sound quite so rhapsodic as its better-known rival, but still came up with a torrent of gushing praise. 'The audience literally stormed the soloist with applause,' the critic enthused. '. . . Haitink and the orchestra gave a splendid account of themselves.' Such notices may not have inspired Haitink to change his outlook on life, but they did no harm and paved the way for his début in March with the Berlin Philharmonic Orchestra, where Claudio Arrau appeared with him.

In the meantime, while Haitink was still in California, his thirty-fifth birthday coincided with the public release of news of a change to his status in Amsterdam. The press release from Philips, in language that would have done credit to the Civil Service, reflected the cautious approach taken in the Netherlands to any alteration in the position of a pillar of the establishment. It read:

> The Management of the Concertgebouw Orchestra have announced today that after a period of two years in which Bernard Haitink and Eugen Jochum have been joint First Conductors of the orchestra, the new contract with Mr Jochum will be framed to accommodate slightly altered conditions. More and more foreign institutions, such as the Berlin Philharmonic Orchestra and the German Opera in Berlin, are now calling on the services of Eugen Jochum. In addition the Management feel the need to place the responsibility for the repertoire, the choice of guest conductors, etc., on one person – Bernard Haitink has been asked to accept these duties. The Management are glad to announce that the above-mentioned decision has been taken with the complete approval of all parties concerned. The relations between Eugen Jochum and the Concertgebouw Orchestra will be continued in such a way that he will act as permanent guest conductor next to Bernard Haitink, in the same way as, in the past, Pierre Monteux, Bruno Walter and Rafael Kubelik have been permanent guest conductors alongside Willem Mengelberg and Eduard van Beinum.

Now with the authority of his position as 'sole First Conductor', Haitink was no longer required to share his enthusiasms with anyone

Family photographs. *Clockwise*: Bernard with his father Willem and sister Laura; aged 7; the young violinist; his parents Anna and Willem in 1952

Bernard Haitink in 1959

America, 1961 *Left to right*: Eugen Jochum, Bernard
Haitink, Marius Flothuis, Piet Heuwekemeijer
(*L. Robert Hafkamp*)

(Philips)
A family group; Marianne was then 2

In May 1969, Haitink was invested with the Order of Orange-Nassau in the Concertgebouw
(Kippa, Amsterdam)

The Concertgebouw Orchestra arriving in America for the 1961 tour, the first tour Haitink conducted abroad. He and Eugen Jochum are in front of the orchestra

(KLM)

else in the matter of repertoire. It is an unwritten rule at the
Concertgebouw that the official conductor directs his choice of works
and the guests then pick from the areas not covered. Although in
practice Haitink maintains that he never blocked repertoire that
other people wanted to conduct, his pre-eminence did mean that he
was able to concentrate far more than before on the mainstream
Austro-German tradition which had previously been to a large
extent the prerogative of Jochum. Although London and Los Angeles
had noticed immediately that Haitink was a natural exponent of
Amsterdam's Mahler and Bruckner tradition, the home audience and
the orchestra had been slower to recognise that potential. And while
the programmes devised by Marius Flothuis had made Haitink's
concerts at the Concertgebouw some of the most interesting that the
orchestra had tackled in years, Haitink's own inclinations towards
the classics had been kept in check. He had been asked to conduct
works which were considered to be 'young man's pieces'; fiery,
modern, and with the emphasis on atmosphere and rhythm rather
than the exploration of symphonic form. With most conductors in
their twenties and thirties this is a sensible approach, since a feeling
for architecture in a work is usually one of the slowest aspects of the
skill to develop. Haitink, however, possessed that sense innately and,
almost from the start of his career, was able to mould the overall shape
of a piece of music so that its directions were clear to the listener even
while the detail was being explored. He had, of course, conducted
many works by Beethoven, Brahms and Mendelssohn with the
orchestra. But his repertoire was far from complete: no Beethoven
Ninth or *Pastoral* Symphonies, for example, or Brahms's Third.
Schumann was almost entirely absent and his experience of Mahler
was only just beginning.

Sole conductorship of the Concertgebouw Orchestra meant that
Haitink was effectively the Netherlands' most senior cultural am-
bassador, and it was in this guise that he travelled with the orchestra in
April 1964 to represent Amsterdam at the celebrations in New York
marking the tercentenary of the city and the opening of the World's
Fair. In fact the trip celebrated two anniversaries: the transition of New
Amsterdam to its present status as New York in 1664, and the
establishment of the first trading-post on Manhattan Island by
Adriaen Block in 1614.

Passing through New York en route to California for his concerts
with the Los Angeles Philharmonic in February, Haitink had prepared
the way for the Concertgebouw's trip by giving an interview to Howard
Klein of the *New York Times*. Klein's article makes intriguing reading a

quarter of a century later, for it gives a particularly detailed description
of Haitink and his opinions at the time, though now he finds them
thoroughly arrogant for a young conductor.

Mr Haitink, a burly, blue-eyed man who at 35 is balding pre-
maturely, was in town briefly before going to Los Angeles to
conduct its Symphony from 25 February to 7 March . . . A bottle of
Scotch, some ice and a few glasses shared the top of the coffee table
with a Mozart symphony score. Mr Haitink, in a brown suit, brown
vest and brown tie, had just finished a phone conversation with his
wife, Marjolein, who had remained in Holland with their three
children (two girls, six and three, and a boy, eight months) and two
dogs (a French poodle and a Labrador) . . .
    Mr Haitink spoke feelingly of his European colleagues. Herbert
von Karajan, the conductor of the Vienna Philharmonic, was the
most exciting one. 'When you hear him do the *Eroica*,' he said, 'you
are electrified. He is a real showman, an extrovert. . . . And his opera
conducting is great, fascinating. His way is not mine, though, nor do
I follow Wilhelm Furtwängler's mystical approach. George Szell
comes closest to my ideal. I don't believe in conducting in front of
mirrors to show how beautifully you are shaping the phrases. I only
study the score so I can, as Dr Szell says, "have the music in my
blood circulation". Then I show the beat clearly and – well,
conduct.'

The interview appeared on 19 April, and his first concert in the
newly opened Philharmonic Hall of the Lincoln Center took place on
24 April. The Dutch work was de Leeuw's *Mouvements rétrogrades*, as
it had been at the Edinburgh Festival the previous September. Also as
in Edinburgh, it finished with Mahler's First Symphony. In between
Daniel Wayenberg was the soloist in Ravel's Piano Concerto in G. The
next night, this time in Carnegie Hall, Haitink conducted the leader of
the orchestra, Herman Krebbers, in the Beethoven Violin Concerto
and followed it with Brahms's Second Symphony. On the Sunday
evening Bruckner's Eighth Symphony was performed, an ambitious
work to mount, for although Bruckner was an immovable part of the
concert tradition in Amsterdam, the New York public regarded his
music as close to impossible.
    On their return from America, Haitink gave two concerts with the
Concertgebouw in May, one entirely of Dutch music, the other entirely
of Beethoven. Then, as part of the 1964 Holland Festival, Haitink gave
a performance which he regards as one of the most important and

memorable of all his concerts in Amsterdam. On 3 and 4 July he shared the task of conducting Britten's *War Requiem* with the composer, Haitink directing the main forces, Benjamin Britten the chamber orchestra. Of particular significance for Haitink was the fact that the soloists – soprano Galina Vishnevskaya, tenor Peter Pears and baritone Dietrich Fischer-Dieskau – were the same as had taken part in the *Requiem*'s first performance, given in the rebuilt Coventry Cathedral as an act of reconciliation in 1962. For Haitink, deeply affected as a boy by the traumatic war years and the period of revenge which followed, the *Requiem* held great meaning. In the event it proved to be his only opportunity to work closely with Britten, but they were performances of which he was proud and which he remembers with a sense of gratitude.

With the return of the Concertgebouw Orchestra from its summer holidays in September 1964, Bernard Haitink started his first complete season as its sole conductor. It began with a mildly peculiar concert on 19 September given to celebrate the 125th anniversary of Netherlands Railways. Pieces by Berlioz, Stravinsky and Mendelssohn were considered appropriate for the gala, together with Peter van Anrooy's *Piet Hein Rapsodie*, which also saw service the following May at another gala, this time to mark Amsterdam Photography Week. No one, it seems, had the nerve to play Honegger's *Pacific 231* for the train birthday!

There was another birthday celebration in October when the Artistic Director, Marius Flothuis, reached fifty. Haitink paid tribute by including Flothuis's *Canti e giuochi* in his second concert of the season. An unstaged performance of Ravel's one-act opera *L'enfant et les sortilèges*, Menuhin playing the Brahms Violin Concerto, and *Antifone* by Hans Werner Henze were the highlights of the rest of the month. In September he had recorded two Haydn symphonies (Nos. 96 and 99) and finished his cycle of Beethoven piano concertos with Arrau. These were followed, before Christmas, by excerpts from Mendelssohn's incidental music to *A Midsummer Night's Dream*, with the appropriately-named Rae Woodland as the soprano soloist, and Haitink's first excursion into Verdi, his overture to *La forza del destino*.

Despite splendid reviews in the English papers for his concert with the London Philharmonic Orchestra in November 1963 – Donald Mitchell, in the *Daily Telegraph*, was 'agreeably reminded of the great days of the London Philharmonic under Beecham' and added, 'Perhaps they will return', while *The Times*'s headline ran 'Conductor

Who Knows His Way' and only the *Guardian*, once again, was sniffy –
Haitink was given no dates with that orchestra in the 1964 season.
Instead he made his first appearances with the BBC Symphony
Orchestra, conducting it in Norwich and then in a broadcast for the old
BBC Home Service on 24 February 1965. A few days later, on 3 March,
the eve of his thirty-sixth birthday, he was in front of it again, this time
at the Royal Festival Hall. Haitink, if he read them at all, must have
had mixed feelings about the reviews littered among the greetings cards
the next morning. Surprisingly, since a fair proportion of his work at
the Concertgebouw that season featured the works of Stravinsky, it
was his interpretation of that composer's *Capriccio* for piano and
orchestra which came in for a measure of disapproval. In the *Financial
Times* Ronald Crichton, who has written some of the most perceptive
criticism of Haitink's British performances over the years, described
Monique Haas's reading of the solo part as

> . . . accomplished but joyless, like an experienced Comédie-
> Française actress handing out an over-familiar Molière role to an
> unresponsive audience. In the orchestra the balance was poor. The
> woodwind could be heard vaguely coruscating; only hints came
> through. Bernard Haitink revealed no conspicuous affinity with the
> music.

He went on, more appreciatively:

> There was no shadow of doubt, on the other hand, about the Dutch
> conductor's affinity with Bruckner, whose Seventh Symphony filled
> the second half of the concert. This was a fine performance. In style it
> came somewhere between the indulgent Brucknerians, who put
> gorgeous sound before formal strength, and the sterner type, such as
> Klemperer, who do the opposite . . . Haitink shaped the symphony
> beautifully and at the same time obtained the most delicately graded
> playing (the BBC strings were in excellent form). It was an unusually
> intimate reading. The big climaxes blazed, but they didn't raise the
> roof. The music seemed suddenly to be full of anticipation of Elgar –
> those chains of falling sevenths in the scherzo . . .

Hugo Cole, writing in the *Guardian*, came up with a comparison
which must have pleased the conductor. Comparing the BBC SO's
pre-war and contemporary sounds, he said of the Brahms *Tragic*
Overture, with which the concert opened, 'Haitink balanced the
interlocking groups as carefully and justly as Boult once did, yet drove

the music on with an impetus that never allowed the thick Brahmsian mixture to curdle.' Only the *Daily Mail* noted his birthday and that he had conducted the massive Bruckner symphony without needing to refer to the score.

Between his recordings in Amsterdam before Christmas and six concerts in the Concertgebouw at the beginning of February (notable for his first performance with the orchestra of Beethoven's Seventh Symphony), Haitink crossed the Atlantic once again. There he conducted several concerts with the Symphony (as they would say in America) in Minneapolis, the orchestra which was the first outside Europe to attempt to appoint him as principal conductor. After his spell working for the BBC he gave a few performances in Belgium before taking the Concertgebouw Orchestra on a short tour of Germany in April. He went there again in June on his own to conduct at the Berlin Festival, and the same month directed the opening gala of the 1965 Holland Festival. This had rather an odd programme, on the face of it something of a stylistic muddle. It began with the première of *Salutation joyeuse*, an occasional piece by Anthon van der Horst; then came Bach's Cantata No.51, with Elly Ameling as the soprano soloist, Schubert's Overture to *The Magic Harp* (not one of his more significant works) and the Suite from *L'Arlésienne* by Bizet. The most unusual date in the schedule for Haitink and the Concertgebouw that year, however – in what had been a season notable for odd dates anyway – occurred on 16 May when they were the star attraction of a Dutch Festival Week at Southend-on-Sea in Essex.

Tours continued into the new season, with a visit to Montreux on 10 September (Beethoven's 'Emperor' Concerto with Artur Rubinstein and Bruckner's Fourth Symphony), followed by concerts in Mannheim and Frankfurt. They all returned to Switzerland at the end of October, this time for a more extensive trip that covered most of the main cities – Geneva, Berne, Zurich and Basle – with another Bruckner symphony, the Ninth, as the main calling-card.

Philips had by then decided that it would be right to record the Concertgebouw Orchestra's performances of all the Bruckner symphonies, in the interpretations of their new conductor, who was plainly being accepted abroad as the most able exponent of the orchestra's traditional repertoire for a generation. The Third had been preserved as early as 1963. In May 1965 the Fourth followed, and in December the Ninth. At the same time, and on rather less reliable evidence of the likely success, it was decided to make the first ever complete recorded cycle of the Mahler symphonies, though this would be an even bigger project and was to be spread over six years. Both were massive undertakings, calling on reserves of musical maturity and, when put together with Haitink's already crowded diary, mental and physical stamina which was, in itself, a challenge.

At thirty-six years of age Haitink, both as an orchestral craftsman and a musical thinker, was probably more appreciated by the public and his record company than by the Dutch critics or the organisation of which he was head. The hint of patronage with which the orchestra had coloured its dealings with him in the first few years had now changed subtly. Those members who had indulged him as an interesting investment now accepted Haitink as the rightful conductor. He was still the local boy made good, though, and was regarded as a youthful talent of whom Amsterdam was quietly proud in a paternal way, while being more than a little aware of his faults (as his elders saw them). Those players who had resented Haitink's appointment were even more set in their dislike now that it was clear that he was well entrenched in his position and, furthermore, seen by the outside world as highly successful. Haitink was becoming tired of being tolerated as a promising juvenile in Holland. The Dutch, as a people, like moderation in all things, including success, and Haitink realised that, if he was to consolidate his authority in his own country, he needed to shake the Amsterdam establishment into wanting his work in a rather more positive way.

At home as a boy Haitink had always been annoyed by the complacent dullness of Dutch life, which he saw as a way of holding everyone to a code of conventional behaviour, stifling excitement and initiative. Success was played down, failure was put to one side, and the most respected level of achievement was that of unhurried mediocrity. He was beginning to sense the same straitjacket at the Concertgebouw. The orchestra liked the fact that, as a result of the considerable rise in standards in the six years that Haitink had been conducting it on a regular basis, it was now seen once again as one of the foremost ensembles in the world. It liked, too, the increase in its number of recordings and the series of successful foreign tours. However, many members were inclined to attribute this success to the natural wonders of the Concertgebouw rather than to the rejuvenated artistic policy associated with its conductor. Haitink, though still young by the standards of his profession, was no longer the shy fledgling who had shuffled into the limelight a decade earlier. He was now an international figure of rising reputation whose abilities were in increasing demand. Much, but not all, the credit for his development could be attributed to the far-sightedness of the Concertgebouw Orchestra in picking him out from the herd in the first place. But he did not need the nannying that he was inclined to receive in the Netherlands. So, when an approach came from the London Philharmonic Orchestra, asking him if he would be interested in succeeding John Pritchard as Principal Conductor and Artistic Adviser, Haitink was determined to accept.

Two cities, two orchestras

THE APPOINTMENT TO the London Philharmonic was announced in March 1966 after protracted and what diplomatic sources describe as 'full and frank' negotiations. Many at the Concertgebouw were horrified that the country's premier orchestra should have to share its conductor with anyone. The idea verged on the unpatriotic. Amsterdam was not only Haitink's home city, they maintained, but the place where his duty lay and where his responsibilites to music should be discharged. The notion that he might find the razzmatazz of the chaotic London music scene attractive was almost inconceivably brash. There were fears, too, that by dividing his loyalties Haitink would be prepared to devote less time to the Concertgebouw, thus making it more reliant on guest conductors and so returning to the unsatisfactory situation that pertained after the death of van Beinum. In that case all the improvements in orchestral discipline and reliability would melt away. Those in the orchestra who disliked Haitink anyway merely had their impression strengthened that he was insufficiently mature and authoritative for an institution as worthy as the Concertgebouw.

The reality of the new arrangement, however, was very different. It was not to be at the Concertgebouw's expense that Haitink's London engagements were to be taken, but at the expense of the rest of the world's orchestras. Instead of subtracting chunks of the time he spent in Amsterdam and transporting those dates to London, he abandoned almost all his guest conducting. The result was that the periods to be spent in London – three weeks in November, three in January and two in March – coincided with the times of the season that he had always been free from commitments in Amsterdam to conduct wheresoever he wished. 'I shall be able to concentrate quietly on my work in Amsterdam and London,' he said at the time. 'I have been guest-conducting for the past seven years in places all over the world. Naturally you gain a tremendous amount of experience in that way, but also the conviction that it can't be kept up for ever. What I have wanted for a long time is a field of activity which gives me just enough to do without all that scramble. The London Philharmonic has provided the opportunity in a very sporting way.' The last remark gives a clue to the truth that the Concertgebouw, once it had accepted that Haitink was determined to take the job in London, won most rounds of the negotiations while the LPO achieved little more than the agreement that Haitink could hold the post it was offering. However, it was agreed that in Britain he would only conduct the LPO, an arrangement that held for over a decade.

Repertoire was another factor in Haitink's decision to take on London. With guest engagements, complete cycles of the Bruckner and Mahler symphonies, and anything between fifty and seventy-five concerts a year with the Concertgebouw Orchestra, he was in danger of becoming swamped with work, leaving too little time to study or assimilate the music that he found most rewarding. This was a problem intensified by Marius Flothuis's belief that Haitink was strongest at that time in the more enterprising areas and he wanted him to be as free as possible from being confined to the standard staples of concert life. Haitink, though, was tiring of conducting the merely interesting and, spurred on by his success in Mahler, wanted to explore the great works of German romanticism. 'I had to fight to do my Beethoven and Brahms,' he said later. 'That was one of the reasons I took the appointment. Amsterdam wasn't very keen on my accepting the post, but I decided I ought to take it. I was right, because it made my life far richer than it would otherwise have been. London is, there is no doubt, a centre of music in a way that Amsterdam will never be.'

Before his tenure in London could begin, however, there were still guest engagements around Europe to be fulfilled. In Germany he conducted in Mülheim and Essen, there was work in Prague, and in August 1966 he appeared at the Lucerne Festival in Switzerland and made his début at the Proms in the Royal Albert Hall. Over the years the Proms have become one of his favourite venues. Haitink is often thought of as an unglamorous conductor who shuns the paraphernalia of showmanship. But at the Proms all his sense of occasion, and often humour, is brought into play so that he has become, rightly, one of the heroes of the Promenaders who throng the red carpet in the summer between the conductor and the fountain.

In June and July 1966 he was to be found as usual at the Holland Festival, though not primarily in his Concertgebouw role. Instead he clambered into the tiny pit at the Stadsschouwburg Theater to make his first foray into the world of Verdi opera, *Don Carlos* – which, one might be forgiven for thinking, is not the easiest place to start. He had conducted only one opera before, another Netherlands Opera production, Mozart's *Don Giovanni*, which had also been the first opera he had seen. However, Haitink was convinced that both attempts were dismal and that he would never be the right conductor for opera. He felt that he 'had no idea of how to convey the dramatic impact of the works', although, since he accepts even now that he finds it difficult to make sense of the music unless he is happy with the production, the relative lack of success may have been as much the producer's fault as his own. Either way, Haitink prefers not to be reminded of the experience and counts as his true operatic début his appearance at Glyndebourne six years later. In the meantime all approaches from German opera companies were turned down with, perhaps, unnecessary firmness. When Haitink was a student, Ferdinand Leitner had wanted to take him to Stuttgart, convinced that one day Haitink would make a better conductor of the operatic repertoire than of the purely orchestral. And Pierre Monteux, attending the *Don Giovanni* performance, had remarked cryptically: 'Thank goodness there's one young conductor who can at least beat!'

Despite the outward impressiveness of his curriculum vitae – conductor of one major orchestra, conductor elect of another and certain of his place in the history of the recording industry – the period that began with the *Don Carlos* performances ('scratch' was how Marius Flothuis described them) and ended with Haitink's first season with the LPO was not an easy one. He was anyway reaching an age which can prove problematic for a conductor; indeed, for many musicians whose career is highly public. At thirty-seven he was too old to be treated as the promising young conductor, yet not old enough to be revered as a master. He was established enough to be regarded as a fair target for criticism and for opposition to consolidate against him, and there were rumbles of discontent from within both the Concertgebouw organisation and the press. Plenty of people still saw Haitink as a jumped-up opportunist, an opinion that was unlikely to be changed by his usually modest and unassuming manner, since that quietness can also translate into a cold aloofness when he finds a person uncongenial. Paradoxically, as was to happen on several later occasions, Haitink's professional problems coincided with a period when his popularity among concert-goers and record buyers in general was steadily increasing. So was his family. In November 1966 his children, Marianne, Ingrid and Willem, were joined by another son, Robert Jan.

The first major crises of his conductorship of the Concertgebouw came to a head in the spring of 1967. Even in London, March had been a less than triumphant month. Two days before his thirty-eighth birthday he had conducted Mahler's Fourth Symphony to a half-empty Royal Festival Hall, and, while receiving praise for that, had been given testy reviews for a lacklustre Mozart performance in the

first half. It was suggested that, however excellent Haitink's interpretation, there was too much Mahler being played in London anyway.
On his return to Amsterdam the row he faced was an internal one. The
Concertgebouw Orchestra's General Manager since just after van
Beinum's death in 1959 had been Piet Heuwekemeijer. While the
orchestra had continued to be run efficiently, his relations with Haitink
had never been as close as Marius Flothuis's. During the season
Heuwekemeijer had put forward a plan that would have changed
radically the character of the orchestra, both artistically and organ-
isationally. His idea was to expand the pool of musicians from which
the orchestra took its membership, giving it a more flexible but also a
more diffuse nature. The move was opposed by Haitink, who feared
that the close contact he had with the players through working with
them on a regular basis would be lost, and by the musicians themselves,
who were worried that their status as full-time members of the
Concertgebouw Orchestra would be diminished by a pooling system.
The orchestral board, which consisted of players, management and
outside directors, voiced its misgivings but Piet Heuwekemeijer
decided to go ahead with the scheme in any case. This was too much for
Haitink. A week before the orchestra was due to leave on its first tour
to the United States for three years and its first to Canada since 1954 (as
part of Expo '67), Haitink announced that he would not be prepared to
conduct if Heuwekemeijer travelled with them. In such circumstances
the board had little choice but to side with the Principal Conductor and
Heuwekemeijer stepped down from his post. It was the sort of
acrimonious dispute that is meat and drink to some, more flamboyant,
artists, but from which Haitink has always shied away. For him such
matters have little to do with his main purpose, the interpretation of
music, and he would rather avoid administration than allow it to
distract him.

The tour went ahead, with a member of the orchestra standing in as
General Manager until a permanent replacement could be found.
Forty-five people applied for the job, but the successful applicant was a
businessman who at that time had no experience at all of the orchestral
world, Dolf van Dantzig. However, he did have an inherent love of
music and great respect for Bernard Haitink, whom he had first seen
when he had taken his eight-year-old daughter to a concert of
Stravinsky's *Firebird* Suite in 1958. Van Dantzig was on Haitink's side
from the moment he met him at the final interview, held in the
conductor's room at the Concertgebouw. He had been so intimidated
by the aggressive questioning of the other members of the board, while
Haitink had remained silent for most of the time, that he was sure he

was not going to be considered further. However, the next morning it was Haitink himself who telephoned to say that he was behind him and that it was almost certain that the appointment would go ahead.

Van Dantzig arrived to find two sources of discontent. On his first day he was visited by the Acting General Manager, now returning to the ranks of the violins from where he had come. It was suggested that Haitink was 'not of the right quality' to lead the Concertgebouw Orchestra and should himself stand down. Van Dantzig was appalled and raised the matter with Marius Flothuis, who was dismissive. There was a perfectly adequate formal procedure, he replied, and if the orchestra wanted a new conductor the members could ask for it. 'Needless to say,' van Dantzig remembers, 'nobody ever asked. The majority would not have thought of throwing him out, but it was not until 1970 that the last "problem" member left.'

The other difficulty van Dantzig faced on his arrival in 1967 was that of the reviews written by the chief critic, H.J.M. Muller, of *De Telegraaf*, the Netherlands' largest newspaper. Muller almost always panned Haitink's concerts and reserved his approval for the other orchestra that shared the hall of the Concertgebouw, the Amsterdam Philharmonic (now amalgamated with the Utrecht Symphony and renamed the Netherlands Philharmonic). A few months after he took over, van Dantzig confronted Muller and asked why he was waging such a relentless campaign against Haitink. His reply was a glorious statement of musical snobbery. 'There are only three possible ways to be a great musician,' Muller said, 'to be a German, a Jew, or both. Haitink is none of these.' The remark was not only insulting, it was, of course, inaccurate, as Haitink's mother could have testified. Shortly afterwards, however, Muller's death brought a change in the critical reaction to Haitink. The more generous notices were also partly a recognition that, with Haitink's appointment in London, Amsterdam musical life had gained a cosmopolitan dimension that it had not had since van Beinum's period with the LPO. Van Beinum had gone on to Los Angeles, but in the 1950s, despite the glamour of Hollywood, Los Angeles was not the booming cultural metropolis that it has become in the last thirty years. Amsterdam, though the nominal capital of the Netherlands, is not the seat of government and so relies heavily on its cultural institutions to provide the atmosphere of a principal city. Haitink's international status was a considerable bonus.

It says much about the English attitude to innovation that, of the five major symphony orchestras based in London, three were founded not out of a philanthropic view of the public good but as the direct consequence of fits of pique, and that those so piqued were, for the most part, plainly in the wrong. The London Symphony came from the first, and most collectively held, fit. In 1904 Henry Wood, tired of finding a different set of players present at morning rehearsal from the one that appeared to play at the evening concert, announced to the Queen's Hall Orchestra – or rather made his manager, Robert Newman, announce – that in future no deputies would be tolerated. Enough players promptly walked out to form the kernel of London's first orchestral co-operative, which employed at the beginning Hans Richter and later Sir Edward Elgar as its conductor.

In 1932 the impetus came from the conductor rather than the players and stemmed from the long-running rivalry between Adrian Boult and Sir Thomas Beecham. Boult was Director of Music at the BBC; Beecham was the country's most charismatic and unpredictable musician. When, in the late 1920s, the BBC declared that it intended to recruit a symphony orchestra, Beecham seemed to many the obvious person to be its conductor. The BBC, however, rightly thought Beecham too mercurial a figure to put up with the quiet discipline of music for radio for very long. In the end, Boult took on the role of conductor as well as the administrative duties of Director of Music. That meant that Beecham, who started more musical enterprises than any other Englishman, was in the paradoxical situation of being the one major conductor in the country without an orchestra he could call his own. So the London Philharmonic Orchestra was born.

Beecham's idiosyncratic ideas of management, which were closer to those of a modern football club or newspaper proprietor than of a principal conductor, together with the dislocations of the war years, eventually brought the partnership to an end. History then, as it tends to do, repeated itself. When Walter Legge decided to form an orchestra to be dedicated to recording, the Philharmonia, Beecham saw himself as the obvious candidate to head it. Once again he was frustrated and once again his creative reaction was to found another orchestra, this time given the even grander-sounding title of the Royal Philharmonic.

Meanwhile, the London Philharmonic survived perfectly well without him under a succession of distinguished conductors. After van Beinum's period it was ironic that the orchestra should have turned to Sir Adrian Boult who, by default, had been responsible for its foundation. When the BBC enforced its policy of compulsory retirement at sixty – plainly an absurd rule when applied to conductors – the LPO was only too pleased to repay the debt and Sir Adrian remained with the orchestra until his death in 1983, becoming President after his time as Principal Conductor. William Steinberg followed and then, in 1962, John Pritchard. Both were solid choices, but Steinberg never really caught the imagination of the London public and Pritchard in his forties had not achieved the reputation that accompanies him today.

The orchestra that Haitink inherited was an improving ensemble, but one which needed an injection of real authority combined with box-office appeal. Its rivals were in strong form. The London Symphony was about to gain the equally young and enthusiastic André Previn; the New Philharmonia (as it was called after being reconstituted as a self-governing body) had Otto Klemperer, and the Royal Philharmonic had Rudolf Kempe, both conductors of towering stature. With Haitink the LPO hoped to climb back up the league. There is fierce competition among the London orchestras – for audiences, grants, recording contracts and the most famous soloists. The reputation as 'the best' is therefore a matter of cash as well as image. The order is always in a state of flux but in 1967 the LPO was not at the top and its morale reflected the fact.

Haitink's first concert as Principal Conductor was given on 8 November 1967 at the Royal Festival Hall. The programme was designed to open his tenure with a flourish of brass and orchestral virtuosity: Berlioz's Overture *Benvenuto Cellini*, Beethoven's Third Piano Concerto with Hans Richter-Haaser, and Bartók's Concerto for Orchestra. The determination and optimism were recognised and appreciated by the reviewers the next morning. 'Music First for Haitink,' announced *The Times*. 'Début with a Ring of Confidence,' said the *Daily Express*. In the *Daily Telegraph* the LPO's Managing Director, Eric Bravington, was quoted as saying: 'This is the fourth or fifth appointment of the kind during my twenty-nine years' association with the orchestra, but I have never known before the enormous enthusiasm and great expectancy there is for this one.'

The Times referred to a remark of Haitink's that 'one of his immediate concerns would be to enrich the string tone'. 'This,' Stanley Sadie pointed out, 'is still to come.' Perhaps the review which best caught the mood was that of Edward Greenfield, who wrote in the *Guardian*:

Some orchestras choose their principal conductors for their magisterial authority, some for their youthful vigour and promise for the future; still others for the mystic rapport they have with the players. The London Philharmonic Orchestra has followed none of these courses. Ever since it started democratically to appoint principal conductors after the war, the players' taste has been very much for great orchestra trainers . . . For its latest appointment the orchestra has followed the same pattern. Bernard Haitink may only be in his thirties still but . . . he has shown how thorough he can be in building up the quality of his band . . . Aptly the work which pointed most hopefully to a bright future was Bartók's Concerto for Orchestra, and never was that much misused title better applied. Every single department of the orchestra has countless opportunities to display its virtuosity, and Haitink ensured that each responded with point and brilliance. Even so it was not a performance based on display for its own sake. I was reminded continually of the first record of the work ever to appear, directed by Haitink's compatriot and mentor, van Beinum, for the straightness and honesty had an undistracting rightness about it while giving full rein to individual expressiveness in the almost continual flow of lyrical solos . . .

Post-Christmas flu laid Haitink low early in the new year, forcing the cancellation of his first London concert of 1968, on 18 January. However, when he recovered and conducted the LPO again on 23 January it was clear that the improvements of the autumn were still progressing. The concert consisted of two of the soundest works in his repertoire, Beethoven's Violin Concerto (with Josef Suk) and Bruckner's Seventh Symphony. The recording that he had made with the Concertgebouw Orchestra in November 1966 had just been released, and inevitably the two ensembles were compared by the critics. The Concertgebouw was famous for the warmth of its string tone – partly generated by the acoustics of the hall itself; the LPO, nurtured in the clinical dryness of the Royal Festival Hall, was thought of as a wind and brass orchestra with a rather thin string sound. This, plainly, was changing, as Andrew Porter noted in the *Financial Times* the next morning when he wrote that Haitink had 'inspired some of the richest playing I have heard from the London Philharmonic for a long time. The strings had uncommon body and fullness.' Haitink found allies for his policy of rejuvenation in his section leaders, particularly the principal cello, the gifted Alexander Cameron, and the leader himself, Rodney Friend, who had taken up the post at the remarkably early age of twenty-four.

The 1967–8 season was one of consolidation for Haitink. There were no major international tours for the Concertgebouw, other than local ones across the border into Belgium and Germany. In Amsterdam the most interesting events were the recording of two Mahler symphonies for the cycle, the Fourth in December 1967 and the Second, the

'Resurrection', in May 1968. In November 1967 Haitink added to his already extensive catalogue of Dvořák when he recorded three works for cello and orchestra with Maurice Gendron and the LPO – the concerto, *Silent Woods* and the Rondo. With the London orchestra the programmes reflected his declared aim to concentrate more on the mainstream classics, though there was also a good sprinkling of Stravinsky. Haitink conducted his first performance in London of Beethoven's Ninth Symphony on 10 March (the soloists being Heather Harper, Anna Reynolds, Alexander Young and Donald Bell) – to general complaints that his tempi were too fast and that, according to *The Times*, he 'seemed to have polished off so many of the rough edges as to erode the rugged strength of the music's utterance'. The two concerts the previous week, in which the main works had been Dvořák's Eighth Symphony and Mahler's Ninth, had gone well, and on his return to London Haitink conducted three programmes that, by his own standards, were glittering. On 9 and 12 May he finished with *The Rite of Spring*, being joined by Claudio Arrau on the latter occasion for both Liszt Piano Concertos. On 9 May Vladimir Ashkenazy had been the soloist in Beethoven's 'Emperor' Concerto, and four days before had played the Schumann in a concert given on behalf of the LPO's appeal fund. This also included the Prelude and 'Liebestod' from *Tristan und Isolde*, Mahler's *Kindertotenlieder* sung by Dietrich Fischer-Dieskau, and Strauss's *Don Juan*.

The next season, that of 1968–9, followed a similar pattern of development; after travelling to Japan with the Concertgebouw, for the second time, in September there were no other major tours with either orchestra, and work was concentrated in the environs of London and Amsterdam. For Haitink this was a particularly valuable period, as it allowed him to work on his repertoire quietly, without having to travel extensively or fit in with the programming requirements of a multiplicity of promoters. When he had signed his initial three-year contract with the LPO, it had been understood that there would be a certain amount of crossover between the seasons of the two orchestras. This had already shown itself in the more regular appearance of Bruckner, Mahler and Stravinsky in Haitink's London programmes – with the attendant growth in the warmth of the LPO's string sound – and Haitink had found the speed with which English musicians learnt in rehearsal an advantage that he would have happily transported back to Holland. Paradoxically, because of the complementary planning, Haitink found that he had more time to include works new to him than he had for several seasons, most notably English music which, as with most musicians based on the Continent, had previously been found as often in his series as a pint of bitter in a French café.

The concerts before Christmas 1968, of which there were only two in London, contained traditional Haitink fare: Mozart, Mahler and Strauss. Those in January, March and May, however, showed a radical change of emphasis. He began, on 16 January 1969, with the first public performance of an overture by Alexander Goehr, *Arden Must Die*, followed by Britten's Violin Concerto (with Rodney Friend, who has made the work something of a speciality) and Walton's *Belshazzar's Feast*. He accompanied Ida Haendel in Elgar's Violin Concerto and, also in March, put together a programme that accurately reflected all aspects of his current enthusiasms: the Symphony No.33, K.319, by Mozart, Bruckner's Mass in E minor and the Fourth Symphony of Vaughan Williams. The Fourth is by far the most spare of Vaughan Williams's symphonies, and one might have thought it odd that Haitink should have started with the most difficult. But he did much the same six weeks later when he launched his interpretation of a composer who was also to increase in importance for him, Shostakovich. Once again Haitink chose the Fourth Symphony, perhaps the most rugged and unashamedly angular of the set.

His first recordings with the London Philharmonic (apart from the Dvořák works with Gendron) also explored what was, for him, peculiar territory. In November 1968 they made discs for Philips of symphonic poems by Liszt. Overall, 1969 proved to be his busiest year ever for recording, with a total of fifteen works. In February came Mahler's Sixth Symphony, in May Bruckner's Second and Brahms's Hungarian Dances, in June Mahler's Ninth and *España* by Chabrier. September was crowded, with the Eighth Symphony of Bruckner and the Fourth of Tchaikovsky, *Háry János* by Kodály, *Peter and the Wolf* by Prokofiev (with Hermann Prey narrating in German) and its perennial coupling in the record catalogues, Britten's *Young Person's Guide to the Orchestra*. Claudio Arrau joined him to record both Brahms Piano Concertos in October, and in November Henryk Szeryng played the Second Violin Concerto by Bartók; the latter being coupled with the Rhapsody No.1. The year's activity in front of the microphone was completed by Mahler's Seventh Symphony in December. In April the first of Haitink's many awards had been announced when, to mark the eightieth anniversary of the Concertgebouw, he was invested with membership of the Royal Order of Orange-Nassau. And in August the LPO promoted him from Artistic Adviser to the more influential post of Artistic Director.

While Haitink was thus active – exploring new ground in London, recording for Philips and forcing the Concertgebouw to recognise his credentials as a conductor of the great standard classics – a row was brewing in Amsterdam which, in view of the sort of programmes he had conducted in the early 1960s, should have been laughable but in fact seriously disrupted the Concertgebouw's season. The affair of the 'Nutcracker Movement' was the single most ludicrous episode of Haitink's period as conductor. It was, in reality, a little local spin-off from the student revolts that had swept Europe the previous year and penetrated into most areas of academic and cultural life. This particular one had not started in Amsterdam at all, but in Tilburg, where the students had objected to what they regarded as the dull and middle-aged programme policy of the Brabant Symphony Orchestra. The Dutch League of Composers had supported their demands and a faction within it argued that the dispute should be broadened to include the policies of all the orchestras in the Netherlands and the Concertgebouw in particular.

A committee meeting of the League took place on 1 November, a Saturday. It was decided that, among other methods of action, the composers would organise the disruption of orchestral concerts of which they disapproved. This put one member of the committee, Marius Flothuis (whose other role was that of the Concertgebouw Orchestra's Artistic Director), in an awkward position. He could hardly be seen to condone the interruption of his own concerts; on the other hand, he was in general agreement with the others that the country's orchestras could do a lot more for contemporary music. He abstained from the vote and next day resigned from the committee, and on the Monday morning he informed the orchestra. The composers had a further demand which affected Haitink more directly, for they wanted him to step down or share his post with the Italian composer Bruno Maderna. Of all their demands this was the least realistic, since Maderna, who had conducted at the Concertgebouw as an occasional guest, was seen by the orchestra as, at best, unreliable and almost impossible to work with over any length of time. Haitink's own opinion of the orchestra's responsibilities was that it had a duty to contemporary music and that such work was essential to the programme but, as he had said in an interview the previous year, 'one must always take care to separate the chaff from the corn . . . we can't turn the Concertgebouw Orchestra into a laboratory. We're doing what we can, more than many other well-known symphony orchestras; more than Bernstein in America and much, much more than the Berliners. But I believe in evolution, not revolution.'

The leaders of the 'Nutcrackers', as they came to be called, were, however, firmly revolutionary in their thinking. All were considerable figures in Dutch musical life. Louis Andriessen, son of Hendrik, the Netherlands' best-known postwar composer, had already heard works of his conducted by Haitink at the Concertgebouw. Reinbert de Leeuw and Peter Schat were both among the more respected experimental composers, and the early-music specialist Frans Brüggen has since become the one most widely known outside the Netherlands. Two weeks after the discussion at the League of Composers, the protests began in earnest. Haitink was conducting a concert of a Quantz Flute Concerto followed by Mahler's Seventh Symphony when demonstrators started to shout and bang from around the hall. The performance duly stopped and the demonstrators demanded to read a manifesto from the platform. The denouement was rather anti-climactic, though, with a suggestion from a member of the audience that Haitink be allowed to continue with the Mahler being accepted, pending negotiations with the Concertgebouw's management. Finally, after much haggling over the appropriate venue, a public discussion was held on 22 April 1970, but, says Marius Flothuis, it resulted in no new initiatives, largely because the 'Nutcracker' group itself was unable to agree in any detail on what it wanted. In the end noises from the gallery, and even the occupation of the orchestra's offices, achieved little more than mild annoyance to the comfortable subscribers. For Haitink, though, it was an ominous way to begin a decade that was to contain a disquieting number of arguments.

Haitink travelled extensively again in the 1969–70 season. He took the Concertgebouw Orchestra to Belgium, Switzerland and Germany, and showed its qualities to his colleagues in Britain. Touring with the LPO for the first time in September and October, Haitink joined the orchestra for the Japanese leg of its trip to the Far East. It had already played in Singapore, Hong Kong, Manila and Seoul under John Pritchard and Jerzy Semkow by the time it arrived in Tokyo on 25 September. Ambitiously the orchestra took seven different programmes, all, with the exception of the one conducted by Semkow, containing British music, by Elgar, Richard Rodney Bennett, Peter Racine Fricker and Sir Arthur Bliss. Haitink's concert in Tokyo on 26 September was attended by the Empress of Japan and was an extraordinary success, with the normally restrained local audience demanding an encore, as Sydney Edwards, the much-respected arts correspondent of the London *Evening Standard*, reported on his return.

Artistically this tour will go down as a triumph in the history of the orchestra. The West spoke to the East in a common language. I wept, literally, at the beauty of the Brahms symphony that first night in Tokyo. I'm sure that some of the Japanese in that audience did too.

Over the following fortnight Haitink conducted the same programme – containing Beethoven's *Egmont* Overture, Bennett's *Aubade* and Bartók's Concerto for Orchestra, as well as the Brahms First Symphony mentioned by Edwards – in Sendai, Nagoya, Hiroshima and Matsuyama, before leaving the orchestra in the charge of Semkow and Pritchard for the last two concerts of the tour in Okayama and Osaka. During his second engagement in Tokyo (on 28 September) he had brought the 'Enigma' Variations and Sibelius's Second Symphony. It was a tour remarkable for the stamina of the LPO, which over the coming years was to set up some impressive mileage records which few of their London rivals could match, and for the absence of any concertos on the schedule, the orchestra relying entirely on its own prowess to draw the audiences.

Haitink rejoined the LPO at the Royal Festival Hall, after a month in Amsterdam, for four concerts at the end of November and the beginning of December. In one of them Janet Baker and Alexander Young were the soloists in Mahler's *Das Lied von der Erde*, and on 1 December, in aid of the LPO's appeal fund, Haitink accompanied Artur Rubinstein in three consecutive piano concertos, by Saint-Saëns, Schumann and Beethoven. For that concert the audience paid between one and five guineas, special gala rates. One looks with envy now at the usual prices for the LPO at London's principal concert hall at the beginning of the 1970s. The top-price stalls cost 30 shillings (£1.50) and ranged downwards: 25s. (£1.25), 17s. (85p), 13s. (65p). The back rows could be occupied for 8s. (40p). This had changed little since Haitink had first conducted the orchestra. The top price had risen considerably but the cheapest seats cost only a few pence more. In 1963 Haitink's interpretation of Schubert's Ninth Symphony could have been heard well for one guinea (£1.05p) or not so well for 7s. 6d. (37p).

In March 1970, again in London, Haitink continued his exploration of English music. He accompanied Leonard Rose in Elgar's Cello Concerto and, after a performance by Vladimir Ashkenazy of Prokofiev's Second Piano Concerto (which the *Daily Telegraph* described as the music of 'a real barbarian'), gave his first account of Holst's masterpiece, *The Planets*, the record of which – made the same month – has become one of his most appreciated.

In his other March concert the main work was Bruckner's Second Symphony, which had joined the rest of the cycle on record the previous May. It was a work which the critics were inclined to treat sceptically as one of the composer's lesser symphonies, but at that performance most were converted, Alan Blyth commenting in *The Times* that Haitink

> made the journey [on one of Bruckner's familiar walks round the countryside] as a committed and loving companion would. The steady flow of its solemn main theme had a breadth of phrasing, an intensity too, that was solid evidence [of] how Haitink had moulded the LPO into a great Bruckner orchestra . . .

The work was also one of the highlights of their concert in New York on 23 April. The sense of occasion in Carnegie Hall was felt by both Haitink and the orchestra, for although he was by now almost a regular, this was the LPO's first appearance on the other side of the Atlantic. Hubert Saal reported in *Newsweek*:

> The musicians, whose average age is thirty-four, played like hungry fighters anxious to make their first engagement count . . . Through-out there was a sense that the enthusiasm and youthful vigor of the orchestra had to be restricted by Haitink to keep it from running away with the symphony.

For Haitink it was an appropriate moment to be presented with the Medal of Honour of the Bruckner Society of America, awarded as much for his recordings of the symphonies with the Concertgebouw Orchestra as for his pioneering work in the concert hall. It meant joining, at the age of forty-one, a list of impressive fellow conductors: Klemperer, Toscanini, Walter, Leinsdorf, Ormandy, Szell, Krips, Barbirolli and Böhm.

Unlike the autumn's tour to the Far East, the concerts in America were all conducted by Haitink himself. There were fourteen between Carnegie Hall, New York, and Charleston, South Carolina. The itinerary covered some of the main cities of the eastern seaboard – Baltimore, Philadelphia and Washington – but, as with his Concert-gebouw tour in 1961, some lesser-known centres as well: Bethlehem and Hershey, Pennsylvania; Athens, Georgia; Durham, Charlotte and Ashville, North Carolina; and Columbia, South Carolina, where the local newspaper became mildly hysterical. Adger Brown declaimed in *The State*:

The British are coming! Welcome news indeed, if by the British one means the London Philharmonic Orchestra, which on Thursday night brought the Columbia Music Festival Season to a triumphant close. Under the baton of Bernard Haitink this ensemble (in the precise sense of the word) gave as faultless a performance as one is ever likely to hear from mortal man!

Praise indeed, but Haitink was past the stage in his career when his brochure required the dubious benefit of hyperbole.

On his return to the Concertgebouw in late May another heavy schedule of recordings awaited him: Brahms's *Tragic* Overture and Third Symphony; Strauss's *Ein Heldenleben*; Tchaikovsky's Sixth Symphony, the 'Pathétique'; and two of Mahler's song cycles with Hermann Prey as the baritone soloist, *Kindertotenlieder* and *Lieder eines fahrenden Gesellen*. He did not remain in Holland for long, though, soon crossing the Atlantic again to conduct at the Blossom Festival, the Cleveland Orchestra's summer home. For Haitink this was an opportunity to revisit the musical base of George Szell, who had been principal guest conductor at the Concertgebouw during van Beinum's last illness in the late 1950s. By 1970 Szell was ill himself but, says Haitink, his influence in Cleveland 'was still paramount'.

'We began by rehearsing *Don Juan*. I thought the playing was so superb, I simply couldn't improve on it. Then we went on to the Bizet Symphony. That was different because it was a work they did not know and I could work with them on that. Then the programme was completed by the *Pictures at an Exhibition*, which again they played marvellously. I returned the following season and I was just as impressed with those players in the Mahler Ninth Symphony.' Haitink found the Cleveland a refreshing change from some of the American orchestras he had conducted which, he said, 'can make a big, fat sound but they are lost when they have to play Mozart or Schubert. In a way, they are still primitive.'

The season that began in the autumn of 1970 was dominated by two people: his fifth child (a third daughter), Tessa, who was born in October, and Mahler. In December Haitink recorded the Fifth Symphony, together with Bruckner's Sixth, in the Concertgebouw. In London that November he had conducted the Third with the LPO at the Royal Festival Hall in a performance that, for many, marked the transition of Haitink from an impressive and sometimes remarkable conductor to a potentially great one. Reviews are not always a sure guide to the reality of a performance, as any musician or, indeed, anyone who has ever reviewed for a daily newspaper knows only too well. Often the pedantry of a critic or an amateurish sub-editor can obscure the balance between subjective impression and honest reporting that the reader requires. Once in a while, however, enough sources are unanimous to lend a measure of reliability to the journalism. The coverage of the concert of 19 November 1970 was one such, with papers as diverse as *The Times*, the *Financial Times* and the *Morning Star* (the journal of the British Communist Party) in agreement. 'If I needed one more proof,' wrote Matthew Quinn in the last, 'that Bernard Haitink was one of the world's greatest conductors, then this concert was conclusive.' In the *Financial Times* Gillian Widdicombe exhausted the index of her thesaurus in the first paragraph.

> Last night's concert was one of those five or six concerts a year that set the critical lexicon of commendatory adjectives into a heady spin. A performance of Mahler's Third Symphony that was great, glorious, magnificent, marvellous, stunning, superb and so on. Or so, perhaps, one might go on to a friend in discussion immediately afterwards. In print the bland repetition looks extravagantly generous; but to say less would be unfair: it was, truly, an exhilarating performance. The Third is the symphony that Haitink does best of all Mahler's; better, perhaps, than all of Bruckner's. It is also, in several ways, the hardest to bring off. The two facts are clearly related, for the exceptional thing about Haitink as a Mahler conductor is his brilliant fidelity to the score; tempo, dynamics, phrasing and all: and only by this can the symphony be made to hold together, to generate taut, emotional excitement all the way through.

In *The Times* Joan Chissell, normally a most reserved writer, was equally enthusiastic:

> . . . never can a conductor have more richly deserved his standing ovation than Bernard Haitink. With the LPO, orchestra and choir (female), plus Norma Procter and the Wandsworth School Boys' Choir, he gave as fine a performance of Mahler's Third Symphony as anyone could ever hope to hear . . . Perhaps the biggest gauge of a conductor's involvement is the way the orchestra responds. These players surpassed themselves in suppleness of phrasing, brilliance of attack, in fact in everything. Their applause for Mr Haitink at the end was proof of their own stimulation and pleasure.

Not surprisingly, it is a performance that Haitink himself remembers with some pride as among the small number that stand out from the thousands he has conducted. It is, perhaps, the one that marks the start of his maturity as a conductor and the peak of his success with the London Philharmonic. When he had begun as that orchestra's conductor four seasons before, it had been near the bottom of the city's league. By now both its attendance figures, averaging around ninety per cent capacity for each series, and the approval of the press indicated that, largely inspired by Haitink, it had climbed to the top. 'I do not take the credit for the rejuvenation,' he says, however. 'I think it was the team that achieved that – and the dedication of all of us. We were all working with the same aim. In London one man cannot achieve miracles – he is simply not there long enough – but together a sensible board and a well-organised administrator with a strong conductor can do things.'

There was further cause for jubilation the following summer when Haitink conducted Mahler's Eighth Symphony, the 'Symphony of a Thousand', in the Concertgebouw. Once again it was a performance that those connected with it regard as a particular triumph, not just for the sense of occasion, but for the musical exhilaration that Haitink engendered. The Concertgebouw Orchestra was, in any case, in an exceptionally positive mood. It had just returned from one of its longest and most far-reaching tours with Haitink: across the United States, then down to Mexico City, Willemstad (the chief town of the Netherlands Antilles) in Curaçao, Caracas in Venezuela, Rio de Janeiro and São Paulo in Brazil and, lastly, Buenos Aires. The atmosphere in Amsterdam on 30 June 1971 was further enhanced by the presentation to Haitink of the Gold Medal of the International Gustav Mahler Society of Vienna. It was the third time that the hall of the Concertgebouw had been used for such a ceremony, since both Eduard van Beinum and Rafael Kubelik had received their medals on the same stage. Just as the performance of the Third Symphony had shown that Haitink was now recognised in London as out of the ordinary, so that of the Eighth in Amsterdam marked his complete acceptance as the Concertgebouw's rightful conductor. It had taken a decade for all sections to be mollified but, for the present, his position was unquestioned. In September 1971 Haitink recorded the 'Symphony of a Thousand' with the same forces as had performed it at the Concertgebouw in June, and put the finishing touches to the cycle with the Adagio from the Tenth Symphony, the only movement from that potentially great work which Mahler had left in anything like a completed condition at his death. The same month Haitink returned to Ravel, for a second time putting his interpretation of the orchestral works on disc (the first had been ten years before). The *Mother Goose* Suite and the two Suites from *Daphnis et Chloé* were followed in December by *Alborada del gracioso*.

So great had been the success in 1970 that the LPO repeated their interpretation of Mahler's Third Symphony the following season on much the same dates (18 and 21 November). Haitink took on considerably more of the Festival Hall concerts than usual that year, conducting thirteen out of a total of thirty. Of the others Georg Solti conducted seven, including a performance of Elgar's First Symphony in February 1972 at which it was announced from the platform that the Prime Minister, Edward Heath, had chosen that evening, with a splendid sense of occasion, to grant Solti British citizenship. From then on he could be known as Sir Georg. Haitink's programmes reflected the orchestra's fresh sense of confidence and adventure. The Britten *War Requiem* was given on 18 January and, two days later, Haitink brought over his two colleagues from Amsterdam, the leader Herman Krebbers and the principal cellist, Tibor de Machula, to be the soloists in Brahms's Concerto for Violin and Cello. British works tackled included Walton's *Improvisations on an Impromptu of Benjamin Britten*, John McCabe's *Notturni ed alba* and (in a somewhat mystical programme with Scriabin's Piano Concerto and *Also sprach Zarathustra* by Strauss) David Bedford's oddly titled, but none the less satisfying, *Star Clusters, Nebulae and Places in Devon*. One concert which the author remembers as being nothing unusual on paper but among the most rewarding in performance included Dvořák's Serenade in E, Beethoven's Second Piano Concerto (with Vladimir Ashkenazy) and the *Pastoral* Symphony, a typical example of Haitink's growing ability to match works on a purely musical basis to build concerts that became more than just the sum of their parts.

By the end of the 1971–2 season Haitink had been in sole control of the Concertgebouw for eight years and of the LPO for five. In that time he had concentrated on them with a determination rare among principal conductors. The result had been a resurgence in both orchestras' prestige at a moment when classical music was becoming more available and more popular throughout the world than ever before. Haitink was to continue to direct them for some considerable time, but he never again devoted quite such a large proportion of his life to the two cities of Amsterdam and London. From the spring of 1972 onwards there was a new element in his career, and the temptation to conduct other great orchestras as a guest would not be denied for much longer.

V
Haitink and twentieth-century music

ALMOST EVERY CONDUCTOR who manages to build a successful career early starts with a reputation for the music of his own age – not necessarily avant-garde or absolutely contemporary music, but certainly that of part of his century. It is assumed that he will be able to 'get away with' the showmanship involved in the more bombastic works of Prokofiev and Bartók, be able to warm the audience with the impressionistic colours of Ravel and de Falla, and convince the listener that nothing is missing from less familiar pieces long before the classics can be gauged and understood. Orchestral managers are not suggesting that it is any easier to conduct Stravinsky than Schumann, only that the audience is less likely to be pernickety about the details of interpretation when listening to works that seem to involve more attention to colour and rhythm than to form. A mature conductor realises, of course, that the arts of transition and shape are every bit as important in a Rachmaninov piano concerto or Bartók's Concerto for Orchestra as in a Brahms symphony. But the noisier, flashier world of the twentieth century, with its emphasis on instrumental texture and orchestral virtuosity, has made it the province of the young conductor.

During his first years at the Concertgebouw and with the Netherlands Radio Philharmonic Orchestra Haitink was saddled for the most part with young man's music. When he did venture into the classics, it was either for symphonies by Mendelssohn or Dvořák, or to accompany a concerto. He had performed the Beethoven Violin Concerto over a dozen times, for example, before he ever conducted the *Pastoral* Symphony in public. Instead his repertoire was built around the works of Ravel, Debussy, Stravinsky and Bartók. Among them were the many works of his own countrymen, which it was the Concertgebouw Orchestra's duty to perform, and Netherlands Radio to broadcast, yet which neither organisation wished to entrust to a conductor of great experience. Haitink's mainstays, performed all over Europe and America in the late 1950s and early 1960s, were the Bartók Dance Suite, Ravel's *Daphnis et Chloé* and works by Hans Henkemans,

74

Ton de Leeuw and Léon Orthel. Since, to a young conductor, all music is new music in the sense that it has to be learnt and mastered for the first time, the work involved in coming to grips with such a variety of styles and idioms was almost defeating. Yet, despite his assertion, often repeated, that he was asked to do far too many works, not often enough to give any satisfaction, he recognises that the glut was a necessary part of his development; that in order to be able to discover the aspects of his art that needed to be refined and polished it was necessary to sample as broad a range as possible. He remains sorrier for the audiences who sat through his early attempts than he does for undertaking them.

Because of this need to conduct everything that was thrown at him early on, Haitink's repertoire has narrowed over the years. He conducts far less contemporary music, and works by Bartók, Kodály, Henze and Lutoslawski rarely appear in his programmes. However, he is not so completely confined to Mahler, Bruckner, Beethoven and Brahms as his reputation would suggest. There are works and composers of this century who have never disappeared or even lapsed from his consciousness. Stravinsky, Ravel and Debussy especially have not only held their places but have influenced his approach to other music, providing a cross-fertilisation which has produced a blend of clarity and romanticism in his favoured sound that is individual and increasingly identifiable.

Stravinsky in particular has been a constant thread. When Haitink first conducted *The Rake's Progress* at Glyndebourne in 1975, several people expressed surprise, since he was not seen as a Stravinsky specialist. In fact the impression could hardly have been more misleading. Since his first performance of *The Rite of Spring* in 1956 persuaded the NRPO that he was a capable conductor, up to and after his recording of a semi-staged reading of *Oedipus Rex* for television with the Concertgebouw in 1985, there has hardly been a season when Stravinsky has not formed a prominent part of his orchestral planning.

At the start of his career the emphasis was, perhaps not surprisingly, on the three great ballets from before the First World War, *The Firebird, The Rite of Spring* and *Petrushka*. Once Haitink was properly in charge at the Concertgebouw, however, less obvious works began to be programmed, among them *Orpheus, Threni, A Sermon, a Narrative and a Prayer*, the *Symphony of Psalms* and the Violin Concerto. The last was often heard and Haitink collaborated on it with both David Oistrakh and Henryk Szeryng. In Britain the *Capriccio* for piano and orchestra opened his 1965 concert with the BBC Symphony Orchestra, and at the LPO, which was far less receptive to the more obscure pieces, he managed to continue performing Stravinsky's music on a regular basis.

In London the counterpart to his activity on behalf of Dutch music was the programming of several new works by contemporary British composers; Nicholas Maw, Malcolm Arnold, Alexander Goehr and Iain Hamilton among them. Perhaps more significantly, he was attracted considerably to the ethereal sound-world of György Ligeti. This was as far as Haitink's taste advanced, though he has ventured to conduct Luciano Berio's music once or twice; even then, he has agreed, not because he was necessarily convinced, but because he accepted the reasoning that it was his duty as Artistic Director or Principal Conductor to perform works by living composers. Paradoxically, as his mainstream repertoire has narrowed in the 1980s, so he has begun to look at the question afresh, and now intends to begin commissioning works in his own right, something which few conductors since Koussevitsky have bothered to do.

His reluctance to incorporate anything but a sprinkling of postwar music into his repertoire reflects his musical background as a listener and a performer. Growing up in wartime Amsterdam, he had very little opportunity to hear much that was more advanced than Richard Strauss. His main source of music was van Beinum's steadfastly conservative Concertgebouw Orchestra, and his own upbringing, solidly middle-class and cautious, distanced him from the radical disillusionment of his contemporaries at college. As a performer, he had only one year's experience before concentrating on conducting, so hardly had the chance to investigate enough new music to make it part of his system. Haitink's temperament, too, put him outside the concerns of the avant garde. The preoccupation with the mechanics of sound, with formal disintegration and mathematical reconstruction, adopted by the young composers of occupied Europe as a response to the collapse of political morality around them, was not Haitink's reason for a fascination with music. Intellectually he is interested in the manipulation and shaping of symphonic form. Emotionally he is a romantic – using music as a means of expressing himself in an uninhibited way which his natural shyness and reserve would normally prohibit him from doing.

This, together with the two qualities he strives for most as a conductor – clarity and warmth – does not make him the ideal interpreter for the more outlandish pieces. However, it does explain his fascination with French music. He has recorded most of Ravel's orchestral output twice and the majority of Debussy's. Through his mother, Haitink has always felt an affinity with French culture, but with Debussy it was the rhapsodic nature of much of the work that first attracted him. He is, he is ready to admit, something of a day-dreamer, and Debussy answered for him the need to let the mind wander, gathering an overall impression without becoming too earthbound by the detail. *La mer* has assumed a particular importance. His house at Bergen, a very private place for him, has kept his love of the sea alive and its sounds constantly with him. For Haitink the two works which most accurately recreate the moods of the wind and water that no one in North Holland can ignore are the Sea Interludes from Britten's *Peter Grimes* and *La mer*. In both cases Haitink invests his interpretations with a passion that is often absent from his normally restrained readings of tone poems.

Ravel, however, he values for the delicacy and the subtle pointing of his orchestration. There are few other composers, he feels, who explore the character of instrumental textures so effectively. A conductor who has an orchestra capable of showing itself to best advantage in works which require such a fine balance between virtuosity and the blend of the ensemble revels not unnaturally in the luminous sound he can achieve. Haitink is more proud of some of his records of French music – Debussy's *Images* and *Jeux* and Ravel's *Le tombeau de Couperin* – than he is of some of his weighty interpretations of the German classics.

The light and shade of French music, its clear wind writing and impressionistic feeling for landscape and dance, have stood Haitink in good stead when he has come to interpret works which lie outside the Gallic tradition. Rimsky-Korsakov's *Scheherazade*, Holst's suite *The Planets* and the symphonies of Vaughan Williams have all lost some of their nationalistic characteristics in Haitink's hands and been lent a new lightness of touch. Both Vaughan Williams and Holst were considerably influenced by Ravel, but the fact is often understated by English conductors who are too concerned with the 'pastoral' tradition. Haitink is able to offer a Continental flavour that makes such composers more firmly part of the general European movement of their time.

While Haitink is most comfortable – or perhaps most rewarded by – the music of the nineteenth century, his style could not be other than of his own time. His clean beat, concern for rhythmic accuracy and lean sound have made the Concertgebouw of the 1980s a very different instrument from the one he, as a boy, heard Mengelberg conduct. 'Warm' sound no longer means thick strings with excessive vibrato and disunited ensemble. 'Interpretation' does not imply that the conductor will take whatever licence he wishes with the composer's markings on the score; nor does a showpiece for the orchestra necessarily mean that Haitink will employ as many instruments as possible. Those changes are as much a response to the expectations of twentieth-century composers as expressions of musical fashion. The ideal sound for an orchestra has changed. When Mengelberg and van Beinum were in charge of the Concertgebouw, it was said to have a 'Rembrandt' sound; lush, mellow and with a tonal richness that differentiated it from the brasher sounds of the American orchestras. Haitink dislikes the label, but 'If you have to talk in terms of painters,' he says, 'my ideal is Vermeer, with his translucent textures and air and clear figures.' It is an approach that owes much to his feeling for Ravel, Debussy and Stravinsky and it has spilled over into the way in which Haitink conducts Mozart, Beethoven and, perhaps most significantly, Mahler.

No conductor putting on the mantle of the Concertgebouw tradition would be allowed to ignore Mahler's music. Long before the rest of the world took his massive canvases seriously, Amsterdam had understood and been uplifted by them. Mahler himself had introduced the city to them when he had conducted the Third Symphony on 22 October 1903. On 25 October he followed it with his First. Almost exactly a year later he returned. In the opening half of the concert he conducted the Fourth Symphony, and then took a seat among the audience to listen to Willem Mengelberg conduct a repeat performance of the same work. From then until 1940 Mahler's works were an integral part of the orchestra's fabric, usually supervised by Mengelberg but, in the 1930s, often led by Bruno Walter, one of Mahler's pupils, who had been appointed First Conductor in 1934. Walter's readings tended to be less eccentric than Mengelberg's, reinforcing the value of the music and making sure that Mahler did not become the province only of the Mengelberg faction. Nevertheless, when Eduard van Beinum took over it seemed unlikely that the tradition would continue to play such an important part in the orchestra's programmes. Van Beinum was a less domineering figure than his predecessor and at first felt uneasy with the emotional demands of the music. However, once the wartime ban on performances had been lifted, it became clear that van Beinum had his own, equally valid, ideas that suited his more straightforward musical approach.

Not unnaturally, Haitink was wary at first of including Mahler in his own programmes. He found the works difficult, both musically and technically. While it was plainly an area he would have to tackle, he was in no hurry to attempt the larger-scale and later symphonies too early, especially in a city that was more familiar with them than any other. He had himself not heard any Mahler in the concert hall until he was seventeen, when van Beinum had performed the Second Symphony ('Resurrection') at the first concert given by the orchestra after the war. Haitink was overwhelmed by it, but when he actually came to conduct the works he had serious qualms. 'I started with the First, and then the Fifth,' he said, 'but it took me years to get inside all the symphonies. I remember that when I first tackled the Sixth it seemed like a completely different world to me. I recall a critic saying "When you think *you* have problems, listen to Mahler's Sixth." That is so true – quite apart from the technical problems he sets!' However, the decision to celebrate the Concertgebouw Orchestra's seventy-fifth anniversary in 1963 in the same fashion as Mengelberg's jubilee in 1920 – with a complete Mahler cycle, but this time on record – effectively left Haitink little option but to master the whole range. It is almost certain that it is not a decision he would have taken so early in his career had the pressure on him to conduct the first-ever complete set not been considerable. 'It took me, I think, ten years to learn to know where the emotions lie. They have to be absolutely right. That is so important. The emotions have to be really properly paced and that is not easy.'

There is a certain paradox in the fact that, as Haitink was working himself into the Mahler symphonies and beginning to understand how to approach them, he was also proving to be their most effective advocate, not only in Amsterdam, but in London as well. For, although Jascha Horenstein and Rafael Kubelik in London (and Sir John Barbirolli in Manchester) had done much to foster appreciation in Britain, it was Haitink who turned that appreciation into a movement that verged on becoming a cult. He found himself known as a Mahler and Bruckner specialist – so much so that the two composers became almost inseparable in the public mind, on the spurious grounds that both wrote long symphonies usually conducted by Haitink. It was a false comparison between two very different artists which is only now being adequately dispelled. Pleased as he was at the obvious enthusiasm, Haitink regarded the Mahler boom with some suspicion. 'There was a phase when any orchestra that wanted to be assured of an audience put on Mahler, and I am not entirely happy with that, maybe because I still like to think of Mahler in a pioneering way. So now I have eased back a little and I am less anxious to conduct the symphonies – except for the Seventh, which I consider to be the one neglected masterpiece.'

Another reason for feeling uneasy about the proliferation is that he believes Mahler can only be played by a first-rate orchestra. 'If you do

his works with a second-class orchestra you really get a terrible shock –
all of a sudden it sounds awful, from every angle. On the other hand, a
good orchestra must play Mahler, because it expands it. I always say
that Mahler is such good "body-building" for an orchestra, but then
the Concertgebouw is like a Rolls-Royce: you can drive it at thirty
miles per hour or ninety and it is just as smooth.'

Recording and performing the works for the first time meant a great
deal to Haitink. 'It was a very big thing in my life,' he says, 'and because
I developed with it, it is very hard to be objective about it any more. I
wonder how my life would have been without Mahler, because that
could happen now, with so much of my attention being given to opera.
For a long time I was very close to the works and I can't deny that I now
feel very familiar with them but, strangely enough, they are not more
important than, say, the Mozart operas are for me now, especially the
three da Ponte's.'

However, they remain a challenge, in emotional and technical terms.
'He is such a controversial man. In one way he was so meticulous in his
scores. You can see that he was a marvellous conductor, because he
knew exactly where all the pitfalls were and he marked "don't slow
down here" and "don't hurry there" with great care. On the other hand
he said that the really important things could not be seen in the notes,
and that is controversial. He leaves something to the musicians and to
the conductor, and that is very important and explains why he is so
difficult to interpret. One has to learn with experience.

'Because of that my "life with Mahler" came in three stages. When I
started I was very inhibited – too cool and detached – because I did not
have the emotional technique to bring the truth out. Then, when I
finally got the confidence, I indulged the emotional side and took
liberties with the music. Now I am in – not a calmer mood, because you
cannot be calm with Mahler – but more as if I am in the mountains and
can see the whole panorama better. It is more disciplined now.' Over
the coming years he will be recording the symphonies again, on this
occasion with the Berlin Philharmonic Orchestra. For two of the works
– the First and the Seventh Symphonies – it will be the third time he will
have put down his thoughts on tape. He is convinced that the changes
will be obvious, particularly in the 'Resurrection' Symphony. 'I don't
want to be remembered for my first recording of that. It was far too
cold. My reading has put on much more weight now; I take the first
movement far more slowly and it has more fantasy and maybe more
freedom. The same is true of the Third Symphony, though to a lesser
extent, and of the Sixth; that too will have a slower first movement.

'You must not be too restrained in Mahler, as I was fifteen years ago,

The Berlin Festival, 1972. The soloist is Kyung Wha Chung

Recording a Liszt piano concerto with Alfred Brendel, May 1972

The rigours of touring with the LPO in Russia, !
(*Colin* !

In the recording studio in 1975 with Volker Strau:
who has been his producer at Philips
since the early 1970s (*Mike Evans*)

Conducting the London Philharmonic Orchestra in Moscow, October 1975

Haitink's first new production at Glyndebourne: *The Rake's Progress* with,
left to right, Don Garrard as Trulove, Jill Gomez as Anne, Leo Goeke as Tom,
Rosalind Delias as Babar the Turk and Donald Gramm as Nick Shadow

Haitink's first new production with the Royal Opera: *Lohengrin* in November 1977.
Centre stage are Anna Tomowa-Sintow as Elsa and René Kollo as Lohengrin

but at the same time you must strike a balance. You must be able to release your emotional currents, which the music puts into you, and not be buttoned-up about them. But if you go over the brink you hurt your musicians and you don't achieve the results you want. This can easily happen if you conduct the symphonies too often. Now I ration myself carefully to one or two each year. If there are two, I place them at either end of the season. Otherwise they would drive me mad. That underlines the emotional pressure you come under when you conduct these symphonies. Maybe that means that I am not a total Mahlerian, yet when I conduct the works I find myself entirely involved in them. It is a marvellous world, but also a dangerous one.

'There is a nice story about Mengelberg. One day he was rehearsing a symphony and in the middle he stopped. The orchestra wondered what was the matter. "Nothing's wrong," he said. "It was simply too good for a rehearsal." It had got too emotional. I sometimes find myself becoming over-involved during rehearsal but I've learnt to recognise the danger signs. To conduct well we have to think with our heart and feel with our brain, and that does not apply only to Mahler. There are two sorts of conductor in the world: one who cries his eyes out during the performance but leaves the audience cold; the other who keeps a cool head but moves his listeners.'

Haitink's repertoire of Mahler's orchestral works now includes the nine symphonies, *Das Lied von der Erde* and the various sets of songs, but not the Tenth Symphony – neither the Adagio, which was the only part Mahler himself orchestrated, nor the complete version reconstructed from the short-score sketches which was built into a performing score by Deryck Cooke. Many conductors find it an acceptable alternative to not hearing the music at all, but Haitink remains unconvinced. 'I have never conducted it and I never will,' he says, 'because Mahler was so meticulous, and changed and corrected before he ever published anything, that you are not allowed to do that sort of thing. I am very puritanical about that. I listened to it and I was not pleased, but maybe I am not objective.

'I am sure that it was a very serious attempt, but I have one experience of the Tenth – with the Adagio, which is not finished either. It lacks certain things. I found conducting it very strange, because in most cases my timings are very consistent. I remember a horrible occasion when I did Mahler's Fifth at the Festival Hall, in two consecutive seasons. A critic who keeps track of these things said "Did you know that you are taking ten seconds longer than a year ago?" and I thought "Oh, God, I am such a computer!" But I did the Adagio on tour and apparently I could not get a grip on it, because there were differences in timing of between two and four minutes. That is a lot. So I decided that there must be something unfinished about it. I could not settle. For me Mahler finishes with the Ninth and *The Song of the Earth*.'

The progression from the symphonies of Mahler to those of Shostakovich might seem an obvious one for a conductor to make. Both composers wrote works of massive scale and universal scope. Both used the form for major, though often ambiguous, public statements and both developed a way of using large orchestras with the deftness and clarity of a chamber ensemble. It is surprising, then, that Haitink himself was slow, and at first unenthusiastic, to perform Shostakovich.

'As so often in my life, I was talked into a thing which I knew very little about. I remember a programme meeting with the LPO in the early 1970s at which someone said "Why don't you do Shostakovich Ten?" I thought, well, Shostakovich is not for me. At that time I thought it vulgar and noisy, and I linked it with unpleasant aspects of the Russian Revolution and I was not interested, but they talked me into it. So I started to look at the score and to learn it.

'It was a tremendous success at the Festival Hall. I had not realised that the audience was so receptive to Shostakovich. Then all of a sudden the LPO management came to me and announced that they could have a contract for all the symphonies from Decca. I thought, "For heaven's sake, this is madness" because I did not know them at all, but again I was talked into it, partly because the orchestra needed the money and the work. I then discovered a totally new world, and after I had given up my post with the LPO I began to conduct the works in Amsterdam as well. There, I remember, when the press got wind that I was doing Shostakovich they reacted with "What is he doing this for, this third-rate composer?"

'The first one that we did in Amsterdam was the Fourteenth. We had Fischer-Dieskau and Varady and it was an enormous success, not only because of the soloists, but because of the music, and from that moment on the audience was fascinated by it. It is such extraordinary music, with those great long periods of pianissimo and those enormous cruel outbursts. It is fascinating to try to shape the thing and keep it under control without losing the impact.

'Shostakovich's two great heroes were Beethoven and Mahler, as I discovered when I stood in his study in Moscow, and that explains a lot about why I am now so attracted to his music.' One of the sad consequences of Haitink's decision to relinquish the conductorship of the Concertgebouw Orchestra is that he will not now give a cycle of the Shostakovich symphonies to mark his own twenty-fifth anniversary in the post, which would have fallen in the 1988–9 season. 'It would have been "old hat" to have done Mahler, because I have done that and Mengelberg did it before me, but Shostakovich: that would have been something!'

Several of the works have dropped out of his repertoire since the recordings were made. 'That is the other story of my life. I do works which then disappear: the Fourth, for instance, I have not conducted since performing it with the Chicago Symphony in 1977. The Fifteenth, too, I have not done for a long time. That is such an extraordinary work. You can almost hear the bones rattling!

'He was very much a man of our time and so I have found it easy to relate to him, though you have to make sense of the "Party music", the parts that he had to write to order. At first I was chary of some of the symphonies, such as the Fourth and Seventh, because neither is without fault – there are some banal passages – but then, others are accepted masterpieces. They are in my system now, though I learned the climate of the works in London and so my approach is probably quite far away from the Russian tradition.

'Shostakovich's symphonies tell you about an artist's life lived in very difficult circumstances, and that is at the heart of their chemistry, for perhaps he could only write through such suffering.' Haitink finds a comparison with the late works of Mahler. Both composers knew they were dying of heart disease and this fact dominated their writing. 'At the end of Mahler's Ninth Symphony, if there is a gleam of hope, it evaporates in the air – it is the end, but not in the way that, for me, Shostakovich's Fifteenth is the end. There a man is dying, whereas in Mahler's Ninth there is something going away for ever, which is a different thing from dying. There is extreme bitterness in the Shostakovich which is not in the Mahler, though the third movement – "To my friends under Olympus" – has a terrible feeling. But the fourth movement has instead moods of withdrawal, of resignation.'

VI

At last to Glyndebourne

TWO DEBUTS DOMINATED the first half of 1972. In February Haitink conducted Haydn and Bruckner symphonies at a subscription concert of the Berlin Philharmonic Orchestra, earning a gale of praise from the German critics: 'By heart and with the heart,' said *Die Presse*. In April he returned with his own Dutch orchestra, bringing Strauss's *Don Juan, Due canzoni* by Otto Ketting, a Mozart Flute Concerto and Brahms's Fourth Symphony. 'Bernard Haitink triumphs in Karajan's Circus,' trumpeted the headline-writer back in Amsterdam. Earlier in February it had been announced by Jacques Duhamel, the French Minister of Culture, that Haitink had been made a Chevalier de l'Ordre des Arts et des Lettres, a decoration that must have especially pleased his mother after her long service to the Alliance Française.

The second début was, for the present at least, more significant. Haitink had always fought shy of conducting opera, partly because he had little opportunity, partly because he did not develop or build on the opportunities that *were* presented. His three attempts for Netherlands Opera in the 1960s (productions of *Don Giovanni, Don Carlos* and, surprisingly since he was never regarded as a Wagner conductor in those days, *Der fliegende Holländer*) were less than successful, or at least were not as polished as his work in the concert hall, and so left him with a strong sense of misgiving about whether he was really suited to opera. However, by 1972, the professional problems of not being experienced in opera were beginning to seem as great as those of tackling the form. 'It is just as dangerous to have a reputation for being a "concert conductor" as it is to be considered an opera specialist,' he wrote ten years later in his essay 'A Foreigner at Glyndebourne' (in *Glyndebourne, a Celebration*). 'Even the word "conductor" is misleading. To be a musician is the most important thing. I felt very imprisoned to be labelled a concert conductor.'

Consequently, when he was approached by Moran Caplat, the General Administrator of Glyndebourne Festival Opera, to conduct the performances of Mozart's *Die Entführung aus dem Serail* in the summer of 1972, his response was more positive than it had been to all the German approaches over the years, and he accepted. The invitation might have come much earlier. Ian Hunter, who had signed Bernard Haitink's rehearsal pass at the Edinburgh Festival in 1948 but was now his London agent, had approached Caplat in the mid-1950s, suggesting that Haitink be employed at the Sussex opera house. They had met in a coffee bar in Wigmore Street, where the two largest musicians' agencies of the time, Harold Holt and Ibbs and Tillett, had their offices. 'I formed an impression,' Caplat wrote in his autobiography *Dinghies to Divas*, 'which was never to change, of a man of taste and culture in whom there ran a sense of humour akin to my own.' There was no immediate offer from Caplat, however, though he did travel to Amsterdam to watch the 1966 production of *Don Carlos*.

Once Haitink was installed as the Artistic Director of the LPO, which had been the resident orchestra at Glyndebourne since 1964, and was clearly more receptive to the idea, Caplat decided the time was right. For the second time the venue for the meeting was a coffee bar in Wigmore Street. Haitink's acceptance was based on two premises. First, he would be working with an orchestra which knew him well and would not add to any problems created by his inexperience of the stage. Secondly, Glyndebourne's long rehearsal times, club-like atmosphere and company cohesiveness meant that he could be sure of his ground and exhaustively prepared before facing the public. There is also a sense at Glyndebourne of quiet experiment, stemming from the number of young singers, the smallness of the auditorium and the relaxed spirit of concentration evoked by the sheltered country setting.

The opening night was on 5 June 1972 and Haitink was able to mark up a quiet triumph, satisfied that, even if all the members of the cast did not win unanimous praise, his abilities as an opera conductor were fully recognised for the first time. *Country Life* compared him to Glyndebourne's founding musical director, Fritz Busch; *The Times* remarked that the LPO played for him as it had for Beecham, called him 'a Mozartian to his baton tip', and, most importantly, noted that 'he is generous in his support of the singers, allowing them the time they need, helping them round crucial corners'. Haitink's singers would have thanked him for that, at least!

The *Entführung* that season was not entirely new, though it had been considerably restaged. The designs by Emanuele Luzzati for the 1968 production had mostly been used again, but John Cox had completely overhauled the action, which had originally been staged by Franco Enriquez with a different cast. Among the singers assigned to Haitink, the men were deemed to be rather more successful than the women: Marius Rintzler as Osmin, Horst Laubenthal as Belmonte, Richard Van Allan as Pasha Selim and the young Finnish tenor, Kimmo

Lappalainen, as Pedrillo. Sylvia Geszty from Hungary sang Constanze and Danièle Perriers impersonated Blonde, neither to much acclaim.

Haitink himself was encouraged but not over-impressed with his own performance. 'I think it was too symphonic,' he says. 'I had little idea of theatre and how to adapt to the needs of the stage, which are different from those of the concert hall, but at least I learnt what opera could be like.' During his time in Sussex that summer he gave an interview to *Records and Recording* which one can read now with a gentle chuckle at the irony provided by hindsight. Ronald Crichton asked whether Haitink, since he was plainly enjoying his new role, would like to run an opera house. 'No,' he replied,

> it's too late, in a sense. I don't mean I'm too old, but to do that successfully one must start very young, work through the whole business from the bottom to the top. I certainly haven't the experience and I don't think I have the temperament for running an opera house – as you know, you need about five extra skins. But I love opera and I would like to do more of it. It's a kind of hobby for me. I don't mean that I want to do it amateurishly, but I enjoy it so much I don't want to spoil it by taking on the administrative side as well.

Haitink's schedule in 1972 was looking far heavier than it had for some years. Apart from his work at Glyndebourne, in Berlin and the normal duties at the Royal Festival Hall and the Concertgebouw, his list of recordings was growing inexorably. In May he completed what was becoming, rather to his surprise, a fairly comprehensive collection of Liszt's orchestral works with the LPO and Alfred Brendel, performing the First and Second Piano Concertos and the *Totentanz*. The same month he finished his work on the Bruckner symphonies by returning to the beginning, the First Symphony, with the Concertgebouw Orchestra. In Amsterdam he carried on with a set of the Brahms symphonies, the Fourth and the First (adding the *Academic Festival* Overture for good measure), and continued his exploration of Tchaikovsky with *Francesca da Rimini* and the *Marche slave*. He also faced the fireworks of the *1812* Overture.

The first ever cycle of Mahler's symphonies for the gramophone had been embarked upon to mark the seventy-fifth anniversary of the Concertgebouw nearly a decade earlier. Haitink had begun with the First Symphony, not so much because that was the obvious place to start as because it had been written in the year of the orchestra's foundation, 1888. Now, with all the symphonies recorded and about to be released, he returned to the First, remaking it with the benefit of coming to know it again after learning all the others. The project had been an extraordinary achievement for Haitink, the producer Jaap van Ginneken and the orchestra itself. As Marius Flothuis pointed out in the *Gramophone* that September, many of the works had needed to be reintroduced to the Concertgebouw's repertoire, and the recording over the same period of all the Bruckner symphonies as well, with the same players, engineers and conductor, was a feat unique in the history of gramophone recording.

The pressure of performance was continued through the summer and into the start of the new season. At the Proms Haitink conducted the LPO in two concerts, on 11 August 1972 recreating the performance of Shostakovich's Tenth Symphony given at the previous year's Edinburgh Festival, and, two days before, directing Bruckner's Eighth once again. It was preceded by a Mozart piano concerto, reflecting a change made as a result of one of the tragedies of the year. Bernard Walton, the LPO's principal clarinet, was to have played the Mozart concerto for his instrument. Sadly he had died of a heart attack while at Glyndebourne earlier in the summer. Walton had been one of the greatest assets of the orchestra throughout Haitink's tenure.

The Promenaders were also denied Haitink's new-found enthusiasm for opera, since Glyndebourne used its music director, John Pritchard, for the concert performance of *Die Entführung* on the previous Wednesday. After that the LPO and Haitink were separated for a few weeks, the orchestra travelling up to Edinburgh as it had the year before, but this time with the conducting being shared between Carlo Maria Giulini and Daniel Barenboim. (The latter's reading of the Brahms *German Requiem*, which had Edith Mathis and Dietrich Fischer-Dieskau joining the Edinburgh Festival Chorus, was promptly recorded by Deutsche Grammophon.)

In the meantime Haitink went home to Holland before rejoining the LPO for its first, and his third, visit of the year to Berlin, whose patrons must have been wondering if there was an orchestra they could invite that did not bring Haitink and Bruckner. The Eighth Symphony was repeated, along with McCabe's *Notturni ed alba*, in the Philharmonie on 19 September, and the next night Haitink conducted works by Vaughan Williams (a month before his centenary celebrations in London), Shostakovich and Mendelssohn, whose Violin Concerto was played by the astonishing young Korean player then storming the world's musical centres, Kyung-Wha Chung.

For the LPO the season was planned to be a triumphant one, marking its own fortieth anniversary which fell on 7 October. The orchestra had good reason to be confident. It was recognised, for the first time since Beecham had stepped down, as the leading orchestra in the capital. None of the others could match its average Festival Hall figure of ninety per cent paid attendance, which in reality meant that almost every concert was sold out. Compared with the half-empty houses Haitink had experienced even for his Mahler performances five years earlier, that in itself was a massive achievement. In 1967 the London critics were blaming over-scheduling of Mahler for the lackadaisical audience response. Now the combination was a recipe for instant box-office success, something that Haitink, whose purpose had been to pioneer the music, was beginning to find a little wearing. Haitink's artistic direction was proving to be almost as important as his conducting, however. He had succeeded in persuading both sceptical audiences and players that programming new music did not mean immediate disaster, and the anniversary schedule contained the London première of Ligeti's *Lontano*, the world première of Iain Hamilton's Concerto for Orchestra (both of which Haitink conducted) and that of Nicholas Maw's Suite from *The Rising of the Moon*. Elsewhere in the season other conductors directed works by Varèse, Miaskovsky, Shchedrin and Humphrey Searle, as well as Schoenberg's *Erwartung*; none of them features of the usually conservative programming policies of the London orchestras. Haitink himself, though, concentrated for the most part on his familiar territory of Bruckner and Stravinsky. The latter's works were played in three of Haitink's total of only eight concerts, most intriguingly in one which combined the Violin Concerto with Mozart's Requiem. Perhaps the evening for which enthusiasts most eagerly hunted tickets was that in which Janet Baker sang 'Parto, parto' from Mozart's *La clemenza di Tito* and Wagner's *Wesendonk Lieder*, and Haitink conducted Mahler's Sixth Symphony.

The orchestra then went on to exhibit its fresh sense of international worth by performing in Haitink's other fortress, the Concertgebouw. For the conductor this was the final act of proof that his much-criticised decision to take on the direction of both institutions had been right. He now had two orchestras, with very different traditions, methods of funding and audiences, running seasons that were complementary, and he had helped to advance the international ambitions of both. However, Haitink's increasing celebrity and the demand for his work was putting a growing strain on his personal life and marriage. He was able to spend less time than ever at the family home, now a house in Blaricum, near Hilversum. His care to separate the personal and professional sides of his life has always been cultivated with determination. By the 1970s, however, it was clear that the professional side was winning and, father of five or not, Haitink could hardly pretend to be an ordinary Dutch suburban husband. The separation from his wife when it came was amicable, though, and it has remained so.

Haitink's policy of working intensely with both the LPO and the Concertgebouw had allowed each to build on the reputation of the other in a way which is rare. There have been plenty of occasions when a conductor has held two posts at once, but usually the result is that he does neither very well. Distance, a lack of local roots and the feeling among audiences that principal conductors are transient beings (even on the few occasions when the public knows their names) all contribute to a sense that the 'hype' of the publicity material is not substantiated by music-making of noticeably individual character. It is that definable individualism that stamped Bernstein's New York Philharmonic, Solti's Chicago Symphony, von Karajan's Berlin Philharmonic and Previn's London Symphony Orchestras. It was Haitink's achievement in the early 1970s that it was possible to think of his Concertgebouw and London Philharmonic Orchestras in that way. The LPO's polish and the Concertgebouw's warmth were seen as distinctive trademarks.

It was paradoxical, then, that it was precisely this sense of identity, encouraged by Haitink, that was beginning to undermine his relations with the LPO. It was, in a sense, the perennial bind of anyone selling his services on a freelance basis. Every employer for whom he works thinks he owns him, but the craftsman knows that his only true loyalty is to his craft. The Concertgebouw Orchestra had always been sure, deep down, that it owned its conductor. The LPO wanted to and was wounded that it could not. It was appreciated that Haitink's period of tenure had brought exactly the benefits of acclaim and recognition which had been so badly wanted in the 1960s. But there was a faction on the board that was starting to resent the insufficient amount of time that Haitink was able to spend with the orchestra and the fact that most of the fringe benefits that went with having a popular figure as conductor – recording work, television and radio broadcasts – seemed to be siphoned to Amsterdam. Too often, it was felt, Haitink was unavailable for engagements which meant a lot to the orchestra. When, during the 1972 season, the LPO gave ten concerts at the Hong Kong Festival and then became the first Western symphony orchestra to visit mainland China (the immediate cultural result for Britain of the opening of relations between President Nixon and Chairman Mao), it was its previous conductor, John Pritchard, who appeared at its head, not Haitink.

The same lack of attention was felt when it came to his availability for recordings. Haitink and the Concertgebouw Orchestra both had exclusive contracts with Philips. Not unnaturally the Dutch company, as much for convenience as nationalism, preferred to give the bulk of its work to Amsterdam, though there were a number of projects pushed in the LPO's direction. However, in the period between Haitink's taking up the appointment with the LPO in 1967 and the end of its fortieth anniversary season in 1973, he had recorded fifty-two works with the Concertgebouw Orchestra and twenty-six with the LPO (with a higher proportion of single records consisting of several works in the LPO's output). Whereas almost all the Amsterdam orchestra's work for the gramophone was done with Haitink, only a small proportion of the LPO's was, and when a new budget label was launched, underwritten by the LPO's principal sponsors, the tobacco firm W.D. and H.O. Wills, it was again Pritchard who took his place on the rostrum. Indeed, although he only conducted one concert in the Festival Hall series that season, when his recording, touring and work as music director at Glyndebourne were taken into account Pritchard was a significant presence in the orchestra's life.

The problem was not one of which Haitink was unaware. 'I did feel that I was not wholly integrated,' he says. 'I would come to London for my concerts, rehearse and perform them as best I could, then leave.' He was, in any case, not particularly interested in the mechanics of orchestral administration in either city, believing that his job was to produce musical results of a sufficient standard, not to run a successful office. This was an attitude that the managers found difficult to accept at times. It has been said that Haitink's obvious boredom and usual silence during committee meetings made them feel that his lack of interest spread beyond the details of administration to the orchestra's affairs as a whole. In fact, Haitink felt strongly about many of the issues but did not consider it a proper part of his role to interfere in matters of a self-governing body that he regarded as being outside the brief of a conductor.

The first three years of the 1970s marked the peak of Haitink's relationship with the LPO. However, for many of the players the artistic triumphs were fine only so long as they were converted into cash through extra or more lucrative sessions. By 1973 opinion on the LPO's Board of Directors – made up entirely of players, unlike that of the Concertgebouw – was fairly evenly divided between those, headed by the principal trumpet, Gordon Webb, who felt that Haitink brought musical dividends that nullified any criticism and those who considered that Haitink simply did not bring the orchestra enough money.

His critics were not being merely greedy. The system of orchestral financing in London is such that no orchestra can remain healthy and solvent without a sizeable amount of work away from the concert hall. In Amsterdam every player had a contract and the Concertgebouw Orchestra's board could be certain that eighty per cent of its expenditure would be met by the public purse, whether local or national. In London each LPO player is self-employed and the proportion of state financing to generated income is precisely reversed. At that time twenty per cent filtered through the bureaucratic layers of government agencies; the rest had to be directly earned. This meant that whereas extra work for the Concertgebouw was a pleasant bonus, for the LPO overwork, few free days and as many sessions as could be crammed in were, and are still, a necessary fact of life. In many ways the lot of the musician has changed little in the century and a half since properly constituted orchestras began to be a regular part of London concert life. The electronic media have ensured that they are invidually better known to the public and have more methods of earning fees, but the need for hectic variety is much the same.

There are sometimes benefits from such a hard-headed view of arts funding. Britain supports the arts with less money per person in state finance, whether given directly or by way of tax concessions, than any comparable nation in the Western world. Yet it has, in London, more orchestras than any comparable city. But this is more a tribute to the initiative and efficiency of the arts managers and the sheer hard work of the musicians than a commendation of the system. Because of the amount of playing needed to keep an orchestra in business, musicians perform a far greater variety of works in a far shorter time than in most other centres. Concerts are usually given only once with a normal maximum of four rehearsals, often only two. The LPO will go from working on Mahler in the morning to recording a film track in the afternoon and then return to the Royal Festival Hall for a performance the same evening. This can bring great spontaneity to the playing. An orchestral musician in London will rarely die of boredom. Fast learning – never making the same mistake twice – late nights, early mornings, a diet of institutional sandwiches, weak coffee and beer, a tendency to forget who conducted the last session or what the music was, and a determined pretence that no performance is ever anything but routine are the qualities that most characterise the players.

Haitink was aware of the problems the orchestra faced and also of the professionalism with which the players dealt with them, but for a conductor who likes slow, contemplative preparation as the basis for his music-making, it was none the less irritating for being understandable. 'I was worried,' he says, 'at the gross overworking of the players, and I was always annoyed if they were doing sessions on the days I wanted to rehearse or even on the day of a concert. The danger in England is that the fight for money will destroy artistic standards. In the end the orchestra as a whole became too commercially minded and conditions, to my mind, deteriorated.

'Although I still think the London system is crazy, there is undoubtedly an excitement about concerts here that is not always obvious elsewhere, and that may have something to do with the dangerous mode of operating, with too much, almost, left to chance. A player in the Philharmonia Orchestra said to me that it was awful the way they worked, but when it went well it was like a stimulating drug. But that is dangerous. Professionals love their music, however tired they may be, but the act is a knife-edge one.'

Haitink's own schedule in 1973 was not much less frenetic than that of his London orchestra. With the LPO in Walthamstow Town Hall he recorded Stravinsky's three great ballet scores complete, *Petrushka, The Rite of Spring* and *The Firebird*. In February he continued his documentation of the works of Mahler, recording *Das klagende Lied* with Heather Harper, Norma Procter and Werner Hollweg in the Concertgebouw. The producer, however, was no longer Jaap van Ginneken, as it had been for the rest of the collection. His death shortly after producing Haitink's reappraisal of the First Symphony the previous May robbed Philips of one half of their most successful artistic partnership. In retrospect it was appropriate that it had been the performance of the Mahler symphony, prior to its recording, which the BBC had chosen to film for a programme on Haitink's work with the Concertgebouw Orchestra, and the record's release was timed to coincide with the screening in February.

From then on Haitink's work for Philips was produced by Volker Straus, who had already been part of the team for several years. Also in February, the re-exploration of the Ravel orchestral works continued. *Valses nobles et sentimentales* was recorded then and *Rapsodie espagnole* followed in September.

May 1973 was the sort of month, as far as his diary was concerned, that Haitink always swore he tried not to encourage. He conducted the Vienna Philharmonic Orchestra at two concerts in the Musikverein, rounded off the LPO's anniversary season with a performance on 4 May that included the world première of Iain Hamilton's Concerto for Orchestra and, four days later, gave an all-Brahms programme, in which Daniel Barenboim played the First Piano Concerto. More Brahms awaited him in Amsterdam. There he recorded the Violin Concerto with Henryk Szeryng – together with that of Beethoven – and the Strauss tone poem which was achieving almost hackneyed status at the time, *Also sprach Zarathustra.*

In April he had spent three weeks in America, one with the Cleveland Orchestra in Ohio and two with the Boston Symphony, the only orchestras in the United States for which he has had any consistent affection. The period in Boston was something of a welcome break from the round of meetings and sessions that cluttered his life in London and Amsterdam. For once he had a reasonable amount of time to himself; his only duties were rehearsing and performing. On his own, and with no responsibilities other than music-making, he could study scores without interruption. This was the good side of being a guest conductor rather than a principal. With the Boston orchestra he was quietly efficient in a way which stood out from the more flamboyant and frequently arrogant attitude of many of his colleagues, especially in America. Abram Chipman wrote in the *New Haven Register* on 20 May:

> When one remembers how the old autocrats used to drill and tyrannize the orchestra, a Haitink rehearsal is the epitome of the enlightened new order. Looking relaxed and at home in Symphony Hall during a first session devoted to Mahler's D major Symphony, Haitink throws no tantrums, exudes no icy condescension, needs no forty-five-minute tune-up exercises and gives no lectures on 'Hoondred Percent Orchester Spieling'. He and the BSO principals discuss problematic passages in a genial, businesslike manner.

At the end of May Haitink returned to England for his second year as an opera conductor at Glyndebourne. Once again the work was by Mozart, restaged by John Cox from the company's old production (first seen in 1963) by Franco Enriquez and Emanuele Luzzati. Unlike *Die Entführung*, however, this version of *Die Zauberflöte* was already among the theatre's most successful and Haitink was given a cast to match his own reputation. He was entrusted with the task of opening the season on 30 May, an evening on which the weather drew more criticism than the performance. As is almost traditional in Sussex, the first night was accompanied by wind, rain and a few minutes of sunshine to lull the frocked and dinner-jacketed audience into a false sense of well-being for the long interval.

As had happened the previous year, it was Haitink's qualities as a

Mozartian that were noticed, particularly in comparison with the less distinguished reading that the opera had been given for its previous run three years before. William Mann in *The Times* was rather liverish in his review, but elsewhere there was happy agreement. 'This year Bernard Haitink dominates the musical performance like sunshine,' announced Gillian Widdicombe in the *Financial Times*. 'The London Philharmonic Orchestra played with more neat elegance than the Glyndebourne pit has heard for a long time, with rhythmic detail cleanly bounced, lyrical lines soft-grained and polished.' On stage the production was notable for the British début of Edita Gruberová as the Queen of the Night and Thomas Allen's Papageno, which was for many the finest interpretation of the role in a generation. It was a strongly cast production in most respects, with Sheila Armstrong as Pamina, Robert Lloyd as Sarastro and Brian Burrows as Monostatos. Only George Shirley as Tamino, by then not quite as vocally secure as he had been in earlier years, was felt to be a weak link.

After Glyndebourne Haitink crossed the Channel once again, giving the last of the season's concerts in Amsterdam for the annual Holland Festival and recording Brahms's Second Symphony in the Concertgebouw before the summer break. With his Dutch orchestra he returned to Britain for two Proms at the beginning of September. The Promenaders had always championed Haitink, according him a place in their lexicon of great conductors while others were still dithering. None the less, the reception he and the Concertgebouw Orchestra were given in 1973 was among the most vociferous of Prom welcomes. Television lights made the temperature in the hall, already over eighty degrees, almost insufferable for the first concert (of Mendelssohn's music for *A Midsummer Night's Dream* and Dvořák's *New World* Symphony). The next night, a Sunday, the impromptu gala continued. For their performance of Bruckner's Fifth Symphony the orchestra were presented with carnations: white for the men's buttonholes, red for the women's dresses (or hair) and pink for Haitink. At the end the applause only subsided long enough for Haitink to make a speech of thanks for the flowers and other gifts presented to them. The Proms are an extraordinary experience for an orchestra on any occasion. The size of the Royal Albert Hall – there are places for seven thousand – the steamy summer atmosphere and the excitement generated when the arena is filled by a standing audience who have queued for most of the afternoon, all create a mood very different from that built by the staid burghers who make up the Continental subscribers. For an orchestra unfamiliar with the experience, the greeting of popping balloons, choruses of wisecracks from the arena and gallery and the closeness of the audience can be daunting. For unseasoned soloists it can be enough to turn the nerves to jelly. They are even more surprised, then, to find that this most rowdy of gatherings can also provide listening conditions more rapt and attentive than almost anywhere else in the world. A successful night at the Proms can make much of the normal drudgery of life in an orchestra seem worth while.

Having brought the Concertgebouw Orchestra from the Continent, Haitink then took the LPO in the opposite direction, beginning its 1973–4 season with a seventeen-concert tour of Germany, Austria, Switzerland and Belgium, which included performances in Hanover, Kassel, Nuremberg and Vienna before finishing at the Europalia '73 Festival in Brussels. The LPO then had Josef Krips, Eugen Jochum and Daniel Barenboim to conduct it until Haitink came back from Holland in November.

In the meantime, at the beginning of November, he made his second visit of the year to the Vienna Philharmonic, a connection that was cemented by a further set of concerts in February and early March 1974. It is an orchestra with which he has always felt at home. The Musikverein hall, like the Concertgebouw, is a glorious example of nineteenth-century acoustical design, lending the strings the same warm glow and the wind a mellowness that suits the music written at the time of its construction. Not being Viennese, Haitink was steered away from the local composers at first – at least from those about whom the Vienna Philharmonic feels particularly protective. 'I suppose my repertory with them has differed a little from that which I do here [in London],' he told Alan Blyth for the *Gramophone* later in the year. 'I have done quite a bit of Haydn with them, Mendelssohn, Strauss's *Zarathustra*, Dvořák, Stravinsky's Violin Concerto – perhaps you could say it's the same but without Mahler and Bruckner.'

Bruckner and Mahler were the composers that audiences elsewhere were still anxious to hear, however, though Haitink himself was starting to find that the labelling was limiting. Mahler especially requires a high degree of nervous and emotional energy which, if over-taxed, can put a considerable strain on a conductor. Now that the recording project of the complete symphonies was fulfilled, Haitink began to ration the supply. Works by both composers were still present in his programmes, though, and in the first half of the season he conducted Bruckner's Eighth and Mahler's Fifth Symphonies in London. However, he was also exploring other avenues, returning to the Dvořák concertos and continuing to learn the major works by Britten. The *Cello Symphony* was heard on 31 January 1975, four days before he conducted the *Spring Symphony*. That concert also gave him the excuse to pair the Britten with Schumann's symphony with the same subtitle, so starting work on repertoire to which he had been a long time coming.

Just as it had taken Haitink twenty years to face Schumann, so it was with a cycle of the Beethoven symphonies. There were two factors in the delay. At the Concertgebouw it was repertoire usually entrusted to the more experienced conductors, and Haitink himself had been reluctant to embark on what is still the most searching test until he felt completely ready. By their very familiarity, with audiences scrutinising each phrase in a way which is suffered by no other body of work, the Beethoven symphonies present an unrivalled examination of a conductor's skills of musicianship and orchestral control. Most interpreters can be persuasive in some of the symphonies, but so great is their range – both stylistically and emotionally – that there are few who can be convincing in all nine. Having waited until two weeks after his forty-fifth birthday to subject himself to such a test, however, Haitink launched himself at the series with the media primed to bring the maximum publicity. As a result all six concerts with the LPO, given between 17 and 31 March 1974, were sold out even before the first had been played.

Between the symphonies a secondary cycle of the piano concertos was being played with Vladimir Ashkenazy. Here Haitink was on more familiar ground, having performed them before as a set with Claudio Arrau, but together the concerts presented a rare chance to hear the works as an integrated collection, the sequence planned to reflect an exploration of musical contrasts rather than merely a consecutive list that pandered to the record collector's passion for boxed sets. The sense of occasion was heightened by the presence of the television cameras for the opening night of the series, on which the third *Leonore* Overture, the First Piano Concerto and the Third Symphony, the *Eroica*, were played. The reviews the following morning pronounced the undertaking a triumph from the start. Joan Chissell wrote in *The Times*:

The playing was worthy of any festival. If this standard is maintained, it will be a cycle to remember. And chiefly because, in the final resort, the hero will be Beethoven. Mr Haitink has the great virtue of bringing up each score with all the immediacy and intensity of a new discovery without making you conscious of an interpreter at work. Whatever he did sounded inevitable.

These sentiments were shared by Hugo Cole in the *Guardian*, who commended the approach as an antidote to the usual run of performances where the symphonies were hastily prepared, 'punished and misrepresented'. He continued:

Haitink's *Eroica* had rare virtues, most of them springing from simple and easily named causes. He observes all pianissimi and fortissimi: crescendi are never anticipated, the vital rhythm of the music never wavers for a moment. Obvious enough, perhaps, but how few can inspire an orchestra to concentrate for fifty-five minutes so that none of these points is neglected?

The series continued in a Sunday-Tuesday-Thursday sequence, concluding on Sunday 31 March with both the earliest work in the form and the last; the First Symphony and the Ninth being juxtaposed to illustrate the extent of Beethoven's development between 1799 and 1823. As soloists Haitink had a quartet that was a mixture of youth and experience: Kiri te Kanawa, Anna Reynolds, Ryland Davies and Donald Bell. At the end of the year the success of the series was recognised when Philips embarked on recording the set. The Seventh and the *Eroica* were taped in November, along with the *Egmont* and *Coriolan* Overtures. In December, with Herman Krebbers, Haitink made his second record of the Violin Concerto in two years, and the rest of the cycle followed in 1975 and 1976.

On the same day as the reviews appeared of the first Beethoven concert, which marked one of the high points of Haitink's conductorship of the LPO, a news paragraph was printed in the *Financial Times* which foreshadowed a development that was to lead to complications later in the decade. It read:

The London Philharmonic Orchestra and its Artistic Director Bernard Haitink have invited Sir Georg Solti to extend his work with the orchestra, and from next September he will conduct up to eight LPO concerts a year at the Festival Hall. At the same time Daniel Barenboim will begin a special relationship with the orchestra, conducting six concerts each season; and, as previously announced, Carlo Maria Giulini will appear three times a season. As principal conductor Bernard Haitink will conduct ten or eleven concerts at the Festival Hall, as well as others elsewhere.

Solti had, for years, been the orchestra's most frequent guest conductor, along with Sir Adrian Boult, the LPO's President. Boult, however, at eighty-five was no longer able to take a major share and

Solti, whose work with the Chicago Symphony was bringing immense international acclaim, had considerable box-office appeal. Since he had ceded the music directorship of the Royal Opera to Colin Davis, he was also anxious to maintain a link with an orchestra in London. At Covent Garden Solti's exciting but erratic performances had earned him a loyal following, though there were many who found his emphasis on rhythmic precision unsympathetic. Certainly his temperament, rehearsal techniques and the sound he expected from the orchestra were all very different from those favoured by Haitink, and over the next few years the LPO was to be split increasingly between those players who preferred the exhilaration of Solti's methods and those who found them intolerable in comparison with Haitink's. The issue raised considerable passion and Haitink himself was less than happy with what he regarded as a devaluation of his role.

After the Beethoven cycle Haitink did not conduct the LPO for the rest of the season, since no spring dates had been agreed and he was not travelling down to Glyndebourne that summer. Instead he concentrated on the Concertgebouw Orchestra, touring with it once again to the Far East in April and May. It was Haitink's fourth visit to Japan, and the orchestra's third.

Haitink began the next season much as he had ended the last, touring the East with the Concertgebouw. This time the itinerary took account of the improving relations with the Soviet bloc, brought about by the process of détente that was then dominating discussions between the superpowers. The orchestra gave two concerts in Prague. Haitink had taken it there once already, just before the Soviet tanks rolled in to kill the process of liberalisation begun by Alexander Dubček. By 1974, however cordial the noises coming from Leonid Brezhnev, the regime that greeted the Dutchmen was the harshest in Central Europe. From Prague they travelled to Russia, reaping the expected applause for their six concerts, three each in Moscow and Leningrad.

On their return the recording sessions began again with, appropriately, given their Russian tour, Tchaikovsky's Fifth Symphony. The Beethoven cycle was continued during his November spell in London, and in December, at home with the Concertgebouw, Haitink made his first foray into the world of Wagner, not a composer with whom he had been associated in the public mind, but whose music he had liked to study in his own time, without the pressures of performance, for many years. The impression was forming in his mind that he should consider starting work on *Lohengrin*, and so the overture to that opera was the first to be recorded, quickly followed by the Prelude and 'Liebestod' from *Tristan und Isolde*, the *Siegfried Idyll* and the Overture to *Parsifal*. Operatic matters were to the fore in the middle of October too, when he conducted the Orchestra of La Scala, Milan – in concert formation. From there he went north-east to Munich for another week with the Bavarian Radio Symphony Orchestra.

Haitink's autumn season at the Royal Festival Hall consisted of three concerts between 7 and 17 November, only the last of which was out of the ordinary. On the Sunday evening he began with Schubert's Eighth Symphony (the 'Unfinished') – by no means a work that often appeared on his programmes – and ended with the Brahms Second Piano Concerto with Claudio Arrau. As the centrepiece, he gave the world première of *Metamorphosis/Dance* by Alexander Goehr. This had been commissioned especially by the LPO, and Haitink demonstrated his commitment to giving new works a decent hearing by repeating it in a different programme in the new year; one of a pair of concerts he gave in London between his annual visit to the Vienna Philharmonic at the beginning of the month and his departure for New York on 26 January.

There, surprisingly belatedly considering his by now secure place in the highest echelons of the musical world and the fact that he had been guest-conducting in the United States for eighteen years, Haitink made his début with the New York Philharmonic Orchestra on 30 January 1975. The programme, as is usual with subscription concerts in both America and mainland Europe, was heard three times, on the Thursday, Saturday and following Tuesday. It perhaps underlines the way in which American audiences are unaware of musicians until they have appeared with the home-town orchestra that the *New York Times* had to qualify its review headline by describing his profession: 'Haitink, Conductor, in Début with Philharmonic.' He had, of course, led tours by both his European orchestras but to New Yorkers he was effectively a new boy, although Andrew Porter was able to tell them in no uncertain terms later that year in the *New Yorker* that 'Mr Haitink must be the conductor most solidly esteemed in Europe today. Solti and Karajan may generate more heat; they are more extravagantly acclaimed, but often with reservation, while Haitink is simply and unanimously praised for his excellence.' After the first concert, which consisted of Bruckner's Seventh Symphony and, an unlikely piece for Haitink, the Symphony in D by Wilhelm Friedemann Bach, the *New York Times*, in the person of Harold C. Schonberg, was more circumspect. 'As a podium figure Mr Haitink is not one of the glamour boys. He does not dance, he does not patronize the best tailor on the

Continent. But he is a dedicated musician . . . an interesting figure and it would be nice to see him around more often.' By and large it was the sort of quiet, sensible assessment that, apart from the remarks about his tailor (for Haitink is a fastidious dresser), he would have appreciated. It was made clear that the New York Philharmonic would be glad to have him back, a re-engagement he fulfilled two years later.

At the Concertgebouw the 1974–5 season saw the most far-reaching change since Haitink had first conducted there in 1956. The orchestra's Artistic Director, Marius Flothuis, retired from the post to take up the professorship of musicology at the University of Utrecht. It had been Flothuis who had drawn the attention of van Beinum to the potential of the young conductor at Netherlands Radio in Hilversum and, when Haitink was installed at the Concertgebouw, had guided the development of his repertoire. There is no doubt that there were times when Haitink found Flothuis's paternalism irksome, and he would have preferred not to have had to battle to convince him that he had a natural affinity with the great classics. On the other hand, without the support and unwavering faith of Flothuis he probably would not have been able to maintain his position with the orchestra during the early years when his reputation was only beginning to be built. Haitink learnt a great deal from Flothuis's experience and musical knowledge as well as his gift for constructing programmes. He relied on the skill and judgement of Flothuis and Dolf van Dantzig, the General Manager, to make sure that the orchestra could look after itself while he concentrated on rehearsal and performance. The efficient team-work meant that Haitink rarely needed to involve himself more deeply in affairs of administration. Paradoxically, had the management been less to his liking at an early stage in his career, Haitink might have found it easier to acquire the habit of imposing his will. However, he has always preferred to veto suggestions which appear unpalatable than to initiate a course of action himself. He trusts those close to him, in most cases, to put forward ideas with which he can concur. For that reason Flothuis's straightforward and civilised approach to his task was invaluable. With his departure Haitink found himself, at forty-five, in the unfamiliar position of being the longest-serving member of the triumvirate at the head of the orchestra's management. For an artist regarded for years as the young pretender, the new role of leader of the establishment was not one with which he readily identified.

The new Artistic Director, who took up his post in September 1974, was Hein van Royen. Younger than Haitink by several years, he had studied law and musicology and was a lecturer in music at The Hague Conservatory. For some time he had been adviser on artistic matters to the Netherlands' rising young conductor, the principal of the Rotterdam Philharmonic Orchestra, Edo de Waart. Van Royen had also been Secretary of the Prince Bernhard Foundation.

As was to be expected after such a long period of stability, there were aspects of the orchestra's affairs which van Royen set out to change and update. Just as Haitink had been unhappy about the high average age of the players a decade before, so van Royen was convinced that it was time for a renewal once again. Over the first three seasons he spearheaded a number of changes in the personnel, particularly among the wind section, which he describes as having been 'painful'. He also felt that, though the orchestra had toured extensively and was directed by a relatively young principal conductor, it had become 'a bit out of touch with the international musical world'. As an organisation it seemed stuffy and complacent, a state induced partly by its comfortable position at the summit of Dutch musical life – a situation reflected in the players' salaries, which are scaled twenty per cent above those of colleagues in the provincial orchestras – and partly by the invariable support of the Amsterdam subscribers, whose attitude was proud but unadventurous.

Another area of the orchestra's work which was in danger of ossification was its recording contract with Philips. In Amsterdam the reverse of Haitink's London situation held true. Whereas the LPO felt that too few of his records were made with them, the Concertgebouw suffered from exclusivity. Because both Haitink and the orchestra were contracted solely to Philips, most of their output was made together. While this limited Haitink's scope to the repertoire thought appropriate in Holland, the orchestra was unable to attract recording work with other conductors whose own exclusive clauses bound them to other companies. This lack of flexibility began to spill over into the day-to-day concert planning, since several conductors with whom the orchestra would have liked to work declined to commit themselves to any worthwhile period of collaboration without the prospect of a potential recording. It was made clear to Philips that patriotic duty to the Dutch recording industry was not enough – especially since it had the smallest market share of the 'big five' companies (the others being EMI, CBS, Decca and Deutsche Grammophon) – and that in future the Concertgebouw would be available to whoever wished to hire it.

Van Royen's taste in repertoire planning reflected a general shift throughout the musical world at the time, which consolidated the range of works played most often within that already familiar to the audience. This, together with an awareness of other, contradictory, fashions meant that he adopted a double-headed policy, narrowing the

number of pieces by composers who formed the backbone of the
schedules but expanding the range at the fringes to take account of the
growing – and largely separate – audience for early and preclassical
music, as well as the equally distinctive audience for contemporary
music. This had the advantage of covering a greater chronological
space while satisfying, at least superficially, a larger section of the
listening population. However, it also meant bringing in specialist
musicians who would tinker with the basic characteristics of the
orchestra's style and sound, a matter about which Haitink was often
less than happy. His own repertoire for the concert hall was by now
well defined, and changed little with the new regime. Mahler and
Bruckner were considered his by right; Beethoven was gradually to
assume a more consistent place; French music remained a firm interest;
Stravinsky was ever-present. He did not insist on any exclusive areas,
though. Van Royen says that Haitink is 'much more generous than
many of his colleagues about releasing repertoire to guest conductors'.
This has led to some strange anomalies: he has rarely conducted
Debussy's *La mer* or some of the Brahms symphonies in the last few
years, not through lack of interest but because they are the works most
often requested for the programme by visiting colleagues.

There were changes of emphasis in Haitink's concerts, however.
Mozart's music began to have a more prominent place as his work in
the opera house expanded, and his increasing interest in Shostakovich
and Strauss was recognised. But relations with Philips began to
deteriorate, as much due to changes in the top management at the
record company as to any decision of Haitink and the Concertgebouw
Orchestra, and both the number and variety of works listed for
recording declined over the following years.

In the spring of 1975 Haitink returned to Glyndebourne to supervise
his first new opera production in England. Stravinsky's *The Rake's
Progress*, the high point of the composer's neoclassical style, had been
mounted at Glyndebourne within two years of its première in 1951.
Whatever Stravinsky's own national origins, it is a peculiarly English
piece, with a libretto by W.H. Auden and Chester Kallman, both
associated closely with Britten's work, and based on William Hogarth's
series of engravings of 1735 which satirised the gin-swilling, bawdy low
life of Georgian London. It was a subject not tackled better since the
ballad operas of John Gay and Pepusch. Glyndebourne had recognised
the cartoon nature of the opera immediately and its first designs in
1953 were by Osbert Lancaster. In 1975, however, the house turned to

an English artist better known for the charm of his paintings and his outrageous lifestyle than for his satire: David Hockney. The choice was inspired, for who better to expose the treachery of fashion than an artist who was himself considered to be at the height of it? Unlike Lancaster, who had set the opera towards the end of the eighteenth century, Hockney used the period and even the graphic texture of the original Hogarth plates. The cross-hatching lines, with which Hogarth achieved his tonal variations, were faithfully recreated, this time in startling colour, however, so that every article on stage, from the chairs to the backcloth and the costumes, maintained the illusion of an illustration come to life. Yet the unreality was preserved as well, with characters and members of the chorus using exaggerated make-up to underline their status as symbols in a morality play rather than flesh and blood (though Hockney and the producer, John Cox, brought out the humanity of the story with telling attention to detail).

For Haitink the production was a breakthrough, awakening his own instincts for the theatre for the first time and so confirming him in the belief that opera could be a natural forum for his work. As he was to prove in later years with Peter Hall, Haitink is at his best when he has been involved in a production from an early stage, so that he feels part of the theatrical process rather than just the director of the music. *The Rake's Progress* was an opera in which he could explore fully his role as an equal partner of the stage team. His thorough knowledge of Stravinsky and his new-found enthusiasm for the visual aspects made the production one of the most remarkable of the decade. He was lucky to have a cast noted for acting ability as much as singing: Jill Gomez (Anne), Don Garrard (Trulove), Donald Gramm (Nick Shadow) and Rosalind Elias (Baba the Turk).

The first night on 21 June set a pattern for the future performances. On his previous appearances in the pit it had been Haitink's qualities that had attracted attention. For *The Rake's Progress*, however, it was the design which was dominant, the startling scenery drawing applause and gasps of astonishment from the audience. The reviewers' art criticism was generally shakier than their music, but most made a gallant attempt, the *Daily Telegraph* finding parallels in Hockney's use of 'pop' representationalism and Stravinsky's pastiche. The same review colourfully described the brothel scene as a 'riot of aphrodisiac attire' which 'provoked stunning feats of coital choreography', an accolade not usually won by opera singers. Luckily not too many people agreed with Rodney Milnes who, in the *Spectator*, wrote off the opera and its production as 'camp hogwash' and 'as pointless as it is puerile'.

Haitink conducted all thirteen performances given that season, and then took the production – or parts of it – to the Proms in the semi-staged arrangement, a compromise between the static presentation of a concert performance and the fully-fledged movement of the theatre, that had become an annual tradition for Glyndebourne at the Royal Albert Hall. The format had the advantage of allowing the music to regain its primacy while letting the audience still become involved in the plot. The Prom, held in grilling heat, gave more people at one sitting than ever before the chance to see what is usually considered a small-theatre work. This time Haitink's contribution was noticed properly. Ronald Crichton wrote in the *Financial Times*:

> Nothing could have been more refreshing, soothing or consoling than these exquisitely controlled and directed jets, trickles and sprays of instrumental sound. For a perfect *Rake* it was, perhaps, a trifle too honeyed and relaxed, but for a packed Promenade in a stifling hall it was ideal. Those edgy, glum, straight-backed readings of the score that one heard in the earlier years of this opera's career seemed leagues away.

As well as being Haitink's first new production for Glyndebourne, *The Rake* marked another début that stands out in retrospect. When it was taken on tour that autumn, the conductor was the twenty-year-old Simon Rattle, making his first appearance in the opera pit.

On 12 August, five days after the Prom, the LPO held its end-of-season press conference, announcing that for the fifth year running it had attracted more people to the Royal Festival Hall than any other London orchestra, though the figure of 82.5 per cent marked the start of a decline in both the national and artistic economy compared with the first few years of the decade. The Managing Director, Eric Bravington, explained that, even with such success at the box office, the gap between costs and income was widening so that 'we shall have to work the orchestra harder than any Continental orchestra is expected to work'. The LPO's budget totalled £800,000, of which £140,000 came indirectly from the state, channelled through the London Orchestral Concert Board (which represented the Arts Council of Great Britain and the Greater London Council); £150,000 was generated at the box office, £80,000 from private donations and business sponsorship, and the remaining money from other promoters, Glyndebourne and the record companies. For Haitink it meant that finance was beginning to dominate the orchestral management's reasoning to the detriment of its artistic judgement.

To underline the problem of trying to square raging inflation with inadequate income, the brochure for the 1975–6 season at the Festival Hall was the first in which the LPO printed a sponsor's name above those of the artists. So Haitink found himself preceded by Commercial Union Assurance, Shiro (UK) and, on two occasions, Philips Electrical, which was celebrating its Golden Jubilee. This last nugget of patronage had its ironic side, since Haitink, like the Concertgebouw Orchestra, had decided not to renew his exclusive recording contract with Philips. While the volume of work for the company had only slackened a little since the peak years of the turn of the decade, the pieces that he was being engaged to conduct broke no new ground and in some cases were merely updates of discs he had made at the start of his career. New management at Philips was less in sympathy with Haitink than had been the case before and was not prepared to consider opera recordings or the English and Russian repertoire in which he was now finding an interest.

This was reflected in his second LPO concert of the season, which consisted of Vaughan Williams's Overture to *The Wasps*, Rachmaninov's Third Piano Concerto and Shostakovich's Tenth Symphony, a collection prepared for the autumn's tour of the Soviet Union. Haitink had conducted in Moscow and Leningrad the year before, but the LPO had not been there since the late 1950s, when it had been the first Western orchestra to visit the country (as it had been to China). It was becoming clear that Haitink's qualities as an interpreter of Mahler and Stravinsky also equipped him well for the music of Shostakovich but, sadly, he did not embark on a complete cycle of the symphonies until after the composer's death. The trip to Russia was as triumphant as that of the previous year with the Concertgebouw. Of the eight concerts, four each in the two main cities, one was memorable for the ovation which brought Haitink back to the stage even after the orchestra had left; another for forcing them to play an encore, something that Haitink usually avoided. Unrehearsed, they launched into Glinka's *Russlan and Ludmilla* Overture, with Haitink, urged on by the leader Rodney Friend, taking it so fast that 'they nearly broke their necks'.

In November the LPO and Haitink made a short tour that was as significant as the one to Russia, though on the face of it less exotic. Funding had not been available for years to allow the LPO to be heard outside London or its handful of regular venues in the South-East of England (many of the Festival Hall concerts were given preliminary hearings in Croydon, Hastings or Eastbourne). Similarly, because Haitink's contract with the LPO forbade him to appear in Britain with any other orchestra (the exception being the occasional visits of the

Concertgebouw), he had not been seen in the North since his concerts with the Liverpool Philharmonic and the Hallé a decade earlier. In Scotland too his appearances had been confined to the Edinburgh Festival. Now, however, the mixed blessing of business sponsorship made it possible for the orchestra to roam the country for five days. Commercial Union Assurance underwrote the deficits and British Rail provided free tickets for the train journeys. Edinburgh, Glasgow, Manchester, Liverpool and Huddersfield were visited, Haitink conducting in Huddersfield for the first time since his English début in May 1959. In Manchester Haydn's Symphony No.95 and Bruckner's Eighth formed the programme, the interpretation of which was described by the author (in one of his first, rather ham-fisted attempts at music criticism) as one of the 'landmarks of today's musical scene'. Sadly the tour did not create a precedent and in future years it was the LSO which took on the duty towards the rest of Britain.

After a few weeks in Amsterdam over Christmas, Haitink returned to the LPO in the middle of January 1976 for three concerts. In the first Sheila Armstrong, Norma Procter, Peter Pears and John Shirley-Quirk joined him for Bach's Mass in B minor, an area of the repertoire which he was allowed to explore all too infrequently. In the second he came to the other extreme of the musical spectrum, giving the world première of the *Concerto for the Instruments of an Orchestra*, commissioned by the LPO from John Mayer. In the same month he continued to record the Beethoven piano concertos with Alfred Brendel (a project started in November) and performed them in public during March. Most importantly for the future, it was announced at the end of January that Haitink would become Musical Director of Glyndebourne from 1979. The notion that he had the wrong background for running an opera house – asserted in many interviews over the years – had obviously been abandoned. While the appointment was seen as something of a coup for Glyndebourne, it did not surprise many people who knew Haitink. His experience with *The Rake's Progress* had left him more than a little stage-struck.

The decision was made public in time for his winter visit to America. A week was spent in Cleveland, which (whatever he thought of the city's environment) nevertheless had his favourite orchestra in the United States. From Ohio he went west to a town the architecture and orchestra of which he had wanted to sample for years, but had never been able to find an opportunity: Chicago. He took in the museums, directed a rehearsal of the Civic Orchestra and, nineteen years after conducting in America for the first time, gave several concerts with the Chicago Symphony in Orchestra Hall. The works chosen for his début pointedly marked the contrast between his style and that of the orchestra's usual conductor, Sir Georg Solti. Thomas Willis wrote in the *Chicago Tribune*:

> The Mendelssohn brought Haitink clearly into view and I have seldom heard a *Scottish* performance so completely satisfying. Haitink has a different ideal sound in mind than most of our great conductors. Strings and wind coexist in a subtly balanced relation- ship with maximum give and take. Some solos stand out more sharply than we are accustomed to hearing, but in other places the strings take on a resonant, blooming tone which brings out the best in the hall.

The picture caption read: 'Low on ambition, high on talent', a remark which was only half true.

Ravel's *Alborada del gracioso* and Mozart's Piano Concerto K.456, in which Judith Burganger was the débutante soloist, made up the rest of the programme given on his forty-seventh birthday. The coming year was not to be one of his happiest, for the outward success masked an increasing dissatisfaction with many areas of his life. One of the subjects weighing heavily on his mind was broached in an interview that week with the *Chicago Daily News*, though the journalist missed its significance. 'I am too full of work,' Haitink said. 'My roots are in Amsterdam but London gives me so much pleasure. I should give up an orchestra now – but it can't be Amsterdam. I have to make a decision.' That decision, like many in his life (for he prefers events to overtake them), was a long time in the making. As a result the intervening period was less than comfortable, either for himself or for those with whom he worked regularly. It was appropriate that his final piece of music for the fortnight with the Chicago Symphony Orchestra was the Fourth Symphony of Shostakovich; an unsettled work, raw and uncompromising, which heralded a transition for the composer that at times brought him close to the brink of emotional catastrophe.

It was a sign of the way things were going that the first production Haitink should conduct at Glyndebourne after the announcement of his future position there should turn out to be one of the most thorough flops of his career, mitigated, according to the press, only by his own reading of the score and the performance of Michael Devlin. The pity of it was that *Pelléas et Mélisande* is such perfect Haitink territory. His inherent feeling for French music, together with an increasing interest in Wagner and the experience with the vast symphonic structures of Bruckner, made him a natural interpreter of the opaque poetry of Debussy's music. The problems began in rehearsal when it became necessary to find a singer for the part of Pelléas as a last-minute replacement. The singer who was engaged, André Jobin, was a less than successful choice whom the critics castigated for failing to master Debussy's style or, rather worse, sing in tune. The production, directed by René Terrasson, from the theatre in Nantes, was a heavily symbolic affair, largely static and dressed up in various uninspiring shades of beige and grey. 'Doomed figures move about almost like zombies in a dun-coloured landscape,' wrote Alan Blyth in *The Times*. 'Gestures are mostly uncommunicative, or else add unnecessary glosses. Essential action is often ignored or misconstrued.'

Haitink himself, judging from his half-hearted defence in interviews at the time, was less than entirely convinced himself. Neither was the Glyndebourne management. After its nine performances, beginning on 6 June 1976, the production was tactfully dropped from the company's repertoire and a veil was drawn over its existence. It was not toured either, and in the official histories of the company it tends to be skipped over by convenient omission. Nevertheless, Haitink's work was at least given a chance to be assessed unencumbered by the producer when it was performed at the Proms on 11 August. In the Albert Hall, Michael Devlin's portrayal of Golaud and Haitink's understanding of Debussy's idiom were able to overcome any of the otherwise weak links in the cast.

Three days later Haitink's feelings of stability with the LPO were weakened further when the leader during his whole time with the orchestra, Rodney Friend, gave his last concert before moving to New York. Six months earlier the New York Philharmonic had begun to sound him out. The post of 'concert master' there offered more money, more security and a less hectic schedule. Both Pierre Boulez and Zubin Mehta, the New York Philharmonic's conductor and conductor elect, had visited him in London, and eventually the prospect of becoming the first British violinist to lead a great foreign orchestra seemed too good an opportunity to turn down. Although it was not realised at the time, his departure, at the end of the orchestra's Prom dates for the season, marked the start of the LPO's gradual descent from the artistic summits that it had conquered in the early years of the decade.

The new leader was David Nolan. As Friend had been when he was given the post twelve years earlier, Nolan was in his early twenties. For a young leader, inexperienced and anxious to survive in a position which usually takes the blame if an orchestra is seen to be slipping, it could hardly have been a more difficult time to arrive. The financial crisis, despite the LPO's continuing health at the box office, showed no sign of abating, and Haitink's worsening feud with the management was by now an open secret. Throughout the autumn and winter, while maintaining, for public relations reasons, that his loyalty to and warmth for the LPO was undiminished, Haitink was dropping hints in the press that three directorships would be too much and that, once he was installed at Glyndebourne, something would have to be eliminated. Since his guest engagements rarely accounted for more than two months each year and he had made it very clear that Amsterdam was his main responsibility, it was not difficult to work out which of his commitments was likely to be axed.

Haitink's suspicions that the LPO's Managing Director, Eric Bravington, was keen to replace him with Sir Georg Solti seemed to be confirmed by the autumn of 1976. Solti was due to conduct six programmes at the Royal Festival Hall during the coming season, Haitink only six and a half, a schedule hardly reflecting his titles of Principal Conductor and Artistic Director. Bravington felt that, having raised the standard of the LPO, Haitink had served his purpose and it now needed a more glamorous figure at its head. 'He believed, quite genuinely,' says Haitink, 'that Solti would bring a new excitement and greater international kudos to the orchestra. I think the idea that you could make the LPO into the Chicago Symphony was mad, just as I never contemplated turning it into the Concertgebouw. Traditions are different in different places and you can't transplant them.' A factor which, unbeknown to any of those involved, was making the situation yet more difficult was that Bravington was suffering at the time from a tumour on the brain.

For the first time Haitink's unhappiness with the situation was spilling over into his day-to-day work with the orchestra. After two warm-up concerts at the Festival Hall, they flew to America. There, on tour to celebrate the bicentenary of the Declaration of Independence, they gave twenty-one concerts in not many more days. One player described it as 'thoroughly unpleasant. We did Mahler's Fifth every other night. Haitink was totally miserable and could hardly bring himself to say "thank you".' The rest of the music was almost as taxing. In the first of the pair of programmes was Mendelssohn's Scottish Symphony (which New York had heard Haitink conduct eleven months earlier with its own orchestra), and Shostakovich's Tenth. In the second programme the Mahler work was preceded by the *Philharmonic Concerto* by Malcolm Arnold, written especially for the tour and given its première in the Festival Hall on 31 October. Arnold, like Bravington, had played in the LPO's trumpet section under van Beinum. The notices were appreciative, rather than euphoric as they had been for the LPO's first visit five years before, the *New York Times* pointing out that it was 'not one of the very greatest orchestras in the world . . .' but 'perfectly serviceable and often rather more than that'.

December was spent in Amsterdam, recording Debussy: *Images* and *Danse sacrée et danse profane*, one of Haitink's most atmospheric interpretations. Five days in Munich at the start of the new year must have seemed a welcome relief from his directorial duties. London had to be faced again at the end of January, however, for two performances of *The Planets* and the London première of Luciano Berio's *La ritirata notturna di Madrid*. The photograph that appeared in the *Guardian* on the day of the first concert pictured him looking pensive and lacklustre, seated on a bean-bag. Press interest was high at the time, in response to the release, to coincide with the LPO's American tour, of the Beethoven symphony cycle. The general feeling, from press, orchestra and Haitink himself, was that it was a useful first statement but, sooner or later, the symphonies would need to be looked at again.

Most of February was spent in New York, where he renewed his collaboration with Rodney Friend. The main initiative of 1977, and the one which pointed to the future more provocatively than he could have imagined at the time, came on his return to London. This time it was not the LPO which demanded his attention, but the Royal Opera House, Covent Garden, where he made his début on 14 March. It was not only his first night there, but also his first in any large theatre of world stature. It was almost as though, shortly after his forty-eighth birthday and having become the complete master of the concert hall, he was beginning his professional life all over again. Prior to 1977 he had conducted three productions in Holland and four in England over a fifteen-year period. That year alone he was due to conduct four more, two of them in new stagings.

As at Glyndebourne five years earlier, he started at Covent Garden with a Mozart revival, this time of John Copley's 1973 production of *Don Giovanni*, re-rehearsed by the staff producer, Ande Anderson. The cast was a strong mixture of youth and experience, with the title role being taken by the American baritone who had been the one outstanding feature of *Pelléas* the previous season, Michael Devlin. As his servant Leporello, Geraint Evans had the security of years in the part, as did Elizabeth Vaughan as Elvira. Gwynne Howell was the Commendatore, Stuart Burrows Don Ottavio and, drawing most praise, Elizabeth Gale Zerlina ('a delectable sweetmeat', one paper called her). The results cannot be said to have been a total success. Haitink did not feel at home with the production and seemed unsure about how to tailor his view of Mozart opera to a house so much larger than Glyndebourne. The rushed nature of rehearsals, the unsympathetic staging and an audience that was a fine example, as the *Financial Times* reported, of multinational philistinism, 'with much whispering, rustling and cases of terminal whooping cough on all sides', was too much a reminder of his first *Don Giovanni* in Amsterdam to be comfortable. For Haitink, with his confidence already at a low ebb, it was something of a setback.

While the experience did nothing to advance Haitink's sense of achievement, it was not wholly wasted. He had established his credentials at the Royal Opera House, tested the system there and reacquainted himself with the work which was to dominate the following months. Having completed the run of London performances, he moved to Glyndebourne, for the same opera, but in very different circumstances. At Covent Garden *Don Giovanni* had been an unadventurous affair. At Glyndebourne it proved to be a landmark for a whole collection of reasons.

Essentially there were two versions of the opera in Sussex that summer. The first was conducted by the retiring music director, John Pritchard, and had Benjamin Luxon as the seducer and Stafford Dean as Leporello; as in the Covent Garden performances, Elizabeth Gale was Zerlina. The production opened the season on the last day of May. Pritchard's Mozartian style was, as usual, gracious and easy-flowing, but it fitted strangely with the vision of the producer, Peter Hall, who had concentrated on the demonic ferocity of Don Giovanni, not his slick attractiveness. His dark approach found a more natural proponent in Bernard Haitink. When he inherited the production on 10 July, there was a feeling that, at the third attempt, Haitink was in charge of a *Don Giovanni* in which he had complete faith and which he could make his own. Almost uniquely, the performances with the second cast had more dramatic and musical unity than those with the first. In theory Haitink's singers had been rehearsed by Stewart Trotter, yet Hall's mark was set more clearly on their acting, and from them and the LPO Haitink drew a view of Mozart that brought him into the forefront of twentieth-century theatre, without being false to the tradition from which the opera sprang. As Don Giovanni himself they had Thomas Allen, an almost angry hero, furiously rampaging towards self-destruction. The same energy drove all the characters. There could be no doubt about their avenging power, unleashed to match Don Giovanni's own. With Richard Van Allan's Leporello, John Rawnsley's raunchy Masetto and Philip Langridge's unusually masculine Don Ottavio, the physical violence inherent in the opera was allowed to spill out. The result of such passion meant that Haitink found himself in charge of a production that became an instant yardstick against which others were judged.

Hall's and Haitink's confidence in the dramatic force of the production was underlined when it became the first opera to be mounted in the new National Theatre in London, where Hall was Director. The Lyttelton Theatre's pit was even more cramped than Glyndebourne's, with the orchestra so far under the stage that the music, as well as the demons that were dragging Giovanni to hell, came from a subterranean fastness. Haitink, squeezed perilously between the front row of the audience and the structure of the stage, could hardly move his arms and it was impossible for his beat to be seen simultaneously by the singers and the timpanist. None the less the feeling was growing by then, 16 August, that the partnership of Hall and Haitink was producing music-theatre of a coherence and in-telligence not seen in England since the days of their precursors at Glyndebourne, Carl Ebert and Fritz Busch.

The exhilaration had been equally strong at the semi-staged performance for the Proms the previous week in the Royal Albert Hall. That night, 8 August, in gruelling heat, Allen's portrayal was re-enacted. Many of the critics opted to stay at home and listen to the radio broadcast, so missing an acting performance that, for its concentrated urgency with the minimum of props and design, would have done the Royal Shakespeare Company's philosophy of 'bare boards and a passion' proud. Haitink, in his favourite forum, enjoyed himself as he had hardly done for eighteen months.

With the launching of his most successful attempt at Mozart and the simultaneous revival of the production of *The Rake's Progress* that had been such a revelation to him two years before, Haitink was finding a satisfaction in the opera house that had deserted him in the concert hall for some time. However, the sense of staleness and *déjà vu* which dogged his purely orchestral work, after twenty-one years as a principal conductor, did not follow him to Glyndebourne. With the LPO and the Concertgebouw his position was one of isolation. In Sussex he was able to merge into a team. There he had ample time to rehearse, collaborators of comparable professional stature and, for him at least, a process of learning which could revive his inspiration. Just as *Don Giovanni* began a fruitful period with Peter Hall, so *The Rake's Progress* launched one with the young soprano Felicity Lott,

(*Phonogram International*)
With Dietrich Fischer-Dieskau in December 1980 for
Shostakovich's Symphony No. 14 in Amsterdam

With Kyril Kondrashin
Phonogram Internationál

(*Guy Gravett/Glyndebourne Festival Opera*)

Peter Hall and Bernard Haitink's production of Così fan tutte for Glyndebourne, which became one of their most successful collaborations. (Bozena Betley as Fiordiligi, Håkan Hagegård as Guglielmo, Stafford Dean as Don Alfonso, Maria Ewing as Dorabella and Max-René Cosotti as Ferrando)

Simon Boccanegra at Glyndebourne in 1986 with Timothy Noble in the title role, and Carol Vaness as Amelia

(*Guy Gravett/Glyndebourne Festival Opera*)

Marianne and Tessa, the eldest and youngest of Haitink's five children, in Sussex in 1986

Bernard Haitink and Ashley Putham at Covent Garden
during the rehearsals for *Jenůfa* in October 1986
(Zoe Dominic)

(Kippa, Amsterdam)

With the Concertgebouw Orchestra

who made her Glyndebourne début that season as Anne Trulove. Flott, as she is universally nicknamed, became an important part of his journey of discovery into opera over the following decade, convincing him, among other things, of the excellence of the English singing tradition.

As important to Haitink's renewed vigour as the success at Glyndebourne was the fact that he had at last made a decision. On 16 July *Classical Music Weekly* reported:

> The LPO has released the following press statement. 'After what will have been a period of twelve years in the position, Bernard Haitink has decided, with regret, to relinquish his appointment as Principal Conductor and Artistic Director of the London Philharmonic Orchestra in two years' time, at the end of the 1978–9 season. He does not intend to sever links with the London Philharmonic Orchestra but he feels that his work as Musical Director of Glyndebourne Festival Opera and Principal Conductor of the Concertgebouw Orchestra requires that he should reduce his administrative and some artistic responsibilities. Mr Haitink will retain a close connection with the orchestra through concerts and recordings in London and opera at Glyndebourne in the years ahead.'

As such statements go, it was a terse one, only just hiding the tension between Haitink and Bravington. The optimism of the final sentence was not borne out in practice, but for Haitink the relief was worth the loss of his London base.

VII
Haitink and the classics

WHATEVER HAITINK'S EXPERTISE in the music of the twentieth century, it is as a conductor of the classics that he would like to be regarded. He approached the works of Mozart, Beethoven and Schumann with great caution in the early part of his career, although Brahms, Mendelssohn and Dvořák were part of his repertoire from the beginning. Even now he feels that he has not yet mastered several of the Schubert symphonies. He did not give Beethoven symphony cycles until he was well over forty, and the four Schumann symphonies waited even longer. It was only with his Glyndebourne experience that he felt completely confident of his approach to Mozart. For all that, however, Haitink is a naturally classical conductor. It was in the classics that his musical taste was nurtured, and the musicians he admired were not the flamboyant figures of opera or new music, but the inheritors of the nineteenth-century Germanic tradition. The Concertgebouw, and Amsterdam music generally, was steeped in this tradition and was in many ways, despite its nationality and location, the most solid bastion of it outside Vienna and Berlin. However much Haitink valued his Ravel and Stravinsky, there was little doubt that, to be taken seriously as a worthy successor to Mengelberg and van Beinum, he had, sooner or later, to become a serious rival to the German school of conducting in its own music.

The first composer whose works encouraged the belief that Haitink was capable of such mastery was Bruckner. These massive works simply do not hold together unless conducted by someone with an intrinsic sense of large-scale musical form, a quality which is often the slowest to develop in a conductor. For Haitink, however, it was just this need for overall shape which most attracted him to the symphonies. Amsterdam is perhaps the only city other than Vienna where Bruckner's music is at the core of the repertoire, and so to a certain extent it was always in Haitink's bloodstream. That should also have been true of Mahler, yet he was comfortable with Bruckner's symphonies long before he felt at home with Mahler's.

'At one of my earliest concerts with Netherlands Radio I was asked to do Bruckner's Ninth Symphony and the *Te Deum*. Some people thought they were crazy to ask such a young man to do that programme but it went well and I never looked back. I did not find the symphonies too hard to learn and I enjoyed them, as I still do. I have always loved the mountains and I found that the sheer spaciousness in Bruckner's music reflected them. Maybe that sounds a bit picturesque, but when you hear it you do have that feeling that you are in some ethereal atmosphere. Then, on a more intellectual level, I have always been fascinated by the architecture of the symphonies; that the movements could be so long and yet maintain a feeling of coherent structure.'

More than any other symphonies of their time, those of Bruckner have been beset by problems of editorial interference, complicated further by the composer's own habit of regular and comprehensive revision. The two main editions are those by Haas, published in the 1930s, and Nowak, published twenty years later. Haitink is a strong believer in the former and does not conduct the Nowak. 'I am against it,' he says. 'The Nowak cuts in the Eighth Symphony, for example, are appalling. They do not help at all!'

Although Haitink says that in Amsterdam, unlike Vienna, there is no undue reverence accorded to Bruckner and admits that there is a section of the audience that still finds the symphonies too long and too Teutonic, the Concertgebouw Orchestra has taken the style required by Bruckner's music as part of its traditional sound. The warmth of the hall itself, the fullness of the string playing and a matching sonority for the wind section characterise and comprise the Concertgebouw's individuality. That too has become closely associated with the sound favoured by Haitink, with appropriate adjustments for the relevant styles in other music.

'I was immediately struck by the sound of the orchestras when I started conducting in Amsterdam, and I well remember my first tour – a very extended one across the United States. Eugen Jochum conducted most of the concerts and so, wherever we were, I was very often sitting in the hall listening. The sound, very warm with weighty strings and woodwind, opened my eyes to the importance of balance, and that awareness has made an imprint on my musical taste. There was one problem then – a very serious one – that the orchestra played everything in the Brahms and Bruckner style. Now that has changed gradually over the years. Ashkenazy has said that the Concertgebouw can now play Prokofiev without always reminding you that it is a Brahms orchestra.'

It was important to Haitink to encourage that flexibility in the orchestra's approach without losing the basic sound of which it was justly proud. The imprint of that sound affected him wherever he worked. In London he strove to enrich the string tone of the LPO and was pleased when critics compared it with that of the Concertgebouw – although, unlike one later Principal Conductor, he was careful not to pit the two orchestras against each other by making comparisons in rehearsal. Nevertheless, in Amsterdam he encouraged something of the stylistic freedom of his London orchestra to become implanted in the Concertgebouw, especially in the wind and brass sections where the LPO's precision and focus was superior. The result of the combination was a distinctive Haitink sound, rich but meticulously clear at the same time, and adaptable to the widest range of symphonic music from Mozart to Shostakovich.

Encouraging this sound was something at which he worked hard, though 'not too consciously and not too obtrusively; it happens with your gesture, with your eyes, with the few words you use to get real results. That is what a conductor can do.' Alexander Cameron, principal cellist of the LPO throughout Haitink's tenure, feels that it was achieved by gentle but constant reminding about a sense of classical style, stopping the strings when there was a false accent and making the players conscious of the need for a rounded, homogeneous tone.

If warmth was what Haitink wanted from the string section, then it was clarity and a sense of line that he required of the wind. This was a matter not merely of the way in which the musicians played, but also, just as importantly, of the number of instruments to a part. The question of doubling is one which Haitink feels is at the heart of his style, especially in Beethoven and Mozart.

'I think I am one of the few conductors,' he says, 'who, after long consideration, refuse to double the wind in Beethoven symphonies, except in the Ninth and, on occasion in London, the Fifth. Riccardo Chailly [Haitink's successor at the Concertgebouw] was very surprised, since he doubles in everything. It is very interesting because I believe that now, with the excellent wind players the orchestra has, and this beautiful hall, it does not add anything to your music-making. On the contrary, it does not make the sound clearer, it makes it more confused, more out of tune. What you gain in the total amount of sound, you lose in focus. The strings have to fight harder, so you lose the subtlety.

'In Vienna they have the same situation as at the Concertgebouw, and the Philharmonic was relieved that I did not double, because the players said that it makes music-making much more complicated and less pleasant. It forces the strings to play unnaturally and you end up ruining the balance. In Berlin, on the other hand, they are used to doubling everything. So was the Cleveland Orchestra under Szell, but Szell had a way of doing it which was his own and very subtle.'

While not a participant in the academic business of experimenting with 'authentic' style, Haitink feels that he realised instinctively that, within the bounds of the Victorian symphony orchestra, there needed to be some reform of performance practice. 'Even without a musicological upbringing, I always tried to conduct classical works in a way which was lighter than that of some of my famous colleagues.' This realisation has made it both easier and more difficult for Haitink to respond to the demands of the 'authenticity' lobby. It is, he believes, impossible for anybody to tell precisely how music was played and, even more importantly, heard two hundred years ago. 'Even if you try to follow the rules of the time,' he says, 'you still have the problem of different instruments, different halls and – it must be said – different ears. The human ear of 1750, for any number of reasons, must be different from that of today. We cannot imagine Mozart, who sometimes could not tolerate even the sound of the trumpet when he was young, listening to *The Rite of Spring*!

'The danger is that if we become too authentic, too musicological, we lose the human touch. We must communicate in a way which makes sense to our listeners today. When I was in New York some years ago I met some people who had, as students, heard me conduct a concert in Boston that I had quite forgotten. It consisted of Mozart's *Serenata notturna*, Ravel's *Mother Goose* and Strauss's *Ein Heldenleben*. They paid me what I considered to be a big compliment. They said each work sounded different from the others and seemed in the right style. So in Mozart I never go for exaggerated dynamics; I avoid rubato or overdone crescendos. The size of the orchestra depends on the hall. In Amsterdam, for Mozart's and Haydn's late symphonies I have twelve first violins, ten seconds, eight violas, six cellos and four basses, and that seems to work well. With less than that the sound can become thin, which I don't like. You get the real string sound and you can still hear the winds; one flute, two oboes. I am very aware now, especially in the last ten years, of the importance of balancing an orchestra correctly; that you must not have loud brass which bursts over the whole string section. I want to hear what is going on.'

Technical decisions about style are central to Haitink's interpretation of the classics, but, he says, 'there are other things which are perhaps more important. If you are working on *Don Giovanni* you become amazed at Mozart's insight into human character and his way of expressing it, so that you forget about mere matters of style. If, for some reason, I could never hear Mahler or Shostakovich again, well, it would be a pity. But if I could not hear Mozart, particularly the three da Ponte operas, that would be really terrible.'

That same indispensability applies to the Beethoven symphonies. Most orchestras and conductors programme Beethoven because the audience is familiar with the music, tickets will sell and the players can produce a respectable performance that will reflect reasonably on the conductor, however uninteresting his interpretation. For Haitink the works are too important for such a mundane approach and he has come to terms with them slowly, only in the last decade reaching a point where he feels sure of his ability to oversee worthwhile performances consistently. Partly because of the doubts of the Concertgebouw Orchestra about the advisability of allowing a young conductor to purvey works which it usually left to the old masters, Haitink's experience of Beethoven was, until the middle of the 1970s, comparatively slender. His first performances of the symphonies with the LPO earned him praise from the critics, as did the box of records that followed, but Haitink himself had considerable reservations, regarding them as preliminary essays. Even in his mid-forties he felt they were 'young man's Beethoven'. He was dissatisfied with some tempi and with a sound that he feels was a little dispassionate and clinical. A few years later his ideas proved to be more settled.

'The breakthrough came with the cycle we performed in Amsterdam and then took to America. At that time everybody thought of the Concertgebouw as a Mahler and Bruckner orchestra and were surprised that we should take Beethoven on tour, but it proved a tremendous success both in New York and Washington. From then on I gained in confidence. I think the danger lies in performing a single Beethoven symphony in isolation. If you do a cycle the whole thing can be seen in perspective. You see the development and the inner growth much better if you play them in a group, and to live with those works for six weeks is an enlightening experience.

'Beethoven is so varied; each symphony is different and that is a mark of the genius of the man. Number six is a unique achievement, and then the changes between seven, eight and nine are incredible. In a way it is superhuman to ask one man to do all nine symphonies equally well. They encompass so many different worlds that one conductor will do number five brilliantly while another will do a very poetic performance of the *Pastoral*, but that is not to say that the same person can do them all. I think we are all frightened of them. You cannot pretend in Beethoven.

'When you remember all those conductors who have recorded the symphonies, you wonder what you can add to that whole heap of knowledge and experience. As a young man you think you should try some unusual interpretation, but of course that is quite wrong. One has to come to a realisation of the works through maturing and growing. Confidence is perhaps the greatest asset one gains with years.

'I think I have changed my overall approach because I am, I hope, more mature and more experienced, and I think that they could all gain from that, both technically and musically. Now the internal changes are less obtrusive. That is an art of its own in classical music, to make transitions so that people do not notice them unduly – that there are no scars on the composition.

'As far as the detail is concerned, I make most of the repeats, except the first-movement exposition in the *Eroica*. If you do that one I feel you lose the intensity of the development. Nor do I repeat the exposition in the finale of the Fifth Symphony. I do not think I have the sheer physical energy for that, though I know Carlos Kleiber makes it; so did Klemperer on his records. But I do not have the stamina to hold the concentration there twice over.'

While Haitink has grown into the Beethoven symphonies slowly and carefully, those of Brahms have been evenly but intermittently spaced throughout his conducting life. The quality of his interpretations, however, he feels has been more erratic, and the recordings of the four symphonies, made between May 1970 and June 1973 with the Concertgebouw Orchestra, reflect this variability. He is still pleased with the disc of the Third Symphony (which marked the beginning of the series), but is less proud of the Fourth, made two years later, which he feels was recorded before his interpretation was ready. 'Number four is not easy to approach. It takes time. It is like old wine which must settle for years and years. You do not automatically have a public success with it, but when I came back to it recently [with the Philharmonia at the end of 1986 in the Festival Hall], having not conducted it for nearly ten years, it was like meeting an old friend.'

If the Fourth is the hardest of the quartet to bring off in the concert hall, Haitink feels that it is almost impossible to fail with the First Symphony. 'Technically it is not simple,' he says, 'but you can get a better result more easily. It is possible to get away with it. You can always have a tremendous public success with it. The First makes an impression. In a way it is safe and solid, perhaps the least subtle and most German of the four. However, having said that, the second movement is extremely beautiful and very difficult to shape properly. But the finale, of course, nearly cannot go wrong. It ends in such a glorious mood, all you need to do is let the orchestra play.' Perhaps because it is such a sure success, Haitink has conducted it relatively infrequently, not out of any perverse objection to popular applause, but because it is often used as a vehicle by guest conductors eager to make an impression. Haitink's preference for remaining with the orchestras with which he had full-time duties meant that the showpiece works were usually ceded to visitors who had more to lose from an unenthusiastic response.

'Perhaps I should have insisted more often,' he reflects, 'but then I was not a real music director in Amsterdam. That was not my title. I was Conductor of the Orchestra. There was a feeling in Amsterdam that the guest conductors should do the classical repertoire and the principal should do works which are more on the fringe of things.'

Of the middle pair of Brahms symphonies Haitink admits that he has 'always had a weakness for number three. It is a wonderful piece, with a mixture of extremely symphonic and chamber music which always fascinated me. But it is also the most difficult to play and to conduct. The reasons are purely technical, for example in the first movement, the 6/4 in 2 and then alternating in 6 at the beat and then leading the musicians into a fluent style without stopping, without too many ritardandos: it is very hard, and rhythmically it is tricky too, making it the most difficult to conduct well.'

Now that Haitink is to be found more often in the opera-house pit than in front of a symphony orchestra, it is inevitable that his repertoire should have narrowed to a core of composers and works about which he feels he has most to say. None the less, there are considerable gaps which he has never tried to fill. He has hardly ever conducted the symphonies of Sibelius or Nielsen, for example, or ventured far into the Russian school – Mussorgsky, Rimsky-Korsakov or Borodin – or attempted much of Grieg or Smetana. He has a general lack of enthusiasm for the nationalist-period works, with the exception of Dvořák whose idiom, for all its Bohemian flavour, is perhaps close enough to that of Brahms and the central culture to fall within his sphere. At the start of his career Dvořák's symphonies, especially the Seventh and Eighth, were among the works Haitink performed most often. The Seventh (then numbered the second) was the first work he recorded, and the Eighth (then the fourth) exists in a rather boxed-in sounding version made in 1963. However, in the last fifteen years even these have fallen into abeyance. This is a great shame, for with Haitink's feel for balance and transition, as well as his insistence on unobtrusive rhythmic clarity, the warm Central European world of Dvořák is natural territory for him. Perhaps because of his growing attraction to opera, his favoured composer from the last decade of the nineteenth century has been Richard Strauss, whose lush tone poems satisfy a streak of unbridled romanticism in Haitink that is often masked by the outward restraint of his personality. *Don Juan, Ein Heldenleben* and *Also sprach Zarathustra* have consistently held their place in his affections, while he regards the performance and recording of the Alpine Symphony as an achievement from which he derived enormous pleasure, though the extraordinary demands that the work makes on orchestral personnel and finances have prevented him from tackling it as often as he would have wished. It is perhaps an obvious point, but his affection for the symphonies of Bruckner and Mahler, together with the Alpine Symphony and Mendelssohn's Scottish Symphony, is stimulated as much by the love for the mountains of a conductor whose home is in the flat and submarinal land of Holland as by appreciation of pure musical form.

It is symptomatic of the differing concerns of record companies and concert promoters that there are a number of works which Haitink has performed successfully for the microphone but never programmed in the concert hall. This is particularly true of the series of Liszt symphonic poems he recorded with the LPO in the 1970s. As with the Shostakovich symphonies, they were works he knew very little about when he signed the contract to record them and, although he found the experience interesting, only a handful of the dozen or so issued on record surfaced at the Royal Festival Hall. They represented an area of the repertoire in which he was uneasy, and he still feels that the performances must have been unconvincing. 'However, there was one piece which fascinated me and still does, but which I was never able to programme: *Héroïde funèbre*. It is an incredibly long piece but it has something special, though I never felt that I was a true Liszt disciple.'

The same is true to a certain extent of Haitink's attitude to Tchaikovsky. Here again he has made a successful and comprehensive set of recordings, yet, with the exception of the Fourth and Sixth Symphonies, the works have never taken a permanent hold on his affections. However, they did give Haitink the opportunity to draw on some of the LPO's finest playing at a time when its string section was at its strongest. As with Strauss and Bruckner, the unfettered romanticism of Tchaikovsky's music is a quality which Haitink can fully nurture without lapsing into tasteless sentimentality. His strength is that he is able to direct the listener into the more searing emotions of the music without losing grip of the orchestral balance or milking the traumatic moments at the expense of the symphonies' overall shape.

This ability to be emotional without being seen to wallow in the more treacle-bound reaches of romantic music is particularly valuable in the works of three composers who have suffered badly over the years from mawkish interpretations: Mendelssohn, Rachmaninov and Elgar. He has, as yet, never recorded the Rachmaninov symphonies, but he has taped the piano concertos with Vladimir Ashkenazy, a collaboration which makes full use of the restrained warmth that characterises their personalities and also marks the style encouraged by Haitink at the Concertgebouw.

This restraint, when applied to Mendelssohn, brings out the classical elements of his music rather than the drawing-room gentility or, in the Scottish Symphony and the *Hebrides* Overture, phoney nostalgia that so often overwhelms Mendelssohn's craftsmanship. When he first began conducting, Haitink tended to overcompensate in his determination not to sound sentimental, and his readings sometimes verged on the impersonal as a result. It is illuminating to compare his 1963 recording of the Italian Symphony, played by the Concertgebouw Orchestra, with the one he made fifteen years later with the LPO. In the intervening years the tempi changed little, only slackening a shade so that the momentum in the 1978 recording is still as forceful, but without the tendency to rush that spoilt the earlier one. The main difference – and the evidence for the benefits of maturity – lies in the way in which Haitink reassesses his orchestral balance. The wind section is better integrated with the string sound, the brass plays with less aggression and transitions within movements are managed more gracefully. There is a realisation that to attack the beginning of a phrase does not mean that it needs to be annihilated in order to maintain the excitement.

It is the same lack of unnecessary gesture that gives substance to Haitink's interpretations of Elgar. He is often complimented on making the 'Enigma' Variations and the two symphonies sound 'Continental'. If that is taken to mean that he avoids the hollow Edwardian rhetoric with which Elgar's works are so often lumbered, and treats the music seriously, then Haitink is pleased to accept the praise. Yet he feels that the remarks betray a certain provincialism in the attitude of the English towards their own music which he believes is misplaced. 'Before I started studying the music I heard only the "grand manner", but I soon found there's much more to it than that. There is tremendous melancholy and insecurity in his music. What attracts me is not the "Crown Imperial" feeling – which I take in my stride – but the loneliness. He is part of the line of Brahms, Dvořák and Strauss, and when I started to look at his metronome marks and his meticulous directions in the score, I found many indications which help you move in that direction. I was astonished to hear so many conductors pulling the music apart, and equally surprised at his own performances which are very true to the score. There is a tradition of English music which crosses the Channel and Elgar is part of it.

'I had to think about the music because it is not in my blood, therefore there is no point in pretending that I see it as an Englishman. People are waving the flag after the First Symphony, but not after the Second, which makes it a fascinating piece. The grand Edwardian gesture is killed, all the time, and then it is such sad and lonely music. It is a shattering piece and also much more difficult to perform than number one. There are many more good performances of the First than of the Second. To achieve the emotions in the 12/8 passage at the beginning is not easy, and there is something of the music of *Parsifal* in the Second Symphony too.

'I came late to Elgar, but now I am very fond of it and it is very special. I cannot stand it when people say there was an amateurish side to him because that is not true at all. He was such a professional musician and his craftsmanship was extraordinary. To be able to take such complex emotions, translate them into music and then write that down is an incredible achievement, and I have the highest respect for the composers who can do that.'

VIII

A knight out of London

B OTH ELGAR SYMPHONIES were included in Haitink's season
with the LPO in 1977–8: a series of eleven concerts at the Royal
Festival Hall, the normal number. For his tenth anniversary
season as Principal Conductor, it included, as well as the Elgar
symphonies, the London première of Lutoslawski's *Mi-parti* and
works by Shostakovich, Britten and Alexander Goehr. The series
opened on 18 September with Mahler's 'Resurrection' Symphony, an
apt choice under the circumstances. The future of Haitink's various
contracts was clear; life had settled on to a more even keel.

November 1977 was a remarkable month for Haitink. His achievements with the LPO were recognised on Tuesday 8 November, when it
was announced that he had been made an Honorary KBE (Knight
Commander of the Order of the British Empire). Had he decided to
relinquish his Dutch citizenship, he would have been entitled to be
addressed from then on as Sir Bernard. Whatever the labelling, he now
had the distinction of being a knight in Britain, a member of the Order
of Orange-Nassau in the Netherlands and a chevalier in France, an
impressive collection for a man not yet fifty. As is usually the practice
with Honorary KBEs, Haitink was not invested with the insignia by the
Queen but by a Government minister. Normally the task falls to the
Foreign Secretary, since the award is a matter of diplomatic relations
involving the agreement of the home government of the nation of
which the new knight is a citizen, but on this occasion the presentation
was made by the Minister for the Arts, Lord Donaldson. Haitink
received the insignia on an appropriate date: 22 November, St Cecilia's
Day.

While the Labour Government was adding to Haitink's collection of
honours, labour relations were complicating his renewed schedule of
engagements at Covent Garden. On 17 November he conducted his
first new production at the country's most important opera house. For
several years he had been hinting that he felt ready to tackle Wagner
and that *Lohengrin* seemed the best place to start. It was a courageous
decision to pick that work for his second appearance at the Royal
Opera, for Wagner productions seem to arouse stronger passions
among their audiences than any other, and Covent Garden's record in

the 1970s had been a patchy one. The boos had tended to out-shout the ovations. Preparations were not made easier by a dispute with the Musicians' Union that disrupted rehearsals. The union was demanding a three-hour limit on 'playing-sessions', a term which was to include performances. Such a limit was reasonable for normal concerts and recordings, but it made nonsense of Wagner operas (and some Strauss and Mozart ones as well).

Despite the tribulations, *Lohengrin* was as great a triumph as *Don Giovanni* had been in the summer. Elijah Moshinsky's production, designed by John Napier, was sensitive and ungimmicky, the two qualities which Haitink has come to value most in a staging. In contrast to his first experience at Covent Garden the previous spring, Haitink was in full sympathy with the producer and singers, an extraordinarily gifted group that included René Kollo as Lohengrin, Eva Randova as Ortrud, Anna Tomowa-Sintow as Elsa, Robert Lloyd as Heinrich I and Donald McIntyre as von Telramund. With such distinction on stage, Haitink produced his best in the pit, as the *Guardian* reported. 'The orchestra played for the new (hon.) conductor knight with the greatest delicacy and splendour. Haitink balanced, caressed the music, nursed the singing, to admiration. No wonder the house roared for him.' The performances continued into December, and in the meantime he finished his LPO engagements for the year before crossing to Amsterdam for Christmas. There he recorded more Debussy and Tchaikovsky with the Concertgebouw, as well as conducting its 'Kerstmatinee', the concert that traditionally takes place on the afternoon of Christmas Day.

For Haitink 1977 had been a strange and eventful year: one that had seen a clear shifting of his priorities. For the first time his operatic commitments in Britain had outnumbered his concerts, and it was apparent that the pattern of his work over the next decade would be radically different from that of his professional life so far. In Amsterdam, Munich, Berlin, and across the Atlantic (in Cleveland, Boston and New York) he would continue to be thought of as a symphonic conductor. But in England he would be seen most at the opera, a fact that would be reflected not only in the periods at Glyndebourne and Covent Garden, but also in records for His Master's Voice (EMI). Nevertheless he did begin a set of the Mendelssohn symphonies with the LPO for Philips in March 1978.

Whatever his disagreements with orchestral management in London, Haitink's position was growing ever stronger in Amsterdam. In 1977 he had led the Concertgebouw Orchestra on its fourth visit to Japan and on other visits to Belgium, England and Denmark. A

project which fulfilled Haitink's ambition to be seen in the Netherlands
as the country's rightful interpreter of the classical repertoire's greatest
works came to fruition in 1978. In his twenty-two-year association with
the orchestra in his home city he had never been able to persuade it to
accept a Beethoven symphony cycle. But quantity made up for the long
wait. From 17 April until 27 May Haitink and the Concertgebouw
played nothing else except Beethoven, the symphonies being inter-
spersed only with the piano concertos, in which the soloist was
Vladimir Ashkenazy. The concerts began with a complete cycle in
Amsterdam, followed at the beginning of May by two evenings at the
Théâtre des Champs-Elysées in Paris, the orchestra's first visit to the
French capital for twenty years. Straight away the bandwagon –
Haitink, Ashkenazy, a hundred and six players and nine staff – moved
to America. On Sunday, three days after the second Paris concert, they
played for one night in Minneapolis. The next morning Haitink took a
car, and the orchestra took three buses, to Ames, a town of only 41,000
in Iowa, where they were the main attraction at the ninth International
Orchestra Festival, held on the concrete campus of Iowa State
University.

On arrival, Haitink gave the local press an opportunity to see him in
an unaccustomed guise. It is not often, perhaps, that Chuck Offen-
burger's 'Iowa Boy' column in the *Des Moines Tribune* creeps into
biographies of leading conductors, but the following is worth quoting
as a portrait of Haitink in the Midwest.

> The room got pretty quiet here Monday afternoon when he was
> ready to perform. Simon van Nispen, the recently appointed Dutch
> Consul-General from Chicago, was looking on. 'This man Haitink is
> very, very highly regarded in my country,' van Nispen said quietly,
> almost reverently.
> There was a serious look on Maestro Haitink's face, a deter-
> mination in his stance, as he reached forward and began the
> performance. The tone he so artfully commanded was good, crisp:
> *Ding! Ding! Boing! Buzz!*
> Huh?
> Haitink, as unflinching in his gaze as he was casual in his red
> pullover sweater, was beating hell out of the Captain Fantastic
> pinball machine in the lobby of the Ramada Inn! When he finally
> looked up to notice that his game was under observation by van
> Nispen, the pipe-smoking government official, the maestro nodded
> at the gaudy board in front of him and said, 'I love these things.'
> His game was good (28,850 points) as he sent the silver balls

smashing into rubber-rimmed islands where there were pictures of buxom young women holding signs saying, 'Buzz Them Buzzers, Champ'. Haitink's skill was evidence that he has killed time in the game rooms of motels and airports and the like before!

Once the orchestra arrived to spoil its conductor's unhindered turn at the machines, recreation became more organised. Beethoven's First and Seventh Symphonies were performed that night, the Fourth and the Fifth the next, the Second and Sixth on Wednesday and the *Eroica* on Thursday. Between the concerts and each morning's rehearsal the players were given farm tours, games of tennis, cycle rides, rounds of golf and parties. Only the last were available for the two concluding weeks of the visit, in Washington DC and New York.

The concerts given in Kennedy Center and Carnegie Hall followed the pattern established in Amsterdam, presenting all the symphonies and concertos in both cities. For the jaded metropolitan audience it may have seemed like an overdose. The *New York Times* (which managed to misspell the conductor's name as Haitnik in its headline) asked: 'Is such a hackneyed series an adornment to the life of a cosmopolitan music center? Probably not.' For the Concertgebouw Orchestra it was a matter of considerable pride, however, and for Haitink it meant that he had conducted all the symphonies in London, Amsterdam, Washington and New York before the age of fifty.

Haitink was entering what, in retrospect, can be seen as his most fruitful period in Amsterdam. His own distinction and that of the Concertgebouw were, after two decades, almost inseparable. To the outside world, conductor and orchestra represented Dutch music with an inevitability that had not been apparent since the finest days of Mengelberg in the late 1920s (when he had been much the same age as Haitink). Only two criticisms could reasonably be upheld against them from then until the mid-1980s. Van Royen could have chosen more adventurous programmes for his conductor, rather than concentrating almost all the out-of-the-ordinary work on guests; and Haitink could have been more determined to be more positive about putting forward ideas for pieces he wanted to conduct rather than waiting for suggestions to come from others. Van Royen considered it important to keep Haitink away from things that did not interest him, letting him concentrate on the music with which he felt most at home. Haitink at the same time did not want to be seen taking repertoire away from conductors who wished to do particular works, or making too many personal demands. However, his own range shrank as a result. He felt confined to a well-worn path and the audience knew rather too easily what to expect from one of his concerts. With regard to the music that was played, though, the partnership between orchestra and conductor was thoroughly productive. The players who had come into the orchestra as Haitink's first intake in the early 1960s were now in their mature prime, while a new balance had been struck between youth and experience so that the average age had dropped to just above forty. As First Conductor – a position that most orchestras would describe as Principal Guest – the Concertgebouw had the Russian-born Kyril Kondrashin. He had always been known as a great orchestral trainer and his repertoire, particularly the works from his homeland and the late-romantic nationalist schools, finely complemented Haitink's more Germanic interests. It is a pity that this peak in the concert hall coincided with a trough in relations with Philips. Consequently the bulk of Haitink's recordings for the company were made in the late 1960s and early 1970s before his work was at its best.

The tour in America caused Haitink to miss the first part of the 1978 season at Glyndebourne, even though he was now Musical Director. There were two new productions, both by Mozart, in which he was involved: *Die Zauberflöte*, designed, like *The Rake's Progress* of three years before, by David Hockney and produced by John Cox, and *Così fan tutte*, produced by Peter Hall. Haitink arrived in time to take charge of the second set of *Zauberflöte* performances and to rehearse *Così* and another revival of *The Rake*. His work with Hall at Glyndebourne and his subsequent engagements with the Royal Opera make such a distinct section in his life that they will be examined in the next chapter.

At Glyndebourne the increasingly sour relationship with the management of the London Philharmonic Orchestra took a turn for the worse. A disagreement with the orchestra's board arose when it wished to sack a player against Haitink's will. Such a decision required a three-quarters majority on the eight-man board, so Haitink was unable to veto it on his own. The decision against him emphasised that his role in the planning and personnel affairs of the orchestra could be little other than a matter of token influence during his last season. It had already been announced that Bravington's bid to replace him with Solti had succeeded and that Sir Georg would head the LPO from the autumn of 1979. Haitink, recognising that his title was a description of a position that he no longer held, resigned as Artistic Director, the announcement being made by sticking a note on the noticeboard at Glyndebourne soon after the opening night of *Così*. Despite an exercise in damage limitation by Bravington, the press sensed a good story and made the most of it, and Haitink made little attempt to hide his disgust at the way he had been treated by the LPO board. The timing of the affair was such that even at Glyndebourne – normally a haven from the arguments of London musical life – the coolness between some sections of the LPO and its Principal Conductor could not be avoided.

It was ironic, then, that in his last season with the orchestra, 1978–9, Haitink should have been committed to conducting more of the concerts at the Royal Festival Hall than in any year of his tenure. Fourteen were planned in all, some reflecting the works in progress for the record companies, two marking Sir Adrian Boult's ninetieth birthday, others retreading familiar ground, as for example in the second programme of the season in which he returned to Mahler's Third Symphony, not heard in London in his interpretation for several years. He conducted no new works, though there were pieces outside his normal scope; among them Britten's song cycle *Our Hunting Fathers*, given in November with Heather Harper as the soprano soloist, Nielsen's Fifth Symphony and Messiaen's *Et exspecto resurrectionem mortuorum*. In January he finally confronted that scourge of London musical life, the terminal cougher of the Festival Hall (there is something about the acoustics which makes audience noise particularly disturbing there). Determined that the finale should not be completely ruined, he shook his handkerchief behind his back to indicate what the offender should do about his problem. Haitink was mellowing. A few years earlier he would probably have walked off the platform, as he had done in Amsterdam when a party of American travel agents had chattered through a performance at the Concertgebouw.

The concerts for Sir Adrian Boult on 9 and 10 April were skilfully planned. They began with Vaughan Williams's Overture to *The Wasps*, which Sir Adrian had heard the composer play through on the piano in the Professor of Music's Oxford drawing-room before it was first performed in 1909. Then came *The Lark Ascending*, which had poignant memories for one of the violinists in the LPO. When Marie Wilson had played the solo part with Boult and the BBC Symphony Orchestra in Canterbury Cathedral shortly after the war, its ethereal ending had been made even more evocative by the birds singing outside. Sir Adrian had retired from the concert platform, without much enthusiasm, in February 1977, after a performance of Vaughan Williams's Ninth Symphony. It was the Ninth by Beethoven, however, with which his anniversary was celebrated. It was a good way, too, for Haitink to end his tenure with the LPO; with the greatest of works, given in tribute to a fellow conductor whom he had first watched forty years earlier. The age gap between the two conductors was thirty-nine years and eleven months, and on 4 March Haitink had reached the milestone of his own half-century.

It was a subject about which he preferred not to think, but the publicity that attaches itself to such events was unavoidable. Even Haitink, though, was forced to admit that his career had fitted neatly into ten-year segments. He told Alan Blyth for the *Daily Telegraph*:

> From twenty to thirty as a conductor you're really still a student – there's so much to learn. From thirty to forty you feel you are just beginning to come to grips with the difficult business of being in charge of an orchestra. Then from forty to fifty you begin to gain some kind of authority and you have the pleasure of finding out that you're beginning to develop as a musician.

Or, as he also said, 'At thirty you wonder how you can get some more concerts. At forty you want to know how you can become more successful. When you're fifty you just want more time to rehearse!' There was no concert with the LPO to mark his fiftieth birthday, but the previous month he had brought the Concertgebouw Orchestra to the Royal Festival Hall on what was becoming its biennial visit to London.

The pattern that seemed to order his life into convenient decades held good and, by the end of the season, that for his sixth was emerging. It was a subtly different one, projecting Haitink no longer as the solid, domestic but quietly aggressive young Dutchman who had held command on either side of the Channel at the end of the 1960s. Haitink was now unmarried and without a family base for the first time in his life. His mother still lived in the house in Vinkeleskade, but Haitink divided his time between a flat in London's Cadogan Place and a retreat at Bergen aan Zee, on the North Holland coast, where he had gone for summer holidays as a child. At Glyndebourne he rented a cottage, like most of its seasonal inhabitants, and cycled back and forth to the opera house. He was also freer professionally. Without a contract binding him to the LPO, he could return to and experiment with the other London orchestras. At the end of May 1979 he conducted the BBC Symphony Orchestra in Mahler's First Symphony at the opening of the Brighton Festival, just a few miles from Glyndebourne. Philips no longer dictated his recording career, and over the next few years he was happy to conduct for Decca, EMI, CBS and Orfeo, as well as his original company. Vienna, Boston, Berlin and Munich once again had regular places in his diary but, as twenty years before, it was only with the Concertgebouw that he toured the remoter musical centres.

Much as he loved the Proms, Haitink asked to be released from conducting the penultimate night of the 1979 series. Having ended his dozen years with the LPO and finished a Glyndebourne season in which he had conducted three productions, he regarded the chance of taking a complete month's rest as a higher priority even than Beethoven's Ninth Symphony. The Promenaders had to make do with James Loughran instead. Haitink re-emerged for the start of the Concertgebouw's season at the end of September. In the same month Kyril Kondrashin, who had been Principal Conductor of the Moscow Philharmonic Orchestra until he decided that artistic life in the Soviet Union in the Brezhnev era was intolerable, was named Permanent Conductor of the Concertgebouw, a title that reflected the growing importance of his involvement in the musical life of his new home country. Also that season, Nikolaus Harnoncourt, who had been working with the orchestra for four years on the baroque repertoire in order to update its playing to a more fashionably 'authentic' style, began to work on achieving the same effect in music from the turn of the eighteenth century. In the long run this was less successful from Haitink's point of view, since Harnoncourt's sound was radically different from his own. As a result the two playing styles became increasingly incompatible and Haitink found it difficult to regenerate his sound after the Concertgebouw had spent a period with the baroque specialist.

Recording work continued with Philips, though at nothing like the volume of previous years. In October 1979 he made discs of three Tchaikovsky symphonies (Nos. 1, 3 and the *Manfred*); in January 1980 four Mozart overtures; and in April Brahms's *German Requiem* and *Schicksalslied*. In general, it was a relatively quiet season. There were six residual concerts to be conducted in London with the LPO, the most interesting of which (on 24 January) combined Mozart's Symphony No.40 with Tippett's Third. Three days later he conducted the Seventh and Eighth Symphonies of Beethoven, the last occasion on which he was to work with the LPO in the concert hall until its fiftieth anniversary season in 1983. Paradoxically, at almost the same time Eric Bravington's illness forced him to retire.

While appearances in London became rarer, those in Amsterdam took on a greater significance. The start of the new decade was productive for the Concertgebouw Orchestra, with visits to France,

England, Belgium, Germany, Austria, Switzerland and Czecho-slovakia, in which Haitink played his part. At the beginning of September 1980 they flew to Mexico, spending two weeks in the capital. Shortly after their return Haitink was married for the second time. His new wife was Saskia Boon, a member of the orchestra's cello section and the daughter of its principal violist at the time of Haitink's first appointment as conductor. This turned out not to have been a wise step, however, and Haitink was soon single again.

In January 1981 Haitink was back in London, once again at the Royal Opera, for nine performances of *Un ballo in maschera*, the first time he had tackled a Verdi opera since his 1960s attempt at *Don Carlos*. He also found a new orchestral home, with the Philharmonia. His two concerts, on 8 and 16 February, re-established his name on the South Bank programme and began a satisfactory guest relationship that has continued ever since. With the Philharmonia, Haitink was able to cultivate a different sound from that of the LPO, with greater emphasis on the gloss of the string playing. It also solved the problem of where in future he would be able to perform the English symphonic repertoire which he had adopted with such enthusiasm. The Philharmonia has traditionally been less of an 'English music' orchestra than the LPO, but with Haitink the Elgar symphonies in particular have become an integral part of its repertoire and it was with that orchestra that he recorded the pair in April 1982 for EMI. It was the Philharmonia, too, that he had been due to conduct at the 1980 Proms, the sad season that was wrecked by the first ever national strike of the Musicians' Union against the BBC.

After Mexico in 1980, the Concertgebouw's major tour in 1981 involved a shorter distance but broke new ground for the orchestra none the less. In September Haitink travelled with it to Finland, Norway and Sweden. Finland and Sweden had not been visited since 1957 and Norway had never before featured on the itinerary. With the Dutch public more receptive to Haitink than ever before and English opera commitments taking up an increasing proportion of his time, Haitink returned by sheer force of work to something like his stable position of fifteen years before, when his guest engagements outside his two home capitals all but dried up. There was little time to conduct in America – although he did make an exception in 1982 when he was asked to take charge of *Fidelio* at the Metropolitan Opera in New York. In Europe he confined his appearances outside Amsterdam to four orchestras, almost entirely: the Berlin and the Vienna Philharmonic, the Philharmonia in London and, most often, the Bavarian Radio Symphony in Munich, with whom he made his first record of opera.

The choice of work and soloists was not too surprising – *Die Zauberflöte* with a cast that included Lucia Popp, Edita Gruberová and Siegfried Jerusalem – but the choice of place was stranger, considering that he had not conducted any opera in Germany.

At the Concertgebouw Haitink's responsibilities were made more arduous for some years as a result of the death of Kondrashin in March 1981. For the orchestra – and European music in general – it was a tragedy, for Kondrashin was just beginning to establish himself as a great conductor in the West, as he had in Russia. The day after he died the commemorative concert was conducted by Haitink, the programme of Shostakovich's Fifth Symphony and Bruckner's Eighth reflecting the strengths of both conductors.

The Concertgebouw was so much 'Haitink's orchestra' in the early part of the decade that it was unthinkable that it should tour with anybody else. His importance as a cultural figurehead for the Netherlands had been further recognised in April 1980 when his Dutch title was upgraded to Ridder (Knight) in de Orde van de Nederlandse Leeuw. That year Haitink instituted a development which was long overdue – the founding of a chorus linked to the Concertgebouw in the same way as is enjoyed by all but one of the London orchestras. For the job of chorus master he turned to one of the most experienced men in Europe, Arthur Oldham, who had performed the same duty for the Edinburgh Festival and the Orchestre National in Paris. This had two benefits. It meant that works with choir could be programmed without having to refer to the availability of outside organisations, and it gave musical amateurs a chance to feel part of the Concertgebouw organisation in a direct sense, offering them a more personal involvement than could be acquired by merely buying a season ticket.

When the orchestra went to America in September 1982 it was at its peak, artistically and financially. Its budget had increased slightly from the thirteen million guilders it had to spend at the end of the 1970s (of which only four million guilders was derived from its own coffers) and although the Dutch government was no longer automatically prepared to foot the bill for overseas visits, the Concertgebouw's reputation was such that, rather to van Dantzig's surprise, foreign impresarios were keen to hire it on a commercial basis. The trip to the United States in 1982 was a case in point. It was the most extensive, as regards distance, undertaken for over a decade. It began in the Arlington Theater, Santa Barbara, on 18 September and ended twenty-two days later in Carnegie Hall, New York. In between the orchestra moved steadily east, visiting Pasadena and San Francisco in California, Salt Lake City (Utah), Denver (Colorado), Ames (though there was no time for Iowa farm tours on this occasion), Chicago, East Lansing (Michigan), Toledo and Akron (Ohio), Washington DC (for two concerts) and Boston. Three programmes formed the staple for the journey: works by Ravel, Tristan Keuris (whose *Movements* represented Dutch music) and Berlioz in the first, by Haydn, Stravinsky and Brahms in the second, the third consisting solely of Mahler's Seventh Symphony. The Mahler was the lynchpin of the season, being performed by the Concertgebouw over twenty times within a few weeks and then recorded for Philips. It was such consistency in artistic planning, combined with a varied but not exhausting schedule and a confidence in the institution of the orchestra that made it, at that time, many people's nominee for the accolade of best orchestra in the world. It was also a younger body than it had been since the war, with the average age down to thirty-eight. The position that prevailed in the early years of Haitink's tenure had been reversed. Youthful players now had a mature conductor, instead of the earlier situation in which an inexperienced beginner had tried to mould a group enjoying the comforts of middle age.

Just as the Concertgebouw reached its highest point in world opinion, however, domestic politicians in Holland started to question its artistic validity and to chip away at its financial base. The Netherlands was facing the same economic problems as the rest of Europe – rising unemployment caused by the collapse of basic manufacturing industries, high fuel prices and a population with advanced expectations and expensive needs relative to its competitors in the Pacific. For the Dutch the situation was made worse by the need to conserve the cheap natural gas that had underpinned its economy, and by the mounting cost of its extensive state benefit system, one of the most comprehensive in the world. Many of the problems found their focal point in Amsterdam, where a chronic housing shortage and an anarchic subculture based on narcotics and prostitution belied the image of dull efficient order that its clean suburbs liked to project. To a hard-pressed central government in The Hague, and an increasingly radical municipal coalition that faced daunting social problems, the Concertgebouw Orchestra – heavily subsidised, well salaried and staffed, playing works of an educated culture to the wealthy (few of whom would be potential left-wing voters) at three out of its four weekly concerts – seemed an irresistible target for any cuts in public spending which had to be made. By 1983 Dolf van Dantzig, the General Manager, had seen half a million guilders lopped off the funding from the city. This was superficially bearable, though even such a cut of a few per cent led to changes in artistic planning. It became clear that some of the world's most sought-after performers were beyond the orchestra's reach – Dame Janet Baker and Carlo Maria Giulini were among them. For an orchestra at the top of the world league it seemed absurd. Far more serious was a proposal from the national government to cut its share of support for the orchestra's wage bill, a move which would have meant the loss of twenty-one players and so put some of the largest pieces of music out of the regular repertoire. To Haitink this was utterly unacceptable and he threatened to resign. It was a measure of Haitink's standing in his own country that the government regarded the idea as a serious challenge which would have led to a major political scandal, and hastily withdrew the plan.

Within a few months, however, Haitink had to reiterate his determination to show that the price of serious decreases in funding would be his own removal. This time further damage was intended by the city council. Philosophically, the coalition of left-wing parties that formed the council majority regarded the Concertgebouw as a temple of privilege. It would have preferred to see less of its subsidy go to the orchestra, already rich in the council's eyes, and more to smaller organisations catering to its own voting constituency. Artistic standards were not so much of a consideration as political orientation. The city did have the excuse that budget restrictions imposed by the central government were forcing it to find savings in its grants ranging from thirteen to seventeen per cent, but it was not a course of action Haitink was prepared to allow to be implemented without a struggle. While the Concertgebouw was playing at the Edinburgh Festival and the Proms in September 1983, he once again proffered his resignation. To a reporter from the *Sunday Times* he made his position clear.

I said then [at the time of the earlier economic threats] that if we have to cut the orchestra, my life with it is finished. That still stands. The Concertgebouw is a family. You cannot cut off an arm or a leg . . . We work very hard and are extremely serious people: we are very Dutch. We know there is a recession outside, that factories are closing and people are being thrown out of work. But what is happening in Amsterdam is that people are exploiting the recession against us for their own political ends. They resent us because we are part of the cultural establishment; but being long-established is, in our case, artistically important.

The article appeared on 4 September. That evening Haitink conducted at the Proms. In the *Guardian* Meirion Bowen wrote:

The Amsterdam Concertgebouw Orchestra began with a performance of Mozart's Haffner Symphony that was as lithe and
delicately poised as could ever be imagined. It was the sort of Mozart
playing we in this country tend to hear only from our finest string
quartets. Indeed, the large string body here sounded just like a
chamber ensemble. Accents, staccato attack, dynamic changes and
all the other details were judged to perfection . . . Haitink's reading
[of Bruckner's Ninth Symphony] was spacious but . . . culminated in
one of the most far-sighted realisations of the final slow movement
that I have encountered. Many performers simply lose their way at
this stage, as Bruckner piles up dissonant harmonies and dense
textures. Haitink's interpretation took the music inexorably towards
a peak of violence and then allowed it to subside surely into the
peaceful closing tonality of E minor. Such music-making had a
maturity which we rarely encounter.

It was such responses that made up the ultimate defence of the
orchestra's status, challenging the authorities to admit that it was an
asset and attraction that the city, for all its prettiness, could ill afford to
lose. Together with its diamond and finance markets, the Concertgebouw and the museums for the visual arts were Amsterdam's main
claims to international recognition. Not being the ministerial capital,
the city had to maintain its place as the cultural capital to be taken
seriously.

Having steered the Concertgebouw through the first phases of its
financial crisis, Dolf van Dantzig retired the following year. This led to
a reorganisation of the management structure. In the past the Artistic
Director and the General Manager had held separate but equal offices.
With van Dantzig's departure, however, Hein van Royen decided to
concentrate both the financial and the artistic strategy planning in his
own hands, appointing an administrator to take over the rest of the
role.

On 3 November 1983 Haitink was conducting the BBC Symphony
Orchestra in the Barbican Hall, opened the year before. Press
photographers were on hand, for it had been announced that morning
that he had been designated the next Music Director of the Royal
Opera House, Covent Garden. For many in the musical world his
decision was a surprise, for he was still seen as primarily a symphonic
conductor. To Haitink, however, it was part of a logical progression.
His late start in opera had been, paradoxically, a result of his love for
the medium. He was doubtful whether he would be able to do it justice,
and it was too important a matter for failure. Glyndebourne had then

given him confidence, proving that the stage held no mysteries which he could not tackle. New productions with Peter Hall inspired his creativity. *Lohengrin* at the Royal Opera proved that he had the same potential in a larger house, and more frequent visits in the early 1980s showed that he could achieve worthwhile results, not only in new productions, but in the everyday repertoire of a major company. With new building developments in prospect and a company that badly needed his blend of approachability and authority urging him to accept, the opportunity was too interesting to turn down.

The changeover was to be a long affair. Although Sir Colin Davis was due to relinquish the post in July 1986, Haitink's contracts with Glyndebourne and the Concertgebouw made a smooth transfer impossible. He was committed to the former until the end of the 1987 season and so could not officially take up the title until then, even though it was clear that, whatever the label, the job would have to begin immediately. Similarly, work with the Concertgebouw still demanded its customary time. His resignation over finances having just been staved off, it seemed certain that he would still be in charge for the orchestra's centenary season in 1988.

Events were turning out differently, however. He was still conducting highly successful concerts with the orchestra all over the world. Mahler's Third Symphony in Amsterdam on Christmas Day 1983, a tour to Salzburg and Budapest, and a performance of the Verdi Requiem the following year all testified to that. In the autumn of 1985 he headed a visit to Brazil and Argentina, following in the footsteps of the Vienna Philharmonic who had travelled the same way a few weeks earlier. In football-mad Rio it was said that the Concertgebouw 'won by three to two'. In Buenos Aires the opinion was that 'the Vienna Philharmonic brought a show, the Concertgebouw brought music'. But for Haitink his relationship with the orchestra was not as close or satisfactory as it had been in previous years. For him the peak, if the pun may be forgiven, had been reached with a performance of Strauss's massive Alpine Symphony in 1983. After that the personnel began to change once more. Many of his most trusted allies among the older players were retiring. With new and not always welcome direction in the management, it no longer seemed to be *his* Concertgebouw in quite the same way. When he had first succeeded van Beinum, his lack of established status had made life difficult; now it was precisely his establishment that distanced him from colleagues. The orchestra no longer seemed to be firmly under his control, so Haitink decided that he should relinquish the conductorship before the start of the centenary celebrations. His period of almost three decades at its head was, after all, a record matched only by Mengelberg. Other challenges beckoned from around the world. The Concertgebouw was no longer automatically the orchestra with which he made recordings. Bruckner's Fourth Symphony and Berlioz's *Symphonie fantastique* were made with the Vienna Philharmonic, and the Berlin Philharmonic, the Bavarian Radio Symphony and the Boston Symphony, as well as the London orchestras, were all anxious for some of his time. Furthermore, the prospect of making the Royal Opera his principal base looked increasingly attractive. Sadly, once he had decided to alter his position in Amsterdam, relations with his home city soured. There were, Haitink found, still remnants of the old attitude that he belonged to the orchestra by right and that too much success abroad was somehow 'un-Dutch'. There was a certain sense of betrayal on both sides which culminated in his not being consulted on the choice of successor. It was an omission that rankled badly. The orchestra's candidate for its fifth conductor was, for the first time, not a fellow Dutchman. Instead the Italian Riccardo Chailly, in his early thirties as Haitink had been, was chosen. Also like Haitink, he was principal conductor of a radio orchestra, though in Berlin. Haitink's decision to leave meant that he had no purely symphonic orchestra of his own for the first time in over thirty years.

IX
Opera

THERE CANNOT HAVE been many opera-house music directors who had conducted so few performances from the pit as Bernard Haitink had done when he succeeded to the post at Glyndebourne. Three half-hearted attempts for Netherlands Opera, two revivals for Glyndebourne, one for the Royal Opera and one new production of *The Rake's Progress* made up his entire tally. The *Don Giovanni* production of 1977 marked the real transition from concert conductor, who had dabbled a little, to operatic musician who understood his role. It also marked the physical handing-over of authority from John Pritchard, who rehearsed and conducted the opening performances, to Haitink, who worked with the second cast, attended the re-rehearsals and, after the end of the Glyndebourne season, travelled with the opera to the National Theatre and the Proms. By the end of the summer it was undoubtedly Haitink's interpretation that remained in the memory, largely because of his own enthusiastic response to Hall's Byronic staging.

In retrospect it can be seen that Haitink's very inexperience was one of his greatest assets when he began to work with greater frequency at Glyndebourne in 1978. He had the humility to realise that he was the beginner in the subject and therefore was not entitled to dictate too much. In any case that was not his style. But he also arrived hungry for the challenge of the stage and without too many preconceptions of how an opera conductor should behave. Having waited so long and so nervously, he had a young man's enthusiasm despite his artistic maturity. Had he followed Ferdinand Leitner to the Stuttgart Opera in 1954, as his mentor had suggested, he would have acquired a very different ideal of opera-house working methods. Instead he arrived at Glyndebourne open to methods which are the very antithesis of those traditional in the German provincial system; co-operative rehearsals based more on the traditions of the English theatre than the Continental 'Staatsoper'. At the same time his expectations, matured in the world's great concert halls, were such that he was not prepared to accept the sloppy standards of singing and orchestral playing which a man who had spent his career in the average opera house would have had to tolerate. His ear had been trained in the recording

139

studio and the Concertgebouw, not in the lower reaches of rep.

For Peter Hall, this combination of lack of authoritarianism and demanding musicality made Haitink the ideal conductor. It was their productions together – of Mozart, Beethoven, Britten and, latterly, Verdi – that formed the kernel of Haitink's best work in Sussex. Hall also feels that the results have been, overall, his own most satisfactory achievements in the opera house.

They first met for any length of time in 1973, when Haitink was conducting the revival of *Die Zauberflöte* and Hall was working on *Le nozze di Figaro*. Haitink took the time to attend some of Hall's rehearsals and they began talking about the ways of staging Mozart. To Hall it was clear even then that they thought along the same lines. Neither feels there is any great secret or mystery about their working methods. The harmony stems from a similarity of approach during rehearsals. Both are good listeners, though outside the opera house their personalities could hardly be more different. From their public image the nervously flamboyant Hall, aggressive with reporters and politicians alike, seems an utterly opposite figure to the quiet and serious Haitink. In rehearsal, however, other more complementary characteristics dominate. There Hall's public bombast disappears, while Haitink's energy and curiosity – humour, too – come to the fore. Perhaps most importantly, he adopts the working methods of the theatre, rather than trying to force it into the patterns appropriate to the world of pure music.

'Conductors are used to inflecting a piece in a few three-hour rehearsals,' says Hall. 'They achieve results very fast. A director works in quite another way. He has to get a group of people together, try and find the right questions to ask, and then get them to find the solutions. Too many conductors become impatient with this process. They want the director to be a super-grade butler: to show the singers on to the stage and make sure they don't bump into each other. They concern themselves only with the music. Haitink, however, comes to production rehearsals to discover what the drama is about. He pitches in with everybody else, and what he discovers affects his music-making.' Often there can be a world of difference between the atmosphere in the rehearsal room, with just a piano accompaniment, and the stage itself, when the orchestra joins the singers. Unless the conductor is completely involved, the addition of the orchestra – which shifts the balance significantly away from the acting – can alter the sense of the production drastically.

To Peter Hall it is the balance between the way the work appears before and after the initial period of rehearsal that makes Haitink such a useful collaborator. Without the consistency in approach, much of the early work can be undone and the production will seem to be losing its way, ill-fitting and incoherent. 'In straight theatre,' he argues, 'the director is responsible for finding the pace and dynamic of a scene. But in opera, if the conductor does not really agree he can control the music in such a way that the original motivation for the scene is no longer there. The singers are being asked to perform in a totally different way.

'Bernard Haitink is pre-eminent because he leaves his ego outside the rehearsal room. We all should, but many conductors are not able to. Collaboration only works if the conductor is secure enough to allow himself to be challenged, which Haitink is. Disagreements must be worked out in public with the singers, because you must come up with something which you can all endorse. Since I don't mind *him* saying that a scene is on the wrong foot and he doesn't mind *me* commenting on the music, this does not become a problem. Because of this I always feel that he brings more out of me than I think is in me.'

The collaboration began in earnest in 1978 when they worked on *Così fan tutte*, which Hall regards, contrary to its popular perception, as being the toughest of the three Mozart operas with librettos by da Ponte. As with *Don Giovanni*, they approached it with a sense of the impending tragedy which is only just below the surface, taking an opera that used to be thought of as a piece of eighteenth-century confectionery and bringing out its kinship with the 'cruel' comedies of Shakespeare. 'The subtitle is *A School for Love*, and in that sense it represents a journey which all four of the lovers make,' says Hall. 'I was tired of seeing productions of the opera which made such fools of the women. The idea I had was that really the men are in love with Love at the beginning, not with the girls, and that their disguise is a revelation of themselves, rather than a covering-up. Being other people releases them and they actually fall in love and learn its true nature. They grow up, and in that case the opera does not make idiots of the women.' It is very like the similar process in *A Midsummer Night's Dream*, which they produced in 1981. 'The work with Bernard revealed the delicacy and ambiguity in the score which I've always imagined to be there but never heard before; the sheer pain and anguish that is there – real pain – and the way the modulations express it. It is not a farce, especially in the second act which, if you do not take it seriously, is in very great danger of being a repeat of the first – only anticlimactic and longer.'

Bernard Haitink feels that his understanding of the bitterness within the opera stems from a remark made by Hall in rehearsal. 'Remember,' he said to the singers, 'that Mozart was in love with two women – sisters – and could marry only one of them!' Hall regards it as a work the importance of which is seriously undervalued, in dramatic and historical terms. 'It is the first modern-dress opera. Suddenly Mozart and da Ponte came up with a contemporary love story which leaves Beaumarchais standing.' Despite the security of that setting, Hall decided to move the action forward thirty years, to the world of Sheridan and Jane Austen, 'largely for the benefit of the women. As with the production of *Don Giovanni*, I wanted to capture that brink point when eighteenth-century enlightenment tips over into ferocious romanticism.'

The main thrust of the production was recognised and welcomed immediately, Peter Heyworth, in the *Observer*, praising the way in which they had done away 'with the pretty-sweetness that disfigures, for instance, Covent Garden's staging of the opera'. For Haitink it made an auspicious start to his term as Musical Director; indeed, the quality of Hall's direction and Haitink's interpretation almost out-shone the singers' contribution, so that it was their teamwork rather than individual arias which made the dominating impression. It was almost as if at Glyndebourne Haitink and Hall were recreating the sense of homogeneity that had marked the Royal Shakespeare Company in its early days. To do so was a return to the ideals that had first inspired Glyndebourne's production policy. Nowadays they would be 'workshop' methods, but the real aim was to move as far away from the operatic circus world of the major opera houses as possible.

It was the same quality of ensemble that characterised Beethoven's *Fidelio* the following season. Two members of the cast did stand out in 1979, however: Elisabeth Söderström as Leonore and Curt Appelgren as Rocco, in thoughtful performances which gave credibility to roles that can disintegrate all too easily into melodrama. Hall and the designer, John Bury, had followed the instructions in the original libretto meticulously. There was no updating or over-emphasis on the political theories of repression and revolution that so often burden the opera. Instead Marzelline did her ironing, as the libretto said she should, Rocco pottered about in a paternal way, and Leonore, dressed as Fidelio, made a believable assistant gaoler. Chickens even scratched about in an ill-managed vegetable patch. The castle was not the focus of world events, but a rather shabby outpost, largely ignored by greater affairs until the significance of its one important prisoner ruffled the homely calm.

'It starts as a conventional Singspiel, a rather domestic little piece,' says Hall, 'and Beethoven burns his way through that into something broader and more metaphysical, and I feel that to do the piece in a place the size of Glyndebourne you are able to get that broadening, whereas if you do it in a big house as a great statement of German culture to start with, you lose its sense of direction.'

Two years later, Haitink and Hall added Britten's *A Midsummer Night's Dream* to their series. Establishing and exploring a line of thought is important to both of them, if their tenure in a post is not to seem haphazard and programming policy a matter of whim. This does not mean that either has a 'boxed set' mentality. They are not interested in performing everything an artist wrote, in chronological order, but believe, rather, that common themes and ideas have to be followed through. So *Così, Fidelio* and *The Dream* all belonged to a pattern. All three are dark comedies. They end happily and have light moments, but they also have a potential for tragedy threatening enough to make reconciliation an outcome for which the characters have to work hard. All three, as well, depend upon disguise which affects not only the plot and the perceptions of peripheral characters, but the emotional state of those being disguised. The lovers in *Così* and *A Midsummer Night's Dream*, Leonore and Marzelline in *Fidelio*, have to come to terms with the consequences of having based their most cherished feelings on assumptions that prove to have no – or at least a subtly different – basis in reality.

Haitink's decision to stage the Britten opera at Glyndebourne was a courageous one, since no work by England's greatest opera composer had been seen at the house since the fledgling English Opera Group had given the first performances of *Albert Herring* there in 1947. John Christie had lost a considerable amount of money backing its European tour of *The Rape of Lucretia* the season before and was, in any case, never convinced that he liked the music. Company founder and composer fell out, and despite the fact that Britten's stage works were usually small-scale and perfectly suited to Sussex, none was performed there for the rest of his life. Five years after Britten's death it was accepted as an absurdity that the alienation should be allowed to continue. In the event *The Dream* was one of Glyndebourne's greatest successes, evoking an atmosphere that made the opera house and its gardens seem as much a part of Shakespeare's enchanted Athens as the set. It was not hard to remember that Kipling's version of Puck's antics had been set only a dozen miles away. Haitink has conducted one other Britten opera: the revival of Elijah Moshinsky's production of *Peter Grimes* at the Royal Opera House in March 1984, when Jon Vickers sang the title role.

In comparison with the comedies, the two tragedies on which Hall and Haitink collaborated at Glyndebourne before 1987, Bizet's

Carmen and Verdi's *Simon Boccanegra*, seemed almost straightforward. The same scrubbed but worn feeling, toned and seasoned
timber, underpinned the sets for *Carmen* in 1985. In the title role Hall
cast his wife, Maria Ewing, whom many thought would have too light a
voice for a traditional portrayal. What was produced, however, was
anything but traditional – though again there was no need to resort to
gimmickry to achieve the effect. What they did decide to do, separating
Glyndebourne's approach once more from that of houses rooted more
firmly in the nineteenth-century tradition, was to strip away super-
fluous music that Bizet had been forced to add after the first
performance. This lightened, shortened and clarified the action,
bringing out the speed and immediacy of the drama. Music, instead of
blanketing dialogue and obscuring rather than illuminating the opera,
could be used as it was first intended when *Carmen* was heard at the
Comédie-Française: as a means of heightening emotional moments.
Even more than *Fidelio* or *Figaro*, both of which have crucial sections
of unaccompanied speech, *Carmen* was a work which used the music
sparingly. This slimline approach allowed Hall to draw out a
performance in which his cast were to a far greater extent singing actors
than in traditional productions. Ewing, in particular, gave an interpretation in which operatic technique was subordinated to energy,
aggression and sensuality that bordered on raw sex. It was an
extraordinary production, which once again demonstrated the
advantage of having both a conductor and a director who had come to
a major work for the first time when they were already well established
in their careers. Experiment and discovery became the motivating
factors, rather than continuance of tradition or the need to generate
reviews useful for the publicity brochure.

The success of Glyndebourne, managed on relatively small budgets
with casts which have not always contained singers of the highest
rank, is a matter of time-scale. Plenty of rehearsals, artists staying in a
community which allows them time to mix and understand one
another, and a sufficient number of performances to enable a
production to mature and develop, are all part of the secret. 'Above
all,' says Hall, 'there is time to question, to admit you don't know. That
is a statement that strikes terror into the hearts of impresarios and
administrators, but unless you can admit it, you cannot begin the
journey that is always entailed. The marvellous thing about Haitink is
that he is prepared to start with an open mind, to admit that he does not
always know the answer, and then to work to discover it.'

Both men feel that their collaborations mark the height of their
achievement in the opera house. This might suggest that they spend

hours in discussion during preparation. In fact, just as Haitink hates to
have anticipated every detail of a concerto with the soloist before the
performance, so he prefers the approach to opera to emerge during
rehearsal. 'Haitink is a doer, not a talker,' says Hall. He watches,
absorbs and then comments or, if satisfied, translates what he has
discovered through conducting rather than conversation. It is in
response to feelings, impressions and spaces that he works, not
through theorisation. His sense of space has been particularly acute at
Glyndebourne, where the small stage, uncomfortable pit and dry
acoustics can seem claustrophobic – indeed, that is one of the
characteristics that Hall has most frequently exploited in his productions for the house. To combat this, Haitink has created a sound
which is definitely different from that achieved at Covent Garden, the
Festival Hall or the Concertgebouw.

'There is so much energy unleashed from a singer and an orchestra in
that small space,' Hall says, 'that one always feels it is about to burst its
bounds. Haitink's Glyndebourne sound is so delicate – he gets a
pianissimo out of the LPO at Glyndebourne which they do not play
anywhere else, simply because it would be inaudible. At the start of
each season, when, after a year of concert work, they are suddenly
squashed down into that tiny pit, the sound is always too loud and
always uncomfortable, and gradually it achieves that silky, delicate
nuance that he wants – and he gets it with his hands.'

Half of Haitink's opera records (and there have only been six so far)
have been made in Munich with the Bavarian Radio Symphony
Orchestra. Since Glyndebourne had apparently been ruled out by
EMI, this was a logical alternative. In the early 1980s Haitink had
agreed to conduct there for four weeks a year – though he had turned
down the Principal Conductor's post – and he was discussing the
possibility of working at the Bavarian State Opera. The first record to
be made was *Die Zauberflöte*, in April 1981. The next was a surprising
choice: Strauss's late one-act opera, *Daphne*. It was a work he had
never come across in performance; indeed, it is almost unknown
outside Germany. However, in the title role it had Lucia Popp, an artist
with whom Haitink works frequently and who performed *Arabella*
with him at Covent Garden in 1986.

One Glyndebourne recording was made in January 1984 to celebrate
the fiftieth anniversary of the opera house. It was sensible to pick *Don
Giovanni*, since not only was it one of the company's most successful
productions – after its first appearance in 1977 it had received forty-

three performances before the recording – it was also Haitink's and Hall's first collaboration; and the cast for the 1982 revival, which formed the basis for the set, consisted largely of singers much of whose reputation had been built at Glyndebourne. Of the eight principals, half had won the John Christie Award for the most outstanding young singer of the season, almost always awarded to a 'home-grown' artist: Richard Van Allan (Leporello) in 1966, Elizabeth Gale (Zerlina) in 1974, John Rawnsley (Masetto) in 1976 and Keith Lewis (Don Ottavio) in 1979. The only change from the 1982 performances at the Festival was that Maria Ewing replaced her fellow American Elizabeth Pruett as Donna Elvira. For the rest, Carol Vaness, enjoying a speedy rise to stardom for a singer in her early thirties, sang Donna Anna, Dimitri Kavrakos was the Commendatore, and Thomas Allen was Don Giovanni himself, the most seductive and malevolent interpretation of the role in his generation. Since then two other Mozart operas, with casts roughly based on Glyndebourne revivals, have followed *Don Giovanni: Così fan tutte* was recorded in February 1986 and *Le nozze di Figaro* in February 1987, the last culminating in a concert performance at the Royal Festival Hall the night after the final sessions.

Haitink has recorded one other opera set, which points to the future. That was of Wagner's *Tannhäuser*, made in Munich in January 1985. Klaus König sang Tannhäuser, and among the other singers were Lucia Popp, Bernd Weikl, Kurt Moll and Siegfried Jerusalem. It will be with a similar team that he will soon embark on a cycle of *The Ring*.

His career at Glyndebourne does, of course, consist of more than just his partnership with Peter Hall, though since Hall has been Artistic Director through much of Haitink's period in office, that partnership has predominated. Almost as important has been the series in which he has worked with John Cox, Hall's predecessor. Apart from *Die Zauberflöte* and *The Rake's Progress*, which the company performed in Paris after the 1980 season as well as at Glyndebourne, Cox was responsible for its line of Strauss operas. The first of these with Haitink was *Der Rosenkavalier* in 1980. This was an extraordinary production, not so much for its musical content, but because it took Cox's predilection for 'designer's opera' to its furthest extreme. The sets and costumes were by Erté, the doyen of Parisian art deco. Erté was eighty-seven at the time (making him the oldest artist Glyndebourne had ever employed) and the settings he produced were works of art in themselves, even more so than Hockney's had been for Cox in previous seasons. They were also, as more than one critic pointed out, 'a long way from Vienna' and so much a feast for the eye that the music and action was almost driven from the stage. One lady was quoted in the *New York Times* as saying that they were 'just what she wanted for the bathroom-dressing room of the country house she was redoing' and the *Sunday Times* felt that the set 'could only be the domain of Ruritanian operetta or of some fairy-tale fantasy in a Christmas number of the *Tatler* between the wars'. Nevertheless it was notable as Haitink's first essay in a genre of opera for which his affinity was as great as for the tone poems.

Julia Trevelyan Oman's designs for the fiftieth anniversary production of *Arabella* in 1984 were less controversial. Felicity Lott was to have graduated from the title role in *Der Rosenkavalier* to that in *Arabella*, but she was having a baby at the time and so English audiences had to wait until the beginning of 1987 to hear her as one of the great Straussian heroines, when she sang the Marschallin at Covent Garden with Haitink. Instead the roles of Arabella and Mandryka were taken from the previous season at Netherlands Opera in Amsterdam; the strength of both Ashley Putnam and John Bröcheler being that they were young and good-looking – a quality even more important at Glyndebourne than at other houses because of the closeness of the audience to the stage.

For their other collaboration, Cox turned to another designer whose credentials were greater outside the theatre, Sir Hugh Casson, then President of the Royal Academy of Arts. The vehicle was Haydn's *La fedeltà premiata*, written in 1780 for the reopening of the theatre of the palace at Eszterháza after a fire the year before. Haitink had felt that the composer's operas had been even more unjustly neglected than the rest of his music and hoped that this would be the start of a 'line of thought', so as to balance the better-known series of Mozart, Strauss and, latterly, Verdi. In the event, however, the problems of staging a work that is dramatically far inferior to its music, with an absurdly complicated plot and ill-defined characters, defeated the long-term project. However, it did provide the occasion for the British début of the American soprano Kathleen Battle; once again a case of Glyndebourne spotting the potential greatness of young singers well before the more traditional houses.

Haitink was dealing with equally quirky material when he agreed to tackle Prokofiev's surreal opera *The Love for Three Oranges*, which for no particularly good reason – since the original was in Russian and English would have been more comprehensible – was sung in French. This too was largely a tour de force for the designer, but in Prokofiev's batty fable the machines, monsters and inflatable giants invented by the New York children's illustrator, Maurice Sendak, were entirely appropriate. Many people were surprised that Haitink was persuaded to conduct the piece, but in fact his interest in Stravinsky made it a reasonable step to take. It was also enormous fun. The singers found themselves saddled with names as unlikely as their costumes. Truffaldino (Ugo Benelli), Tchélio (Richard Van Allan), Sméraldine (Fiona Kimm) and Fata Morgana (Nelly Morpurgo) all cavorted about the stage in a bizarre blend of *commedia dell'arte*, gothic horror and high camp.

Nothing can have been further from this romp than Haitink's other new production of 1983, Mozart's static and sombre early opera *Idomeneo*; it was directed by Trevor Nunn and was his first opera staging, despite his eminence as Artistic Director of the Royal Shakespeare Company. The design, by John Napier, tried to suggest both the stillness of the classical style and the violence of the age by investing the setting of ancient Crete with a hint of Japanese simplicity as well as Minoan artefacts. Its dramatic challenges have rarely been satisfactorily met by producers, but the music provided Haitink with an opportunity to indulge both his passions: Mozart opera and romantic musical architecture. It was a score that he found particularly rewarding, lavish yet restrained, delicate in its detail yet demanding a sense of scale that brought him close to the worlds of Wagner and Strauss. It also provided, once again, an opportunity to exhibit the Glyndebourne genius for vocal blending, with Philip Langridge as Idomeneo, Carol Vaness as Electra and Margaret Marshall as Ilia.

During his period as Musical Director at Glyndebourne, Haitink conducted only three operas at Covent Garden up to 1986, when preparations were already in progress for his accession to the same post there. The first of these, in 1981, pitched him directly into the sort of crisis that can occur in the life of a metropolitan opera house. The revival of Otto Schenk's production of *Un ballo in maschera* was to be the highlight of the season. It was to include the talents of Luciano Pavarotti, Renato Bruson and Montserrat Caballé. However, in the new year the headline in the *Sunday Times* accurately described the feelings of the Royal Opera's General Director, Sir John Tooley. 'Nightmare at the Opera,' it read. All the bad news came within hours on 5 January. At ten-thirty in the morning Caballé rang from Barcelona to say that she was suffering from Hong Kong flu and would almost certainly be too ill for the first night. An hour later Bruson, in Parma, announced that he had a serious throat infection and had been ordered to rest completely for three weeks, which meant that he would miss the rehearsals and the first two nights. At half-past four Pavarotti called from New York to say that his father was seriously ill and would have to undergo surgery on 15 January, two days before the production was due to open. The problems continued during rehearsal when another member of the cast, Forbes Robinson, collapsed and had to be taken to hospital. Replacements were found, though it meant scouring the world for available, able-bodied and acceptable singers. Matteo Manuguerra stood in for Bruson, Juan Lloveras found himself having to live up to Pavarotti's reputation and Paul Hudson replaced Forbes Robinson. Montserrat Caballé bravely decided to sing, though she was plainly ill and could not produce her best. Through all this Haitink relied on his reserves of Dutch stoicism and tried to make what sense of the mangled rehearsal schedule as he could. The show duly went on, though the salvage operation could hardly be ignored. It was decided that, in the circumstances, most of the critics should be invited to the second performance, not to the potentially disastrous first night. In the event the opening passed without mishap, but by the second Caballé too was close to collapse. Whatever the disasters on stage, however, the audience did have a performance to watch and, as one critic wrote, it was redeemed by 'the remarkable orchestral playing (including a lovely cello solo for Amelia's moving third-act aria) and the sombre, challenging, heavyweight conducting of Bernard Haitink'.

Two years later he returned to the Royal Opera House for more Verdi. In March 1983 he was in charge of the revival of Visconti's old 1958 production of *Don Carlos*, staged by Chris Renshaw. It was a work he had tackled with Netherlands Opera, but not in its French version. This time matters ran smoothly and the cast reflected the sort of mixture between excellent local performers and international celebrities picked for their appropriateness, rather than their box-office appeal, which was to become the hallmark of his directorship. Of the former there were Jean Rigby, John Tomlinson, Thomas Allen and Robert Lloyd (as Philip II). Of the latter there were Livia Budai (Princess Eboli), Romayne Grigorova, Peyo Garazzi (Don Carlos) and Stefka Evstatieva (Elisabeth de Valois). A review in the *Daily Telegraph* suggested that either Peter Stadlen had been let into a secret, or that the gossips of Fleet Street had good information. 'The orchestra,' he wrote, 'played for Bernard Haitink with delicate accuracy and shattering expressiveness, and maintained immaculate liaison with the stage, all of which may have increased his chances as one of the rumoured nominees for the position of the Royal Opera's next Music Director.'

X
The conductor's year

THE YEAR 1986 was one of transition for Bernard Haitink, almost of limbo. It had been announced that he was giving up some of his appointments and he was due to take up the work, but not the title, of another. He was still Musical Director at Glyndebourne and Conductor of the Concertgebouw Orchestra, but in both cases there was a sense of withdrawal. With 1988 fixed as the year in which he would leave both, there were no new decisions to be made, no long-term plans to set in motion, only commitments to carry out. In London only five concerts were to be given, three with his old orchestra, the LPO, a pair with the Philharmonia. At the Royal Opera House he was officially a guest conductor with the ambiguous duties of Music Director Designate. Sir Colin Davis was not due to bow out until July and Haitink was not to assume the title until the autumn of 1987. Unofficially he was already the occupant of the Music Director's office high up in the Opera House, next to the amphitheatre, looking down into Floral Street. The orchestra, stage and administration staff treated Haitink as the boss, whatever it said on the headed notepaper. It was to him that problems were brought for resolution and from him that opinions which mattered were canvassed. However carefully he reiterated that he was not in the job yet, it was a point regarded as semantic by almost everyone except himself. So throughout the year there were weeks set aside in his diary for meetings and auditions.

At the start of 1986 it became clearer than ever before that Haitink was now principally a man of the opera. Between his arrival in England at the beginning of February and his return to the Concertgebouw in April he gave no concerts at all. Instead the full two months were devoted to Mozart and Strauss: *Così fan tutte* and *Arabella*. The last fortnight of February was spent, for the most part, in the huge Studio One at Abbey Road in London's St John's Wood, opened originally by Elgar. EMI had agreed to continue the project begun in 1984 with *Don Giovanni*, recording all three of Mozart's operas with libretti by da Ponte, in their Glyndebourne productions. It is a project much cherished by Haitink, for, of all his work in the last decade, these operas have come to mean the most to him. All three were to be conducted during a twelve-month period. As with *Le nozze di Figaro* to follow, the

150

cast for the EMI recording of *Così* was largely, but not entirely, the one put together for the 1984 season at Glyndebourne. The two sisters were the same, played by the American singers Carol Vaness and Delores Ziegler, and Claudio Desderi was again Don Alfonso. John Aler had sung Ferrando in 1979, though not in 1984, and Lillian Watson had played Despina in the previous Glyndebourne production in 1976. Only the Guglielmo of Dale Duesing was completely new to Glyndebourne.

The recording was completed on 27 February, and the next day Haitink spent at a preliminary rehearsal for *Arabella* at Covent Garden. His part in the proceedings started in earnest ten days later when music rehearsals began on 10 March. It was not a new production, but although Haitink had conducted the work at Glyndebourne he had never done so in London. At its heart were two performers who had worked with him on his recordings in Munich, Lucia Popp as Arabella and Bernd Weikl as Mandryka, and the supporting couple – David Rendall's Matteo and Marie McLaughlin's Zdenka – were well cast. In many ways it was a typically strong Haitink list, reflecting his preference for lyrical voices and good acting over the need for volume and established reputations. In Popp and Weikl he had singers who were stars because of their musicality, not their lifestyle or temperament.

The first night was scheduled for 27 March; a week before, most of the hard work had been done. On the Friday and Saturday mornings Haitink ran through the opera with orchestra and costumes. For a while he made little comment, letting the singers accustom themselves to the conditions. 'It was a bit loose,' he said afterwards, 'but I wanted to see what they could do.' So on the Saturday he stopped more often, corrected details and was fussier in a quiet way, prepared to make the orchestra play a passage two or three times until he was satisfied. His diplomacy and understanding of the conflicts of interest that complicate a singer's life was shown when David Rendall found he had been double-booked. He was due to rehearse Matteo at Covent Garden and *Carmina Burana* at the Festival Hall with the LPO at the same time. Since Haitink had only three rehearsals with the stage and orchestra at his disposal, it was a measure of his confidence that he allowed Rendall to leave. 'Producers have so much time compared with conductors,' he lamented. 'But they can't do anything on the night! Some conductors assert themselves by being unpleasant. But with British musicians, especially orchestras, you have to be very good indeed if you want to be nasty. Then if you are good there is no need, since they will respect you anyway.'

The dress rehearsal took place on the Monday afternoon. It is a well-worn maxim in the theatre that a bad 'dress' heralds a good first night, but Haitink does not believe in it. 'You should work up to it slowly,' he says, 'each rehearsal being a little better than the last. By the dress it should be nearly right, because the better it is the less nervous everyone will be on the first night when it is up to them.' Whatever happens at the opening, though, the second night can feel flat. If the reviews have been bad, the singers will be depressed and lacking in enthusiasm. If they have been good, there is a tendency to relax too much. 'Then it is up to the conductor,' says Haitink, 'because he is the only one in control at that stage who can lift the performance.' In the event, what criticisms there were in the reviews were levelled more at Strauss and the original production than at the performers. Lucia Popp radiated Viennese warmth, which is almost the only point of the opera. After five performances, the last on 10 April, Haitink could go back to Holland well pleased with the start of what was, in effect, his time in control of the Royal Opera.

In Amsterdam Haitink's two weeks with the Concertgebouw in April were filled with an almost indigestible amount of music-making. Two programmes were given in five concerts and recording sessions took every spare moment, leaving him with the sort of schedule which is the perfect answer to those who think of the life of a leading conductor as an easygoing and leisurely round of glamour and applause. A glance at his timetable for the week beginning Saturday 18 April proves the point. That evening he conducted a subscription concert of Mahler's Rückert Lieder and Second Symphony (the 'Resurrection'), with the singers Ashley Putnam and Jard van Nes (both of whom appeared with Haitink several times during the year). Sunday was a rest day, but on Monday morning he was back in the Concertgebouw to record Beethoven's Fifth Symphony for Philips. That was completed by mid-afternoon, and so the first takes were recorded of the opening movement of the Sixth Symphony (the *Pastoral*). More work was needed on the movement the following day, but by lunchtime the second movement was finished and the third begun. Tuesday afternoon was given over to meetings, but on the Wednesday morning the remaining movements of the *Pastoral* were completed. That evening Haitink conducted the second performance of the Mahler programme, and gave it again on the Thursday night. In the meantime he had directed rehearsals of Bruckner's Third Symphony for Saturday's concert. On the Friday there were more rehearsals for the Bruckner and for Beethoven's Fifth Piano Concerto (the 'Emperor'), with Murray Perahia as soloist, which they were due to record for CBS the following Monday. After a final rehearsal on the Saturday morning the concert was given that evening, and again on the Sunday afternoon. In eight days Haitink had been standing in front of the orchestra for something over thirty-five hours. Perhaps the most extraordinary aspect of such a week is that in the case of all six of the works performed, whether on the concert platform or for the microphone, Haitink and the orchestra produced music that was consistently of the highest standard.

That standard was not achieved without effort, however. Part of Haitink's gift as a conductor lies in the sense he imparts to his performances that the music has somehow grown inevitably and naturally out of the players, without his intervention. Just how illusory that is can be seen at his rehearsals and recording sessions. The work is still done through gesture rather than words, but the organisation and discipline is all the more concentrated for the lack of verbal interruption. Furthermore, arriving in Amsterdam for that fortnight with such a workload involved more than just slotting back into his relationship with the orchestra.

Haitink had not conducted the Concertgebouw since Christmas Day. In the meantime it had been directed by different artists with very different styles from Haitink's, including, immediately beforehand, its Conductor Elect, Riccardo Chailly. After such an absence Haitink needed time to coax his individual sound from the orchestra, a task which usually, he believes, takes him at least a week. In this case he had just four days available before the first concert, a position that was further complicated by the need to work with the chorus as well.

By the second day of recording, the Haitink sound was beginning to emerge again. At ten o'clock they reworked the first movement of the *Pastoral* that they had laid down the previous afternoon. The first take showed the signs of being an early-morning one: a little lacklustre, with the odd patch of rough ensemble, the strings not quite together, the flutes needing a little more precision. Haitink was aiming for a natural flow to pervade the music, but the initial attempt was a shade too relaxed and when he strove for pianissimi it was rarely quite quiet enough. However, hearing it in conjunction with the material recorded the day before, the producer Volker Straus felt that he had enough to work with. Gradually the sense of ease and lightness of touch came through as they worked on the second movement, and this time the recording went smoothly, each take being a genuine improvement on the one before.

That evening Volker Straus returned to his control panel, without Haitink, to mark up his score and do the preliminary editing for the conductor to hear early on the following day. In some ways Straus's approach to recording is an unfashionable one. While he falls in with Haitink's preferences for long takes, sometimes of a complete movement, sometimes of just a logical section, he is meticulous in the editing-room, using the advantages of digital equipment to the full to select fragments of the music from one take to superimpose on another, where there is an unsatisfactory moment. He is a perfectionist, finding fault with phrases that sound quite reasonable, even to a trained ear. His patience and discrimination is matched by his skill, however, and the version he presents to the conductor before the next day's session is seamlessly coherent; a tribute, too, to Haitink's ability to pick the same tempo each time a passage is recorded. Many record producers prefer to capture the sound with as few microphones as possible, so that a natural balance emerges that reflects the conductor's priorities, not those manufactured in the control room. Straus, though, uses a forest of microphones that gives him complete control over the sound. This is not just a matter of recording philosophy. It is partly dictated by the difficulties of recording in the Concertgebouw, for although the hall is almost acoustically perfect when an audience is present, it has some very peculiar characteristics when it is empty. 'It can play tricks,' Haitink confirms, 'as producers from companies who do not record there often soon discover.' Straus adjusts his balances so that the sound recorded is as close as possible to that experienced when the hall is full, without letting the warmth of the acoustic cloud the detail.

On the Wednesday morning Haitink arrived early in the control room – a makeshift affair set up on piles of equipment cases in what is usually the dressing-room for artists appearing in the smaller recital hall – so that he could listen to the previous day's work and prepare the next session before the orchestra arrived. It was decided that more work was needed on the scherzo. However, once again the first take of the day was not a success. This time the playing was clearly unsatisfactory. At this point Haitink's professionalism was most in evidence. Many conductors would have criticised the players, pointed out the faulty details and exhorted the orchestra to pull themselves together. For Haitink that was unnecessary. Instead he called the section principals into the control room to listen, trusting their musicianship to alert them to the problems. He was rewarded by an embarrassed glance or two, the odd groan, and a mildly depressed silence. At the end he smiled, shrugged his shoulders and just said, 'So! Let's do it again.'

Back in the hall, the opening of the movement was tackled four more times before Haitink and Straus were satisfied, but the effect of concentrating on the short section until it was as near perfect as possible paid excellent dividends. For the rest of the session the playing was both more disciplined and better integrated, with Haitink achieving a graceful inevitability in the transitional passages that led the symphony forward without any sense of being forced. The *Pastoral* is one of the hardest of Beethoven's works to conduct well, partly because of its familiarity, but partly because of the need to evoke an atmosphere without over-indulging in impressionistic picture-painting. That Haitink's tempo for the last movement seemed uncannily natural turned out to have a simple explanation. His beat fell at a pace almost exactly equivalent to a second.

At Glyndebourne Haitink almost relaxed. He arrived in Sussex at the beginning of May, when stage rehearsals were already well in progress, and within a few days he was visibly more at ease than he had been amid all the strains and stresses of Amsterdam. Not only were the traditional working methods of Glyndebourne more in tune with his own preferred pace, they were also to a far greater extent within his control. There he is music director in all its senses, whereas in Amsterdam there was always an underlying feeling that the orchestra and his home town owned him; that it was his duty to make music as a matter of obligation to Dutch culture. Any deviation from the obedient and the expected would be an affront to the convenient homogeneity of the city's social life. His loyalties were seen as being first to the Concertgebouw and its subscribers, second to Amsterdam, and third to the music. At Glyndebourne the order of priorities was reversed and his only true obligations were to the proper staging of opera.

  Glyndebourne is not designed to nurture anxiety. And while its gardens and homely character, apparent to all its audience, are part of the charm, for those working there the real benefits are both more subtle and more pervasive. Outside the strict hierarchy of the rehearsal room and auditorium there is a sense of equality and community that is unrivalled in the opera world. In the Courtyard Café that is at the centre of backstage life it is only an arrogant person who demands special treatment. Everybody is an artist and important, however small the role or low the salary. The company atmosphere is not an excuse for false bonhomie, but a natural way of ensuring that it is the opera that receives the lion's share of the attention, not the egos of insecure divas. It also gives Glyndebourne an almost collegiate air. Many of the performers are relatively young and for them the place is as much a laboratory as a source of employment. The long rehearsal periods, the intensive coaching and the opportunities to talk informally with colleagues of greater stature and experience, make it an ideal place for young artists to develop. Because so many come from abroad or just cannot face the trek back to London each night, the cast stay in cottages in the surrounding countryside or find digs in nearby Lewes. So for most of the spring and summer the company is truly resident. As a result the social life tends to be as close-knit, and hectic, as the working relationships. Parties abound, and Glyndebourne is as famous among singers for its love affairs as it is for its music. In good weather, breaks in rehearsal or the time before a performance can be spent sunbathing in the gardens, sauntering by the lake or playing tennis, of which Haitink is an enthusiastic exponent.

Most of all, perhaps, it is at Glyndebourne where Haitink's methodical approach to rehearsal comes into its own. He has the time to work his way into a score, knowing that the first night is just the start of a journey of discovery and that rehearsals can be a matter of preparatory development rather than a frantic rush to have something presentable for when the curtain rises.

The new production for May 1986 was something of a departure from Glyndebourne's normal repertoire. It had been decided to begin a Verdi cycle, with Peter Hall as producer, and to start with *Simon Boccanegra*, a daring choice since it is one of the grandest of Verdi's works, needing a chorus and cast of soloists that is rather too large for the house's modest stage. It is also, Haitink believes, very much a musician's opera. 'The mood and the intrigue is almost too dark, too oppressive for the audience.' Making *Boccanegra* work in such a small space required all Hall's patience and ingenuity, and from Haitink an even greater than usual awareness of the need to maintain the balance between the singers and the large Verdi orchestra. The staging was inevitably complicated and, even with Glyndebourne's generous schedule, rehearsal time seemed all too short. However, it is not in Hall's nature to rush matters. 'He watches and listens for a time before making up his mind,' says Haitink. 'He likes to stand back and look at developments. He doesn't say much for a week or so. To some people it looks as though he doesn't know the opera, but I realise that we work in very much the same way. My ideas are not fixed before I make the music either.'

For ten days Haitink went to production rehearsals, worked with the singers individually and prepared the ensembles with only piano accompaniment. Then the orchestra arrived and for several days

Haitink worked with them alone, fashioning the Verdi sound as though it were a symphony. The London Philharmonic had not worked with Haitink since the previous autumn. By 1986 the tensions and misunderstandings that had spoilt the last years of his directorship had been long since buried and he was greeted with a cheer as he appeared in the Lily Davis room, its double doors open to the sunshine streaming in from the garden. 'Letting Haitink go was the biggest mistake this orchestra ever made,' remarked one player in the courtyard afterwards.

Proper preparation for rehearsal is as important to Haitink as for a performance. 'I do the groundwork in my study,' he says, 'and then it helps me tremendously to go out for a walk and think about the work, about what and how I want to rehearse. I feel that the orchestra realises that this gives a purpose to the work if I know where I want to go.' His method is deceptively simple. He starts at the beginning and works his way to the end, without jumping around in the score too much or lifting sections of the music out of context. This not only gives shape to the rehearsal, it allows the performers to retain a sense of the opera's coherence and progress. Neither does Haitink try to spend too much time on a small segment, perfecting it before moving on. He prefers to let the orchestra play through a reasonably long section, almost as a warm-up. Then he drills the opening until the orchestra's playing is at its most disciplined, with ensemble perfect, ears attuned and a palpable air of concentration. With that established he moves on, taking another long passage before correcting details. One of Haitink's great attributes as an orchestral trainer is his ability to judge when the players are getting tired and need to relax for a moment. He will either break off for a few minutes or just lighten the atmosphere with some gentle wit. Towards the end of one *Boccanegra* rehearsal he was attempting to tighten up the rhythmic clarity of the trumpet part and resorted to humming it. 'Is this what you want?' the principal asked.

'Yes, that's it.'

'Well, it's not what you sang.'

Haitink grunted: 'What do you expect? I'm only a conductor!'

Just as important as Haitink's musical insight is his awareness of the reality of orchestral playing. He realises that all parts of the score, however great, are not necessarily fascinating to play all the time. 'I know this is a bit boring for you,' he told the violinists after a particularly prolonged passage of ostinato, 'but it really is beautiful music – when they sing well!' A few bars before, there had been a change in tempo that required sensitive negotiation. 'This is the sort of place,' he said, 'where all sorts of things could happen between the tenth and the fifteenth performance, so I'm afraid you will have to watch me.'

'His changes of tempo are always smooth,' says Alexander Cameron, 'and he has unerring intuition in heavily scored passages if something is not quite right. He never gets embarrassed if things go wrong. As a player you can feel secure with him because he is so reliable. You know just what you have to do in the performance. But he knows, too, when to trust the orchestra and encourage freedom of expression from the soloists without making too many little demands which would have an inhibiting effect on us. He is also aware of just how much rehearsal is needed and when to break.'

Once the orchestra and soloists were ready to be put together in the theatre, it became clear that Haitink had matched his orchestral sound with his singers cleverly. The production had a particularly formidable quartet of baritones and basses – John Rawnsley (Paolo Albiani), Geoffrey Moses (Pietro), Timothy Noble (Boccanegra) and Robert Lloyd (Fiesco) – and Haitink complemented the dark tone of the voices with a warm string sound and a lightness of touch that prevented the prevailing texture from becoming too sombre. This care also enabled the richness of Carol Vaness's Amelia to be supported with an orchestral balance that would have been impressive in a recording studio and was much more so in the dry acoustic of a small opera house.

Haitink conducted fifteen performances of *Simon Boccanegra* between 28 May and 11 July. Then, after a week's rest, he returned for a short run of performances of *Don Giovanni*, in the Peter Hall production that they had been reviving since 1977, but which still seemed as fresh and as satisfying as ever. In the cast were singers who were a regular part of Haitink's company for the year: Carol Vaness again (Donna Anna), Richard Stilwell (Don Giovanni) and Felicity Lott (Donna Elvira).

On 17 August Glyndebourne's *Simon Boccanegra* travelled to the Proms. There, in the spaciousness of the Royal Albert Hall, the power and force of Timothy Noble's singing and the scale of his acting could be appreciated in a way which had been difficult in Sussex. There, too, Haitink could allow the orchestra and chorus to have their heads without worrying about the volume. They were rewarded by a standing ovation – an event that would be regarded as a formality at the Concertgebouw (where an ovation just makes it easier for the subscribers to scuttle away early), but which is rare in London, even in the euphoric surroundings of the Proms.

Haitink and the LPO returned to the Proms at the end of August for concerts of Elgar's 'Enigma' Variations, Shostakovich's Tenth Symphony, Beethoven's Third Piano Concerto (with Murray Perahia, who had performed and recorded the work earlier in the year in Amsterdam) and Strauss's *Ein Heldenleben*. They were Haitink's last engagements before taking a summer holiday, which he spent partly in the Highlands of Scotland. However, he was back with his old orchestra at the beginning of October for a concert at the Festival Hall. The programme included Tchaikovsky's Suite No.3 and Vaughan Williams's Second Symphony, the *London*, the latter being recorded over the next two days.

For the six weeks that followed, Haitink was in residence at the Royal Opera House. Although he was still referred to as Music Director Designate, he was in fact fully in charge for the first time. The production that launched his tenure was both controversial and, for Haitink, a new departure in the repertoire. Although he had been conducting opera seriously for fourteen years, he had never before tackled anything by Janáček. *Jenůfa* had not been seen at Covent Garden for nine years, and Haitink was determined that the production of an opera he regards as one of the greatest of the century should give an indication of the direction in which he wanted the Royal Opera to develop. At Glyndebourne he had found a style, principally in collaboration with Peter Hall, which combined a high degree of dramatic integrity, whether the music was taken into account or not, with singing chosen for its possibilities of homogeneity and singers picked as much for their physical eligibility for the roles as for their use in drawing an audience. The Russian Yuri Lyubimov was chosen as *Jenůfa*'s producer. This was an inspired but potentially dangerous choice, for Lyubimov's reputation as a brilliant but autocratic director ensured that there would be nothing ordinary about the production. However, the choice of such an internationally recognised theatrical figure immediately gave Haitink's new regime credence, and the first sign that changes were to be expected in Floral Street emerged when he accepted the withdrawal from the production of Gabriela Beňačková, who was to have sung the title role, when it became clear that she had ideas of the duties of a visiting 'star' which were very different from his own. She was replaced by the American soprano Ashley Putnam – younger, undisputedly beautiful (as the prettiest girl in the Czech village of the story should be) and used to working with producers who demanded more than a good voice.

Working with Lyubimov, as Haitink soon discovered, was not the exploratory and amiable business it was with Peter Hall. Lyubimov arrived at rehearsal with most of his decisions on movement and interpretation already made, moving his cast around the stage as if they were chessmen, and interested in little in the way of suggestions. Haitink concentrated on the music. The production that emerged was, none the less, a strong one; Paul Hernon's designs were bare of any inessential props or scenery, so that the drama was enacted in a stark and unforgiving landscape.

With such an uncompromising staging, the focus inevitably fell on the quality of the acting, and it was a mark of its success that the strongest performances came from the singers with the most intense roles: Philip Langridge as Laca, and Eva Randová who, as the Kostelnička, scored one of the greatest triumphs of her career. There was no doubting, either, the enthusiasm with which Haitink's reading of the score was greeted, and it was clear that the audience, from the stalls to the gallery, was determined to demonstrate that his appointment had a large reservoir of public support, whatever the problems that would beset him.

The first night of *Jenůfa* took place on 17 November, and just how intractable some of the problems were likely to prove had been indicated six days earlier when the Royal Opera House released its Annual Report. The failure of the company's grant from the public purse to keep in line with inflation meant that it had to dig deep into its contingency funds to make the books balance. It was clear that Haitink was inheriting an opera house in circumstances which were straitened even by the dismal standards of the previous few years, and the Chairman, Sir Claus Moser, found himself warning that 'the implications of this for our future artistic activities . . . are likely to be serious'. It was not the first time Sir Claus had made such a statement in his twelve years in the post, but on this occasion his demeanour was even more despairing than usual.

In between performances of *Jenůfa* there were two concerts with the Philharmonia Orchestra, one given over to Brahms (the Serenade No.1 and the Fourth Symphony), the other to Rachmaninov (Rhapsody on a Theme of Paganini) and Bruckner (Fourth Symphony). Between them he was joined by Vladimir Ashkenazy for a recording of the Rachmaninov Rhapsody for Decca.

Jenůfa's run ended on 6 December, and Haitink left immediately for Amsterdam to begin his winter season with the Concertgebouw. It was shorter than in most years, with one concert in The Hague and five in Amsterdam. Ashkenazy followed him over so that a Rachmaninov concerto cycle could be completed with a recording of the First, which also formed the central work in the opening programme. After it was placed Prokofiev's cantata *Alexander Nevsky*, and before it Brahms's *Tragic* Overture. Because of inadequate rehearsal time the last piece was drafted in to open the next programme as well, replacing Debussy's *Marche écossaise*, which the orchestra had not played for several years with Haitink.

The twenty-fifth anniversary of Haitink's appointment as Joint Principal Conductor of the Concertgebouw was marked in 1986. In celebration he wanted to commission a new work from the composer who had been the orchestra's Artistic Director at that time and who had first picked out Haitink as an impressive young conductor, Marius Flothuis. He responded with Three Songs for Mezzo-soprano and Orchestra, and Haitink gave the world première on 17 December. Only the middle song, *Santa Espina*, was in fact new. The other two, *To an Old Love* and *Sonnet*, had been written forty years before. However, it was something of a tribute to the consistency of Flothuis's style that the three songs fitted together seamlessly and the older pair sounded fresh and undated. Flothuis is not a man given to exaggerated expression, but he was plainly pleased with the subtlety of Jard van Nes's singing and with Haitink's interpretation. 'I was impressed with how quickly he understood the different moods of my songs,' he said. 'He went to the heart of them from the beginning.' Flothuis cast a paternal eye over his protégé's progress over thirty years. 'His technique has simplified. Now his gestures are extremely clean, whereas at the beginning he was a bit over-active. But from now on he is going to be seen increasingly as a very great conductor.'

The Songs were performed twice more: on the Thursday night, when they were broadcast by Netherlands Radio, and on the following Sunday, with Beethoven's *Eroica* Symphony forming the second half. Haitink's final concert of the year was the 'Kerstmatinee', the traditional concert for the afternoon of Christmas Day, in which Mahler's Fifth Symphony was broadcast live on television to the whole of Europe (thus delaying Christmas lunch for all those who do not share the Dutch tradition of leaving the celebratory meal until the evening).

At the start of the new year Haitink was back at the Royal Opera House for a revival of Strauss's *Der Rosenkavalier* in John Schlesinger's production of 1984. In the Siberian temperatures of a particularly bad winter, it was a struggle to hold rehearsals. Haitink was uncertain each morning whether his orchestra would be able to fight its way to Covent Garden and, if so, of which sections it would consist. There were moments when an arrangement for string quartet seemed the most realistic solution. Although he inherited the production, the casting reflected Haitink's concerns for vocal blend and physical appropriateness. Felicity Lott sang her first Marschallin in Britain, and for once the role's regality was both credible and vulnerable enough to be an obvious inspiration to Octavian, played with great subtlety by Ann Murray, who was also appearing in the part for the first time in London. With a group that included Hans Sotin (Baron Ochs), Barbara Bonney (Sophie), Robert Tear (Valzacchi) and Eirian James (Annina), Haitink was able to secure the sort of rounded performance that can prove most musically satisfying. When he conducts, this production suggested, the Royal Opera can be seen to be moving away from the 'circus' system in which the major parts are expensively cast and the minor ones are distributed among minor singers.

Before leaving Covent Garden for the season, Haitink had one important innovation to make. On 12 and 14 February he conducted the first concerts the Orchestra of the Royal Opera House had ever given on the stage of the theatre. Since he was no longer to have a full-time symphony orchestra at his disposal, that of Covent Garden was now the only one he could call his own, and he was determined that it should no longer be the only orchestra of a first-rate European opera house not to give concerts in its own right. In Munich, Milan, Vienna and Paris the opera orchestra can be heard outside the pit, so why not in London? One reason in the past has been the unsuitability of the theatre's stage, the problem being that most of the sound would disappear up the fly-tower without being bounced back into the auditorium. To circumvent this a special acoustic shell was built, to be lowered behind the orchestra for Haitink's concerts, its construction sponsored by the Friends of Covent Garden and IBM, so that the sound could be focused towards the audience and the theatre could become more like a concert hall (even boasting chandeliers). The sound was still a little too dry, but it was acceptable and it meant that the orchestra could now feel as much at the centre of the Royal Opera House's activities as the opera and ballet companies with which it shared the building.

In the future Haitink plans to commission new works for the orchestra itself and to widen its repertoire to rival those of the more established London orchestras, but for the first concerts the music had operatic connections – the Symphonic Suite from Britten's *Gloriana* and two Mozart vocal works: the aria *Vorrei spiegarvi, o Dio* and the motet *Exsultate, jubilate*, with Kathleen Battle as soloist. In the second half, though, Haitink moved firmly away from music for the theatre when he conducted Shostakovich's Fifth Symphony. Anthony Payne wrote in the *Independent*:

> It was the performance of the symphony which produced the peak of the evening's music-making. Mr Haitink's assured grasp of the composer's panoramic discursive style, allied to the orchestra's increasingly rich and integrated sonority . . . and their growing ensemble precision, combined to unfold the work's heroic vision with style and conviction.

There was one more project for Haitink during the winter in London, which was the completion of his set of the Mozart and da Ponte operas for EMI. As with *Don Giovanni* and *Così fan tutte, Le nozze di Figaro* was to be based on the Glyndebourne production, in this case that of 1984 in which Claudio Desderi played Figaro and Richard Stilwell was the Count. Now, though, the perky Cherubino of Faith Esham was to be contrasted with the stately Countess of Felicity Lott, with Gianna Rolandi remaining as Susanna. The sessions began in Abbey Road Studios on 16 February, and ten days later John Fraser, the producer, was able to announce to a tired group of singers that they had finished. It was well into the evening when the two-hundred-and-thirty-third take – a small section of recitative – proved to be the last.

The orchestra, as always for Glyndebourne over the previous quarter of a century, was the London Philharmonic. It was twenty years since Haitink had first become its Principal Conductor, and there were those in its ranks who counted their own best professional years from the time when he took up that post. Then, Bernard Haitink had been known for his youth and the speed with which he had advanced to the top of the profession, as much as for his insight as a musician. Now, though, in terms by which conductors are measured, he is still comparatively young at fifty-eight. It was his musicianship and understanding that made him stand out in a profession desperately short of conductors with something more than moderate talent. Alfred Brendel describes Haitink as 'one of the few who conduct from a position of calm energy and whose technique is united with his musical personality'.

To many, he is the antithesis of what a great conductor should appear to be. He does not hurl insults at orchestras, make singers with the severity of his judgement or parade his earnings with glamorous mansions. His clothes are comfortable but not overtly expensive. He avoids flying around the world as much as he decently can, without neglecting his obligations. Haitink appreciates the strains under which musicians work and still has the humility to be excited by the work of his colleagues and in awe of composers. He is, however, no saint. He can be moody, rude and exasperatingly indecisive. Yet this is rarely tinged with malice. When he is difficult it is often a result of tiredness or because he is in a position in which he would rather not be and is failing to find a polite way of extricating himself. Many writers over the years have commented on his shyness and modesty. He is certainly shy, though not as much as he was as a young man, and he is modest about his own importance. About his ability as a musician, though, he is thoroughly proud. However, he sees his task as being to coax the best from the singers and players around him so that the stature of the music is clearly exhibited. He is not concerned with proving to the audience that he finds the music moving, or with trying to express it through his movements like a dancer, or living up to the popular image of a Great Artist for the benefit of media publicists. He is a musician's conductor first, and only once that has been established do the supramusical needs of the public concern him. For this reason, despite acres of newsprint devoted to him over the thirty-five years of his professional life, his is not yet a household name. Most people, asked to think of a famous conductor, would suggest von Karajan, Bernstein, perhaps also Solti and (in Britain at least) Previn. Of Haitink too many otherwise intelligent and well-informed people are ignorant.

Those who attend the performances that he conducts, however, have a different perspective, as audiences at Covent Garden, the Proms, Glyndebourne, the Concertgebouw or the Royal Festival Hall demonstrate. As the cast gathered in the control room at Abbey Road after the recording of *Figaro*, Haitink apologised to them for the fact that they would have to perform it all over again at the Festival Hall the following night. Exhausted as they were, he was the only one who seemed alarmed at the prospect. Indeed, when they gathered again the next evening, there was almost a party atmosphere on stage. It seemed fitting that, after coming together first for Glyndebourne, then for the microphone, they should end with a celebratory concert. Although in theory they were not staging the work, in practice they knew their parts so well that they were almost incapable of not acting. Faith Esham ignored her music entirely, as she had even during the recording, and dressed for the part in tunic and breeches. Claudio Desderi as Figaro bantered as much with his eyes and nimble footwork as with his voice. As Haitink signalled the end of the exuberant finale, there was the prospect to enjoy that the next time he conducted *Figaro* in London it would be as Music Director, in title as well as fact, at Covent Garden.

Ferdinand Leitner's prediction that one day Haitink would be as great a conductor of opera as of the symphony was in the process of fulfilment.

Discography

Abbreviations:

BRSO (& C) Bavarian Radio Symphony Orchestra (and Choir)
CGO (& C) Concertgebouw Orchestra, Amsterdam (and Choir)
GLC Glyndebourne Chorus
LPO (& C) London Philharmonic Orchestra (and Choir)
NRC Netherlands Radio Chorus
VPO Vienna Philharmonic Orchestra
VSOC Vienna State Opera Chorus

Recording date	Composer	Work	Orchestra and soloist	Record company
Sept. 1959	Dvořák	Symphony No.7 (2)	Concertgebouw	Philips
,,	Dvořák	Slavonic Dances Nos. 1, 3, 7 & 8	,,	,,
May 1960	Tchaikovsky	Violin Concerto	CGO: A. Grumiaux	,,
,,	Mendelssohn	Violin Concerto	,,	,,
,,	Beethoven	Romances for violin & orchestra	,,	,,
,,	H. Andriessen	Symphonic Etude	Concertgebouw	,,
,,	Mendelssohn	Hebrides Overture	,,	,,
Sept. 1960	Bartók	Concerto for Orchestra	,,	,,
,,	Bartók	Dance Suite	,,	,,

166

Recording date	Composer	Work	Orchestra and soloist	Record company
Sept. 1961	Ravel	Daphnis et Chloé, Suite No.2	Concertgebouw	Philips
„	Ravel	Pavane pour une infante défunte	„	„
„	Ravel	Alborada del gracioso	„	„
„	Ravel	Rapsodie espagnole	„	„
„	Tchaikovsky	Capriccio italien	„	„
„	Smetana	Vltava	„	„
„	Stravinsky	Firebird Suite	„	„
„	Dvořák	Scherzo capriccioso	„	„
July 1962	Beethoven	Symphony No.8	„	„
„	Bruch	Violin Concerto No.1	CGO: A. Grumiaux	„
Sept. 1962	Mussorgsky	Pictures at an Exhibition	Concertgebouw	„
„	Saint-Saëns	Danse macabre	„	„
„	Berlioz	Overture: Carnaval romain	„	„
„	Mahler	Symphony No.1 (Titan)	„	„
„	Dvořák	Slavonic Dance No.4	„	„
Feb. 1963	Handel	Music for the Royal Fireworks	„	„
„	Mendelssohn	Symphony No.4 (Italian)	„	„
June 1963	Dvořák	Symphony No.8 (4)	„	„
„	Dvořák	Slavonic Dances Nos. 2 & 6	„	„
„	Stravinsky	Violin Concerto	Lamoureux: D. Oistrakh	„
„	Mozart	Violin Concerto, K.207	„	„
Oct. 1963	Bruckner	Symphony No.3	Concertgebouw	„
April 1964	Beethoven	Piano Concerto No.4	CGO: C. Arrau	„
June 1964	Beethoven	Piano Concerto No.1	„	„

167

Recording date	Composer	Work	Orchestra and soloist	Record company
June 1964	Beethoven	Piano Concerto No.5 (Emperor)	CGO: C. Arrau	Philips
"	Tchaikovsky	Overture: Romeo and Juliet	Concertgebouw	"
Sept. 1964	Haydn	Symphony No.96 (Miracle)	"	"
"	Haydn	Symphony No.99	"	"
"	Beethoven	Piano Concerto No.2	CGO: C. Arrau	"
"	Beethoven	Piano Concerto No.3	"	"
Dec. 1964	Mendelssohn	Music for A Midsummer Night's Dream	CGO & NRC: H. Watts, R. Woodland	"
"	Verdi	Overture: La forza del destino	Concertgebouw	"
May 1965	Bruckner	Symphony No.4 (Romantic)	"	"
June 1965	Schubert	Music for Rosamunde	"	"
Dec. 1965	Bruckner	Symphony No.9	"	"
"	Glinka	Overture: Russlan and Ludmilla	"	"
May 1966	Mahler	Symphony No.3	CGO & NRC: M. Forrester	"
"	Dvořák	Slavonic Dance No.5	Concertgebouw	"
July 1966	Bruckner	Symphony No.0	"	
Sept. 1966	Bruckner	Te Deum	CGO & NRC: E. Ameling, A. Reynolds, H. Hoffmann, G. Hoekman	
Nov. 1966	Bruckner	Symphony No.7	Concertgebouw	"
Nov. 1967	Heppener	Eglogues	"	Donemus
"	Dvořák	Cello Concerto	LPO: M. Gendron	Philips
"	Dvořák	Silent Woods	"	"
"	Dvořák	Rondo	"	"

Recording date	Composer	Work	Orchestra and soloist	Record company
Dec. 1967	Mahler	Symphony No.4	CGO: E. Ameling	Philips
"	Weber	Overture: Euryanthe	Concertgebouw	"
May 1968	Mahler	Symphony No.2 (Resurrection)	CGO & NRC: E. Ameling, A. Heynis	"
Oct. 1968	Bartók	Music for Strings, Percussion & Celesta	Concertgebouw	"
Nov. 1968	Liszt	Symphonic Poems	London Philharmonic	"
"	Liszt	Les préludes	"	"
"	Liszt	Orpheus	"	"
"	Liszt	Tasso: lamento e trionfo	"	"
Feb. 1969	Mahler	Symphony No.6	Concertgebouw	"
May 1969	Bruckner	Symphony No.2	"	"
"	Brahms	Hungarian Dances	"	"
June 1969	Mahler	Symphony No.9	"	"
"	Chabrier	España	"	"
Sept. 1969	Bruckner	Symphony No.8	"	"
"	Tchaikovsky	Symphony No.4	"	"
"	Kodály	Háry János Suite	"	"
"	Prokofiev	Peter and the Wolf	CGO: H. Prey	"
"	Britten	The Young Person's Guide to the Orchestra	Concertgebouw	"
Oct. 1969	Brahms	Piano Concerto No.1	CGO: C. Arrau	"
"	Brahms	Piano Concerto No.2	"	"
Nov. 1969	Bartók	Violin Concerto No.2	CGO: H. Szeryng	"
"	Bartók	Rhapsody for violin & orchestra No.1	"	"
Dec. 1969	Mahler	Symphony No.7	Concertgebouw	"

Recording date	Composer	Work	Orchestra and soloist	Record company
Jan. 1970	Liszt	Mazeppa	London Philharmonic	Philips
"	Liszt	Hamlet	"	"
"	Liszt	Hungaria	"	"
March 1970	Holst	The Planets	"	"
May 1970	Strauss	Ein Heldenleben	Concertgebouw	"
"	Brahms	Symphony No.3	"	"
"	Mahler	Lieder eines fahrenden Gesellen	CGO: H. Prey	"
"	Mahler	Kindertotenlieder	"	"
"	Brahms	Tragic Overture	Concertgebouw	"
"	Tchaikovsky	Symphony No.6 (Pathétique)	"	"
Sept. 1970	Brahms	Concerto for violin, cello & orchestra	CGO: H. Szeryng, J. Starker	"
"	Beethoven	Romances for violin & orchestra	CGO: H. Szeryng	"
Nov. 1970	Liszt	Ce qu'on entend sur la montagne	London Philharmonic	"
"	Liszt	Hunnenschlacht	"	"
"	Liszt	Von der Wiege bis zum Grabe	"	"
Dec. 1970	Mahler	Symphony No.5	Concertgebouw	"
"	Bruckner	Symphony No.6	"	"
Sept. 1971	Ravel	Mother Goose Suite	"	"
"	Ravel	Daphnis et Chloé, Suites 1 & 2	"	"
"	Mahler	Adagio from Symphony No.10	"	"
"	Mahler	Symphony No.8 (of a Thousand)	CGO, Toonkunst Choir, De Stem des Volks, Collegium Musicum, Kinderkoor St Willibrord, Amsterdam: I. Cotrubas, H. Harper, H. van Bork, B. Finnilä, M. Dieleman, W. Cochran, H. Prey, H. Sotin	"

Recording date	Composer	Work	Orchestra and soloist	Record company
Nov. 1971	Liszt	Festklänge	London Philharmonic	Philips
,,	Liszt	Die Ideale	,,	,,
Dec. 1971	Bruckner	Symphony No.5	Concertgebouw	,,
,,	Ravel	Alborada del gracioso	,,	,,
Jan. 1972	Rimsky-Korsakov	Scheherazade	,,	,,
May 1972	Liszt	Totentanz	LPO: R. Friend	,,
,,	Liszt	Piano Concerto No.1	LPO: A. Brendel	,,
,,	Liszt	Piano Concerto No.2	,,	,,
,,	Elgar	Enigma Variations	,,	,,
,,	Mahler	Symphony No.1 (Titan)	London Philharmonic	,,
,,	Bruckner	Symphony No.1	Concertgebouw	,,
June 1972	Brahms	Symphony No.4	,,	,,
,,	Brahms	Academic Festival Overture	,,	,,
Sept. 1972	Tchaikovsky	Overture: 1812	,,	,,
,,	Tchaikovsky	Marche slave	,,	,,
,,	Tchaikovsky	Francesca da Rimini	,,	,,
Dec. 1972	Brahms	Symphony No.1	,,	,,
Jan. 1973	Stravinsky	Petrushka	London Philharmonic	,,
Feb. 1973	Stravinsky	The Rite of Spring	,,	,,
,,	Mahler	Das klagende Lied	CGO & NRC: H. Harper, N. Procter, W. Hollweg	,,
,,	Ravel	Valses nobles et sentimentales	Concertgebouw	,,
May 1973	Brahms	Violin Concerto	CGO: H. Szeryng	,,
,,	Beethoven	Violin Concerto	,,	,,
,,	Strauss	Also sprach Zarathustra	Concertgebouw	,,

Recording date	Composer	Work	Orchestra and soloist	Record company
May 1973	Strauss	Don Juan	Concertgebouw	Philips
June 1973	Brahms	Symphony No.2	,,	,,
Sept. 1973	Ravel	Rapsodie espagnole	,,	,,
Nov. 1973	Stravinsky	The Firebird (complete)	London Philharmonic	,,
Dec. 1973	Brahms	Piano Concerto No.2	CGO: A. Brendel	,,
Sept. 1974	Tchaikovsky	Symphony No.5	Concertgebouw	,,
,,	Brahms	Variations on St Anthony Chorale	,,	,,
Nov. 1974	Beethoven	Symphony No.3 (Eroica)	London Philharmonic	,,
,,	Beethoven	Symphony No.7	,,	,,
,,	Beethoven	Overture: Egmont	,,	,,
,,	Beethoven	Overture: Coriolan	,,	,,
Dec. 1974	Wagner	Overture, Preludes: Lohengrin	Concertgebouw	,,
,,	Wagner	Prelude and Liebestod: Tristan	,,	,,
,,	Wagner	Overture: Parsifal	,,	,,
,,	Wagner	Siegfried Idyll	,,	,,
,,	Beethoven	Violin Concerto	CGO: H. Krebbers	,,
April 1975	Ravel	La valse	Concertgebouw	,,
,,	Ravel	Boléro	,,	,,
,,	Ravel	Le tombeau de Couperin	,,	,,
Aug. 1975	Beethoven	Symphony No.4	London Philharmonic	,,
,,	Beethoven	Symphony No.5	,,	,,
,,	Beethoven	Symphony No.6 (Pastoral)	,,	,,
,,	Beethoven	Overture: Prometheus	,,	,,
Sept. 1975	Mahler	Das Lied von der Erde	CGO: J. Baker, J. King	,,
,,	Schubert	Symphony No.5	Concertgebouw	,,

Recording date	Composer	Work	Orchestra and soloist	Record company
Sept. 1975	Schubert	Symphony No.8 (Unfinished)	Concertgebouw	Philips
,,	Brahms	Hungarian Dance No.5	,,	,,
,,	Beethoven	Symphony No.1	London Philharmonic	,,
,,	Beethoven	Symphony No.2	,,	,,
Nov. 1975	Beethoven	Piano Concerto No.1	LPO: A. Brendel	,,
,,	Beethoven	Piano Concerto No.2	,,	,,
,,	Mozart	Overture: The Marriage of Figaro	London Philharmonic	,,
,,	Mozart	Overture: Così fan tutte	,,	,,
Dec. 1975	Schubert	Symphony No.9 (Great C major)	Concertgebouw	,,
Jan. 1976	Beethoven	Piano Concerto No.4	LPO: A. Brendel	,,
March 1976	Beethoven	Piano Concerto No.5 (Emperor)	,,	,,
,,	Mozart	Overture: The Magic Flute	London Philharmonic	,,
April 1976	Mahler	Lieder from Des Knaben Wunderhorn	CGO: J. Norman, J. Shirley-Quirk	,,
May 1976	Beethoven	Symphony No.8	London Philharmonic	,,
,,	Beethoven	Symphony No.9 (Choral)	LPO & C: H. Bode, H. Watts, H. Laubenthal, B. Luxon	,,
June 1976	Tchaikovsky	Violin Concerto	CGO: H. Szeryng	,,
,,	Mendelssohn	Violin Concerto	,,	,,
July 1976	Brahms	Serenade No.1	Concertgebouw	,,
,,	Ravel	Menuet antique	,,	,,
,,	Ravel	Pavane pour une infante défunte	,,	,,
Dec. 1976	Debussy	La mer	,,	,,
,,	Debussy	Prélude à l'après-midi d'un faune	,,	,,
,,	Debussy	Rhapsody	,,	,,
,,	Debussy	Marche écossaise	,,	,,

173

| --- | --- | --- | --- | --- |
Jan. 1977	Beethoven	Triple Concerto	LPO: Beaux Arts Trio	Philips
"	Mozart	Overture: Don Giovanni	London Philharmonic	"
"	Mozart	Overture: Idomeneo	"	"
"	Shostakovich	Symphony No.10		Decca
April 1977	Beethoven	Piano Concerto No.2	LPO: A. Brendel	Philips
"	Beethoven	Choral Fantasia	LPO & C: A. Brendel	"
May 1977	Strauss	Don Quixote	CGO: T. de Machula, K. Boon	"
Sept. 1977	Bizet	Symphony in C	Concertgebouw	"
"	Bizet	Jeux d'enfants	"	"
Oct. 1977	Tchaikovsky	Symphony No.2 (Little Russian)	"	"
Dec. 1977	Debussy	Images	CGO: V. Badings	"
"	Debussy	Danse sacrée et danse profane	Concertgebouw	"
"	Tchaikovsky	The Tempest	"	"
"	Tchaikovsky	Elegy for String Orchestra		"
March 1978	Shostakovich	Symphony No.15	London Philharmonic	Decca
"	Mendelssohn	Symphony No.1	"	Philips
"	Mendelssohn	Hebrides Overture	"	"
"	Mendelssohn	Overture: Calm Sea and Prosperous Voyage	"	"
"	Beethoven	Overture: Leonore No.3	"	"
Oct. 1978	Tchaikovsky	Symphony No.6 (Pathétique)	Concertgebouw	"
"	Bruckner	Symphony No.7	"	"
Nov. 1978	Mendelssohn	Symphony No.3 (Scottish)	London Philharmonic	"
"	Mendelssohn	Symphony No.4 (Italian)	"	"
"	Mendelssohn	Symphony No.5 (Reformation)	"	"
Dec. 1978	Tchaikovsky	Symphony No.4	Concertgebouw	"
"	Brahms	Serenade No.2	"	"

Recording date	Composer	Work	Orchestra and soloist	Record company
Jan. 1979	Shostakovich	Symphony No.4	London Philharmonic	Decca
April 1979	Berlioz	Symphonie fantastique	Vienna Philharmonic	,,
May 1979	Debussy	Nocturnes	Concertgebouw	Philips
,,	Debussy	Jeux	,,	,,
Oct. 1979	Tchaikovsky	Manfred Symphony	,,	,,
,,	Tchaikovsky	Symphony No.1 (Winter Daydreams)	,,	,,
,,	Tchaikovsky	Symphony No.3 (Polish)	,,	,,
Nov. 1979	Shostakovich	Symphony No.7 (Leningrad)	London Philharmonic	Decca
,,	Shostakovich	The Age of Gold, ballet suite	,,	,,
Jan. 1980	Mozart	Overture: Die Entführung aus dem Serail	,,	Philips
,,	Mozart	Overture: La clemenza di Tito	,,	,,
,,	Mozart	Overture: Der Schauspieldirektor	,,	,,
,,	Mozart	Overture: Lucio Silla	,,	,,
,,	Shostakovich	Symphony No.1	,,	Decca
,,	Shostakovich	Symphony No.9	,,	,,
April 1980	Brahms	German Requiem	VPO & VSOC: G. Janowitz, T. Krause	Philips
,,	Brahms	Schicksalslied	VPO & VSOC	,,
Oct. 1980	Brahms	Hungarian Dances Nos. 1-10	Concertgebouw	,,
,,	Beethoven	Symphony No.9 (Choral)	CGO & C: J. Price, B. Finnilä, H. Laubenthal, M. Rintzler	,,
Dec. 1980	Shostakovich	Symphony No.14	CGO: J. Varady, D. Fischer-Dieskau	Decca
Jan. 1981	Shostakovich	Symphony No.2	London Philharmonic	,,
,,	Shostakovich	Symphony No.3	,,	,,

175

Recording date	Composer	Work	Orchestra and soloist	Record company
April 1981	Mozart	Die Zauberflöte	BRSO & C: S. Jerusalem, L. Popp, E. Gruberová, W. Brendel	EMI
May 1981	Shostakovich	Symphony No.5	Concertgebouw	Decca
"	Bruckner	Symphony No.8	"	Philips
Nov. 1981	Bruckner	Symphony No.9	"	"
"	Schumann	Symphony No.3 (Rhenish)	"	"
"	Walton	Symphony No.1	Philharmonia	EMI
"	Brahms	Nänie	BRSO & C: O. Wenkel	Orfeo
"	Brahms	Gesang der Parzen	"	"
"	Brahms	Alto Rhapsody	"	"
"	Brahms	Begräbnisgesang for chorus & wind	"	"
Dec. 1981	Strauss	Till Eulenspiegels lustige Streiche	Concertgebouw	Philips
"	Strauss	Tod und Verklärung	"	"
Feb. 1982	Shostakovich	Symphony No.12 (The Year 1917)	"	Decca
"	Shostakovich	Overture on Russian and Kirghiz Folk Themes	"	"
April 1982	Elgar	Symphony No.1	Philharmonia	EMI
"	Elgar	Symphony No.2	"	"
Oct. 1982	Brahms	Piano Concerto No.2	VPO: V. Ashkenazy	Decca
Nov. 1982	Strauss	Daphne	BRSO & C: L. Popp, O. Wenkel, K. Moll, P. Schreier	EMI
Dec. 1982	Shostakovich	Symphony No.8	Concertgebouw	Decca
"	Mahler	Symphony No.7	"	Philips
"	Strauss	Don Juan	"	"
"	Keuris	Movements	"	Donemus
Feb. 1983	Schumann	Symphony No.1 (Spring)	"	Philips

Recording date	Composer	Work	Orchestra and soloist	Record company
Feb. 1983	Schumann	Overture: Manfred	Concertgebouw	Philips
April 1983	Mahler	Symphony No.4	CGO: R. Alexander	,,
May 1983	Shostakovich	Symphony No.11	Concertgebouw	Decca
June 1983	Mendelssohn	Violin Concerto	CGO: I. Perlman	EMI
,,	Bruch	Violin Concerto No.1	,,	,,
Dec. 1983	Shostakovich	Symphony No.6	Concertgebouw	Decca
,,	Shostakovich	Six Poems of Marina Tsvetaeva	CGO: O. Wenkel	,,
,,	Shostakovich	From Jewish Folk Poetry	CGO & C: E. Söderström, O. Wenkel, R. Karczykowski	,,
Jan. 1984	Schumann	Symphony No.2	Concertgebouw	Philips
,,	Mozart	Don Giovanni	LPO & Gl.C: T. Allen, C. Vaness, M. Ewing, E. Gale, K. Lewis, R. Van Allan, J. Rawnsley, D. Kavrakos	
April 1984	Shostakovich	Cello Concerto No.1	CGO: L. Harrell	EMI
,,	Bloch	Schelomo	,,	Decca
Sept. 1984	Rachmaninov	Piano Concerto No.2	CGO: V. Ashkenazy	,,
Oct. 1984	Shostakovich	Symphony No.13 (Babi Yar)	CGO: M. Rintzler	,,
Dec. 1984	Rachmaninov	Piano Concerto No.4	CGO: V. Ashkenazy	,,
,,	Schumann	Symphony No.4	Concertgebouw	Philips
Jan. 1985	Strauss	Alpine Symphony	,,	,,
,,	Schat	Symphony No.2	,,	Donemus
,,	Wagner	Tannhäuser	BRSO & C: K. König, L. Popp, B. Weikl, K. Moll	EMI
Feb. 1985	Bruckner	Symphony No.4 (Romantic)	Vienna Philharmonic	Philips

Recording date	Composer	Work	Orchestra and soloist	Record company
Aug. 1985	Rachmaninov	Piano Concerto No.3	CGO: V. Ashkenazy	Decca
Oct. 1985	Vaughan Williams	Sinfonia antartica	LPO & C: S. Armstrong	EMI
"	Beethoven	Symphony No.7	Concertgebouw	Philips
Feb. 1986	Mozart	Cosi fan tutte	LPO & Gl.C: C. Vaness, D. Ziegler, C. Desderi, J. Aler, D. Duesing, L. Watson	EMI
April 1986	Beethoven	Symphony No.5	Concertgebouw	Philips
"	Beethoven	Symphony No.6 (Pastoral)	"	"
"	Beethoven	Piano Concerto No.5 (Emperor)	CGO: M. Perahia	CBS
"	Beethoven	Piano Concerto No.3	"	"
Oct. 1986	Vaughan Williams	Symphony No.2 (London)	London Philharmonic	EMI
Feb. 1987	Mozart	Le nozze di Figaro	LPO & Gl.C: C. Desderi, F. Lott, G. Rolandi, F. Esham, R. Stilwell, A. Mason	"
April 1987	Mahler	Symphony No.1 (Titan)	Berlin Philharmonic	Philips

Index